ADVANCED BAKERY AND CONFECTIONERY

ADVANCED BAKERY AND CONFECTIONERY

Anandam Lahiri
Vikrant Vyas

NAMAN PUBLISHER & DISTRIBUTORS
NEW DELHI

Published by
Sangeeta Jain for Naman Publisher & Distributors
7360-B, Prem Nagar,
Gali No.1, Shakti Nagar,
Delhi-110007
PH: 23823642, MOB.: 09013478302
E-mail: rajivjain72@ymail.com

First Published – 202

ISBN–978-81–920935–4-3

Published in an association with **HLDC**, Agra.

SOLE DISTRIBUTOR
JINDAL BOOK SERVICES
LG-4A, Ganpati Bhawan,
4675-B/21, Ansari Road,
Darya Ganj, Delhi - 110002

Jacket Designed by :
S.M. Graphics

Printed by:
Sachin Printers, Delhi, India

Preface

Baking is an art and science, and mastery in baking allows the baker to be creative in exploring new and quality products from inconsistent ingredients and process conditions. Baking is the technique of prolonged cooking of food by dry heat acting by conduction, and not by radiation, normally in an oven, but also in hot ashes, or on hot stones. It is primarily used for the preparation of bread, cakes, pastries and pies, tarts, and quiches. Most bakery items are made of the same ingredients: flour, water, sugar, eggs, leavening agents, and fat. Sometimes the difference between two products is simply the method of preparation used in assembling the ingredients. Ingredients play special role in baking and cooking process. Some functions are critical to the success of the finished product. Some of these ingredients can be substituted with other ingredients and produce the same outcome but many times substitutions will have some affect on the end product.

Confectionery in a broader sense implies the preservation of sweet-meat preparation in the form of candies, caramels, chocolated, processed cocoa products and traditional Indian confections. A practical guide for elementary ingredient of baking, tracking of informations about food ingredients, fruits and vegetables in baking, additive, emulsifier, tarts, candy, non-candy confectionery and so on useful in confectionery and bakery industries.

This book is designed and presented in an easy to read and easy to understand format. It will be beneficial to both aspiring professionals and those already in the industry.

We hope this text book meets its intended purpose as a practical resource, and serve as a vehicle for promoting the professionalism of this important segment of the Hospitality Industry.

ANANDAM LAHIRI
VIKRANT VYAS

HERITAGE

LEARNING & DEVELOPMENT CENTER

Heritage Learning and Development Centre (HLDC) is an extended arm of Heritage Institute of Hotel & Tourism (HIHT). Heritage Institute of Hotel & Tourism is an Institute of excellence of the upcoming chain of Management Institutes, founded by D. K. Singh, President. At HIHT, our endeavour is to take education to the higher domains of never ending success. Heritage Institute of Hotel & Tourism provides the best possible infrastructure for pursuing best quality Hotel Management Education. HIHT has three campuses Agra, Shimla and Goa and proposed campuses at Kolkata, Pune, and Singapore.

In the modern era, Hospitality Industry is a reality, fighting for extremely challenging phase and getting into a stability mode. There are SMILES everywhere and this is relatively controlled and guarded, a sign of maturing and learning of Hospitality, which is cyclic in nature. The Hospitality Industry reflects a bright future. Earlier days, hospitality was synonymous with only hotel industry, but today this industry holds its important place with tourism. Hospitality academic in India is still in its nascent stage when compared to the west.

HLDC has been developed through the inputs from the industry and experts from the academics. This panel of experts have gone through the book and made suggestions which were incorporated. Every attempt has been made to thoroughly cover the day to day problems faced in the profession. In this field, as in most any other, it is prudent to remember the old adage, actions speak louder than words. The information given in this book makes the students fit for the industry. It provides about technical skills, personality and soft skills and ability to think and make decision.

This book is designed and presented in an easy to read and easy to understand format. It will be beneficial to both aspiring professionals and those already in the industry.

We hope this text book meets its intended purpose as a practical resource, and serve as a vehicle for promoting the professionalism of this important segment of the Hospitality Industry.

Contents

1

Techniques of Baking

Baking is the technique of prolonged cooking of food by dry heat acting by conduction, and not by radiation, normally in an oven, but also in hot ashes, or on hot stones. It is primarily used for the preparation of bread, cakes, pastries and pies, tarts, and quiches. Most bakery items are made of the same ingredients: fl our, water, sugar, eggs, leavening agents, and fat. Sometimes the difference between two products is simply the method of preparation used in assembling the ingredients. Other times the difference is the proportion or amount of each ingredient in a formula.

Because small differences in method and in proportion of ingredients can have a large effect on the quality of baked goods, it is crucial that bakers and pastry chefs follow methods of preparation carefully and measure ingredients properly. Otherwise, a product may turn out unexpectedly, or worse, it may turn out unacceptable or inedible. For example, if too much shortening and too few eggs are added to a formula for moist, chewy oatmeal cookies, the cookies will likely turn out crisp and dry. If the same error is made with cake batter, the result will likely be a complete failure, since eggs provide structure and volume. In fact, bakers and pastry chefs require a higher degree of accuracy when measuring ingredients than do culinary chefs in the kitchen.

When the kitchen chef prepares a pot of soup, it doesn't really matter if a little less celery is added or an extra onion is included. The chef still has a pot of soup, and if the fl avor is off, adjustments can be made along the way. Bakers and pastry chefs cannot make adjustments along the way. If too little salt is added to bread dough, it will do no good to sprinkle salt onto the bread once it is baked. Instead, ingredients must be weighed and measured accurately at the beginning. This means that, more so than kitchen chefs, bakers and pastry chefs are chemists in the kitchen. As with chemists, creativity and skill are important for success, but so is accuracy. If a formula calls for two pounds of fl our, it doesn't mean around two pounds, more or less. It means two pounds.

Working in a professional bakeshop is different from baking at home, however. Production in a bakeshop is on a larger scale. It takes place day in and day out, sometimes under severe time pressures, in uncomfortably hot and humid conditions, and over long hours. Despite the discomforts and pressures, product quality must remain consistently high, because that is what the customer expects. It takes specialised knowledge and practiced skills to accomplish these goals successfully.

It helps to be attentive to the sights, sounds, and smells of the bakeshop. Experienced bakers and pastry chefs, for example, listen to the sound of cake batter being beaten in a bowl, knowing that changes in sound accompany changes to the batter itself. They push and pummel bread dough to feel how it responds. They use smells from the oven to judge when baking is nearly complete, and they sample their fi nished products before presenting them to the customer. Experienced bakers and pastry chefs rely, too, on tools like timers and thermometers, because they know how time and temperature affect product quality. They also rely heavily on accurate scales.

Balances and Scales

Formulas used in the bakeshop are in some ways like recipes in the kitchen. Formulas include a list of ingredients and a method of preparation (MOP). Unlike recipes used by the kitchen chef, however, formulas include exact measurements for each ingredient, and these measurements are usually given in weights. The process of weighing ingredients is called scaling because pastry chefs use scales to weigh ingredients.

The standard scale used in the bakeshop is a baker's balance scale. It measures ingredients by balancing them against known weights. It is an investment that should be selected for its durability and its precision. A good baker's scale can weigh amounts as large as 8 pounds (4 kilograms) or more and as small as ¼ ounces (0.25 ounce or 5 grams). This provides the precision needed for most quantity food preparation.

Bakers and pastry chefs sometimes use digital electronic scales. While many affordable electronic scales provide the same or better precision than baker's scales, it is not necessarily the case. The precision of a scale—either baker's scale or electronic scale—depends entirely on the scale's design and construction.

Most digital electronic scales provide information about precision—also called readability—and capacity on their front or back panels. For example, a scale that is marked 4.0 kg × 5 g has a capacity of 4 kilograms, meaning it can measure quantities as large as 4 kilograms (about 8.8 pounds). The readability of this scale is 5 grams. Five grams is equivalent to just under 0.2 ounce, which is similar to the 0.25-ounce precision of a good baker's scale.

Consider another electronic scale, one marked 100 oz. × 0.1 oz . This scale has a capacity of 100 ounces (6.25 pounds or 2.84 kilograms) and a readability of 0.1 ounce

(3 grams). The smaller value for readability indicates that this scale provides better precision than a typical baker's scale, making it useful for weighing small quantities of spices or fl avorings.

Just as baker's scales need to be checked periodically for accuracy, so too must digital scales. Digital scales typically come with a brass weight calibrated for accuracy.

If the scale's reading does not match the mass of the brass weight, follow the manufacturer's instructions to adjust the scale. Because a scale is an important piece of equipment in a bakeshop, it is best to check its calibration at two different points (200 grams and 2000 grams, for example). The scale will need adjustment or repair if either of these two readings is off.

How an ingredient is added to a digital scale can make a difference in the accuracy of the reading. For example, multiple small additions will sometimes read lower than the identical amount added all at once. This can happen because scales are generally designed so that they don't fl uctuate excessively with air movement, and the scale cannot necessarily differentiate a small amount of product from air movement. Vibration, heat currents, cordless and cell phones, and static electricity should all be avoided, since they can affect the ability of a scale to read consistently.

Units of Measure

Digital and baker's scales measure in either standard U.S. common units (pounds and ounces; imperial units in Canada) or in metric units (kilograms and grams). Some versatile digital scales switch at the touch of a button from U.S./imperial units to metric units. Most countries throughout the world have adopted the metric system. This provides a means of sharing formulas more easily across national borders. More importantly, the metric system is simpler to use once you become familiar with it. With the metric system, for example, fewer math calculations are needed when converting a formula to a new batch size. Since 1 kilogram in metric equals 1,000 grams, you simply move decimal points to convert from one size unit to another. For example, 1.48 kilograms is equal to 1,480 grams, and 343 grams is equal to 0.343 kilograms. Try converting as quickly from pounds to ounces, or ounces to pounds! This ease of use is probably the main reason why more bakers and pastry chefs in North America are adopting the metric system for use in the bakeshop.

Using the metric system, for the most part, does not require tedious math conversions from ounces to grams or pounds to kilograms. This makes it much easier to use the metric system than most people believe.

Weight and Volume Measurements

Home cooks in North America use volumetric measurements—measuring containers and measuring spoons—for all ingredients, including dry ingredients. This is a problem when measuring certain ingredients. For example, fl our settles over time. When fl our settles, there is less air between particles. Density increases, and more fl our is needed to fi ll a container. On the other hand, if fl our is sifted before it is measured, there is more air between particles. Density decreases, and less fl our is needed to fi ll a cup.

To avoid these inconsistencies, pastry chefs and bakers do not use volumetric measurements for fl our and other dry ingredients. Instead, they weigh dry ingredients—and most liquid ingredients—for accuracy. Density does not affect weight measurements the way it affects volume measurements. A pound of sifted fl our weighs the same as a pound of unsifted fl our, regardless of the density. They both weigh 1 pound! While some pastry chefs and bakers weigh all ingredients using a scale, others measure some liquids volumetrically. They use measuring containers for water and for liquids that have about the same density as water. While practices vary from bakeshop to bakeshop, ingredients that are often measured volumetrically include milk, cream, and eggs. Table 1 indicates why.

Table 1. A comparsion of the approximate weights of 1 Pint and 1 Half Liter (500 Milliliters) of various Ingredients

Ingredients	*Approximate weight per U.S. Pint (in weight ounces)*	*Approximate weight Per half litre (500 ml) (in Grams)*
Splenda	4.0	120
Ginger, ground	6.0	180
Flour, sifted	8.2	245
Flour, unsifted	9.2	275
Sugar, granulated	14.1	420
Oil, vegetable	14.8	445
Cream, heavy	16.4	490
Water	16.7	500
Milk, whole	17.0	510
Eggs, whole	17.2	515
Orange juice	17.4	520
Coffee liqueur	17.5	525
Simple syrup (equal parts sugar and water)	20.6	615
Honey, molasses, and glucose corn syrups	23.0	690

Notice that the weights per pint (or per half liter) of milk, cream, and eggs are around the same as that of water. Measuring 1 pint of each of these ingredients yields about a pound or so (while these ingredients do not weigh exactly 1 pound per pint, they are approximately so; notice, however, that in the metric system, 1 half liter—500 milliliters—of water at room temperature does weigh exactly 500 grams. This is not a coincidence). Many other liquids, including honey, corn syrup, and oil, have densities much different from water. These liquids must be weighed, because 1 pint will not weigh 1 pound.The Difference between Density and Thickness

Density is a measure of the compactness of particles or molecules in a liquid or solid. If the particles or molecules are loosely packed, the liquid or solid is not dense, and the weight per cup or per liter of that ingredient is low. If the particles or molecules are closely packed, the liquid or solid is dense, and the weight per cup or weight per liter of that ingredient is high.

Viscosity or consistency is a measure of how easily a liquid fl ows. If a liquid's particles or molecules slide past each other easily, the liquid fl ows easily and is considered thin. If the particles or molecules bump or tangle with each other, the liquid will not fl ow easily and is thick. This is the case with fruit purees. Tiny pulp pieces in fruit purees bump and tangle with one another, preventing water and pulp particles from fl owing easily past one another. This makes the puree thick. Some common liquids—honey and molasses, for example—are both dense and thick. The molecules are close together, making these liquids dense, and the molecules do not slide easily past each other, making the liquids thick. But consider vegetable oil. Vegetable oil is thicker than water, yet it is less dense than water. Notice how the density of a liquid cannot be judged by looking at its thickness.

Weight Ounces and Fluid Ounces

The term ounce represents a unit of weight or mass. It

can also represent volume or capacity. That is, there are weight ounces that measure weight, and there are fl uid ounces that measure volume. While 1 fl uid ounce sometimes does weigh 1 ounce, it is not necessarily so. Consider feathers and bullets. No one expects 1 cup of feathers to weigh the same as 1 cup of bullets. Likewise, food ingredients vary in how much they weigh per cup. Refer back to Table 1, which lists several ingredients—arranged from less dense to more dense—and their weights per pint (2 cups) and per half liter (500 milliliters). Notice the large range in values. This shows that the expression "a pint's a pound the world 'round" is not only false for feathers and bullets, but it is also false for many common bakeshop ingredients. It is approximately true for water and for ingredients with the same density as water. Because 1 fl uid ounce of water (and ingredients with the same density as water) weighs about 1 ounce, and 1 milliliter of water weighs 1 gram, for practical purposes it doesn't matter whether water is weighed on a scale or measured volumetrically.

Baker's Percentages

Formulas, especially bread formulas, are sometimes expressed in percentages called baker's percentages. With baker's percentages, each ingredient is expressed as a certain ratio or percent of the total amount of fl our in the formula. Flour is used as the basis for baker's percentages because it is typically the predominant ingredient in most baked goods. Since the total amount of fl our is designated as 100 percent, the percentages of all ingredients add up to more than 100 percent. Table 2 provides an example of a bread formula expressed in weight and in baker's percentages. Notice that more than one type of fl our is included in this formula, but that together the weight of the fl ours adds up to 100 percent.

Table 2. Whole wheat bread formula expressed in weight and in Baker's Percentages

Ingredient	*Pounds*	*Ounces*	*Grams*	*Baker's Percentage*
Flour, bread	6		3000	60%
Flour, whole wheat	4		2000	40%
Water	5	10.0	2800	56%
Yeast, compressed		6.0	190	4%
Salt		3.0	95	2%
Total	16	3.0	8085	162%

For formulas that do not contain fl our, each ingredient is expressed as a percentage of the predominant and characteristic ingredient. In the case of a date fi lling, for example, each ingredient is expressed as a percentage of the amount of dates. For baked custard, each ingredient is expressed as a percentage of dairy ingredients—milk and cream. Baker's percentage—sometimes called formula percentage or indicated as "on fl our weight basis"—is different than the percentages commonly taught in math classes. In the more common type of percentage, each ingredient is expressed as a certain percentage of the total batch size. In this case, ingredient percentages add up to 100 percent.

Controlling Ingredient Temperatures

The fi nest ingredients can be selected, they can be accurately weighed and properly mixed, but if temperatures are not carefully controlled, there is still a chance for failure. Why? Many ingredients change properties with temperature. Think of fat, especially fats that melt easily, such as butter. Butter must remain within a narrow temperature range (65–70°F; 18–21°C) as it is spread onto croissant dough. If it is too cold, it will not spread properly; if it is too warm, it melts into the dough and fl akiness is compromised.

Often, ingredients that are at widely different temperatures must be carefully combined to avoid damaging one ingredient with the shock of the heat—or cold—of another. In making vanilla custard sauce, for example, cold yolks cannot be added directly to hot milk, or the yolks could curdle. Instead, in a technique called tempering, small amounts of hot milk are stirred into the yolks, diluting them. The diluted yolks can now be safely added to the bulk of the hot liquid.

Tempering is also necessary when stabilising whipped cream with a gelatin solution. Warmed gelatin hardens into tiny rubbery balls if it is added too quickly to a cold ingredient like whipped cream. The addition of a small amount of whipped cream to the warm gelatin dilutes the gelatin, so it can be added safely to the bulk of the cold whipped cream.

Notice that in the first example of tempering, a small amount of a hot ingredient is added to a cold ingredient, to prevent damage to the cold ingredient. In the second example, a small amount of a cold ingredient is added to a warm ingredient, to prevent damage to the warm ingredient. Many other examples demonstrate the need for controlling ingredient temperatures and for carefully tempering ingredients.

Baking Ingredients

Ingredients play special role in baking and cooking process. Some functions are critical to the success of the finished product. Some of these ingredients can be substituted with other ingredients and produce the same outcome but many times substitutions will have some affect on the end product.

Dry Ingredients

Baking Powder

A combination of baking soda, an acid and a moisture absorber, which together form a leavening agent. Just the right amount of acid is added to the baking soda so that when the baking powder is added to moist ingredients, there is a reaction that releases carbon dioxide bubbles. This reaction is what makes the batter or dough rise.

Baking Soda

An ingredient used as a leavening agent. When it is mixed with an acidic ingredient and then comes in contact with liquid ingredients, a chemical reaction occurs. The chemical reaction releases carbon dioxide gas and causes the rising action in dough or batter. Some of the acidic ingredients that cause the reaction with baking soda are vinegar, lemon juice, orange juice, buttermilk, sour milk, sour cream, honey, chocolate and molasses. The chemical reaction begins as soon as the liquid is added, so the dough or batter should be baked as soon as possible after it has been mixed. If too much time passes before baking, the gases can escape and the product will not rise properly when baked.

Bran

Bran is the outer layer of a kernel of grain. Bran is added to cereals and baked goods to increase the nutritional value and to add fiber.

Bread-crumbs

Breadcrumbs are used to add texture and body to foods. They are added in with other ingredients or they can be used as a coating for meats, fish and vegetables. Breadcrumbs are used fresh or dried, and are used in different degrees of coarseness. Fresh breadcrumbs are handmade. Dried breadcrumbs can be made by hand but are also sold in food stores already dried and prepackaged.

Brown Sugar

Granulated sugar that has molasses syrup added to it. The molasses syrup softens the texture of the sugar. Brown sugar is available in a light and dark variety. The darker has a more intense flavour. Use light brown sugar unless dark brown is specifically specified in the recipe.

Canning & Pickling Salt

A fine-grained salt that does not contain any additives, which prevents the brine from becoming cloudy when canning and pickling food. It is used when canning and pickling vegetables and meats. It can also be used in the same manner as table salt but it may start to clump when exposed to excessive humidity.

Cocoa Powder

An unsweetened powder made from the leftover chocolate liquor that has had the cocoa butter removed. The chocolate liquor is made from cacao beans and about 75% of it is extracted as cocoa butter and the remainder is dried and ground into cocoa powder. Cocoa powder is used to add chocolate flavouring to baked goods.

Corn Meal/Flour

Made from ground dried corn. It is available coarse, medium or fine ground. Corn flour is ground finer than fine ground corn meal. Corn meal or flour will not form gluten so products made from them have a more coarse, dense texture than products made from some of the other flours. Corn meal and corn flour provide a corn flavour to products it is used in.

Cornstarch

A thickening agent used in sauces, gravies, soups and desserts. It is finely ground from the heart of the corn kernel and has twice the thickening power of flour.

Tartar Cream

A white powder made from the acid deposits that form on the inside of the wine barrels during wine making. It is added to egg whites to give them more volume and stability. It also helps to stop sugar syrups from crystallising and makes creamier frostings and candies when it is one of their ingredients. This acidic powder is also added to baking soda to create commercial baking powder.

Flour

Generally, flour is the ingredient that gives baked goods their form and structure. When the flour is mixed with water, the proteins in flour interact with each other to form gluten. Gluten is what gives the dough its elasticity and the ability to stretch as the leavening agent produces the carbon dioxide gases that cause the dough to rise. Different types of wheat flour contain different amounts of proteins for forming gluten. Soft wheat have a lower protein content than hard wheat. A flour with higher protein content is more desirable for yeast breads, whereas lower protein content is better for cakes, pastries, and quick breads to produce a more tender texture.

All-Purpose Flour

All-purpose flour is a multipurpose flour made from hard and soft wheat. It can be used for all baking purposes. It is available bleached and unbleached.

Arrowroot Flour

Arrowroot flour is a fine powder ground from the arrowroot plant. It does not have any flavour and its texture is similar to cornstarch. It is used as a thickener for sauces, gravies, puddings and dessert fillings. Arrowroot flour has approximately 50% more thickening power than flour.

Bread Flour

Bread flour is a hard wheat flour that is higher in gluten forming protein. It is used with yeast breads because the higher gluten content produces bread that is lighter, has more volume and is less crumbly.

Cake Flour

Cake flour is a soft-wheat flour with a fine-texture and a high starch content. It contains a lower level of protein than bread flour. When mixed with moisture, the protein in flour turns to gluten that gives the baked goods strength and structure. Pastries and cakes need only a limited amount of gluten. Since the pastry flour contains less protein it creates tender pastries and cakes. Cake flour is also referred to as pastry flour.

Oat Flour

Oat flour is ground from rolled oats. It provides a nutlike flavour and has a high protein content. Oat flour does not form gluten like the wheat flour, so it must be used in combination with a wheat flour so that the bread will rise. When using oat flour, about 1/3 of the flour can be oat flour and 2/3 should be wheat flour.

Pastry Flour

Pastry flour is a soft-wheat flour with a fine-texture and a high starch content. It contains a lower level of protein than bread flour. When mixed with moisture, the protein in flour turns to gluten that gives the baked goods strength and structure. Pastries and cakes need only a limited amount of gluten. Since the pastry flour contains less protein it creates tender pastries and cakes. The higher level of protein found in bread flour is required to create the structure of the bread crumb. Pastry flour is also referred to as cake flour.

Potato Starch Flour

Potato starch flour is a non-gluten forming flour that is ground from dried, cooked potatoes. It is a fine textured flour that has a mild potato flavour. Potato starch flour must be used in combination with a gluten forming flour, such as a all-purpose flour.

Rice Flour

Rice flour is a flour made from finely ground long or short grain rice. It is used as a thickening agent to thicken puddings, desserts, and sauces. It is also used to make noodles. It does not form gluten, so it can be substituted for wheat flour in some recipes to be used by people that do not tolerate gluten.

Rye Flour

Rye flour is ground from grains of rye grass and has a slightly sweet-sour flavour. It does not contain enough protein to develop the gluten necessary for the bread to rise sufficiently, so it must be combined with wheat flour. Rye flour produces a denser and darker loaf of bread and is available in light, medium and dark varieties. The darker the flour the darker the loaf of bread will be. When using light rye flour in combination with wheat flour, you can use about 40% rye flour. When using the medium or dark rye flour, the amount of rye flour must be decreased.

Self-rising Flour

Self-rising flour is an all-purpose flour into which baking powder (a leavening agent) and salt have been added. When used in a recipe in place of all-purpose flour, the baking powder and salt are omitted from the other ingredients.

Semolina Flour

Semolina flour is ground from hard durum winter wheat. Semolina flour produces stronger dough because it contains a high level of gluten, which adds elasticity to the dough. Dough made from semolina flour is too hard to handle when rolling out by hand because of its stickiness but when mixed with unbleached white flour it produces a strong dough that is easier to handle. Semolina flour is used when making pasta and some breads.

Soy Flour

Soy flour is flour ground from hulled and roasted soybeans. Soy flour cannot form gluten and contains no starch, but it is very high in protein. It is generally used to increase the protein in baked goods but you must be cautious as to how much you use because it will affect the taste and cause increased browning if too much is used. The flour is produced as natural (defatted), which has the oils removed, or full-fat, which retains the soybean oils.

Triticale Flour

Triticale flour is ground from the man-made grain triticale. Triticale is a high protein man-made grain produced by crossbreeding wheat and rye. The man-made grain was produce in effort to duplicate the protein and bread-making qualities of wheat and the durability and high lysine content of rye. Triticale flour provides a nutty flavour similar to wheat and rye, and generally contains more protein than wheat flour. Because of its durability, it handles better than rye flour but not as well as wheat flour. It can be substituted in equal portions for recipes requiring either wheat or rye. Yeast dough made with triticale flour should be fermented for less time than dough made with wheat flour.

Wheat Flour

Whole wheat four is ground from the full wheat kernel, including the bran, germ, and the endosperm. Whole wheat flour is brownish in colour and is much more nutritious than refined white flour. It is often added to white flour to improve the nutrition of baked goods. Whole wheat flour is available in fine, medium and coarse ground. As the coarseness of the flour increases, the coarseness of the baked good's texture increases.

Due to the higher unsaturated oil content in whole wheat flour, it has a shorter shelf life. Food products made with whole wheat flour have a higher potential of becoming rancid if kept for long periods of time. The life of the food product can be extended if stored in the refrigerator. If substituting whole wheat flour for part of the white flour when making yeast and quick breads, each cup of white flour that you replace should be replace by 1 cup plus 2 tablespoons of whole wheat flour. Bread made with whole wheat flour will produce a smaller, denser loaf.

Granulated Sugar

Fine or extra-fine sugar crystals made from refined beet or cane sugar. It serves several purpose in baking. It provides sweetness, adds tenderness, and helps in the browning of baked goods. When added to yeast dough, it helps the yeast begin producing the gas for the dough to rise and helps to retain the moisture in the bread. It is also referred to as white sugar.

Fat Ingredients

Butter

The semi-solid product that is produce from churning cream. It is at least 80% milkfat and is available in salted or unsalted varieties. The unsalted variety is often used when cooking because it allows the cook to have more control over the seasoning. Butter creates flaky pastries, and it provides flavour, tenderness, crispness, and a golden-brown colour to many foods. It is used when frying and sautéing food, as a spread for baked goods such as breads and rolls, and as a flavouring for cooked vegetables. When eaten, it does not leave a greasy feeling in your mouth because it melts at body temperature. It is an ingredient in hundreds of recipes including breads, pastries, cakes, entrees, and sauces.

Lard

Lard is pork fat that has been rendered. In rendering, the fat is heated, causing the connective tissues to brown and turn crispy. They are then strained from the fat to purify the lard. Lard provides a slightly nutty flavour and because of its richness, it creates very tender, flaky pastries and pie crusts. It can be used in place of butter in baking recipes, but the amount should be reduced by approximately 25 percent.

Margarine

Margarine is made from partially hydrogenated vegetable oil, water, milk solids, salt and generally colouring. It is similar to butter in appearance and texture. Its flavour is also similar to butter but is not as rich. In addition to regular margarine (containing 80% fat), it is available in several other varieties, such as reduced fat (containing 60% fat), low-fat (containing 40% or less fat), and fat-free (containing less than half a gram of fat). It can be used in most recipes in place of butter but there will be a slight loss of flavour. For best results when substituting margarine, use regular margarine and not one of the reduced fat varieties. Margarine will create a softer dough but butter should be used when making pastries to provide the most flakiness.

Oil

Oils are extracted from seeds and fruits such as corn, cottonseed, soybean, sesame, sunflower, safflower, olive, and avocado. Some oils are extracted from nuts such as peanut, walnut, almond, and hazelnut. Oils are used to fry and sauté foods, for making salad dressings, and as an ingredient in baking. Some of the common oils used for these purposes are vegetable oil, corn oil, canola oil, olive oil, sunflower oil, soybean oil, and peanut oil. Oil is used in recipes for breads, cakes, cookies and muffins. Oil can be used in place of butter or margarine in most recipes by using 7/8 cup of oil for each cup of butter or margarine that is called for. Substituting the oil will result in the finished product having a heavier texture. Because oil has a higher smoke point than butter or margarine, it works better for sautéing, frying, deep-frying and stir-frying.

Kosher Salt

A coarse grained salt that does not contain any additives. It is preferred for its texture and flavour. Because it is coarser grained, it takes up more space when measuring. When using it in place of regular salt, you will need to increase the amount called for in the recipe. Add an additional 1/8 tsp. of kosher salt when the recipe calls for 1 tsp. of salt.

Oatmeal

A cereal ground from hulled and cleaned oats. It can be

cooked to eat as a breakfast cereal or it can be used as an ingredient for baking. Oatmeal is available as old fashioned rolled oats, which are larger flakes that take approximately 15 minutes to cook or as quick-cooking oats, which are smaller cut flakes that take approximately 5 minutes to cook. Both types can be interchanged when baking. It is also available as an instant oatmeal, which is oatmeal that is made up of very small cut flakes that are precooked and dried. They require minimal cooking but are not recommended for use in baking.

Pearl Sugar

Large, smoothly polished crystals of sugar, which are used for decorating purposes.

Pepper

A savory spice that has been ground from peppercorns. Pepper is available as whole peppercorns that can be freshly ground and can also be purchased cracked or in ground form.

Powdered Sugar

Granulated sugar that has been finely ground into a powder. It is used to make creamy frostings and to add a decorative coating to baked goods. Cornstarch is sometimes added to the powdered sugar to prevent it from absorbing moisture and forming clumps. Also referred to as confectioner's sugar.

Salt

Salt is a seasoning that sharpens the flavour of other ingredients. If the amount of salt called for in a receipe is reduced, other seasonings should be increased to compensate for the flavour loss. Salt will also enhance the sweetness of a food. The salt in yeast dough slows the fermentation of the yeast, so reducing the amount of salt used will affect the finished product. The loaves of bread that will rise to quickly, which will affect the flavour and shape of the loaves.

Salt Substitute

Generally a salt substitute consists of potassium chloride. It is bitter in taste but provides for a lower sodium intake. It should not be used in baking. There are also salt substitute mixtures available which consists of a mix of potassium chloride and sodium chloride.

Sea Salt

Sea salt is produced through the evaporation of sea water. It is available in fine and coarse grained crystals. It is preferred for its fresh, distinctive taste, which will vary depending on the location it is from.

Spices

Spices are taken from a variety of plants. Spices are found in the stems, roots, buds, bark, seeds, and fruit of plants. They have strong aromas and strong flavours that are used to add flavour to baked and cooked foods. Most spices are available in both whole and ground form. Ground spices will lose their potency faster than whole spices. Some of the spices you will find are allspice, aniseeds, caraway, cayenne pepper, chili powder, cinnamon, cloves, coriander seeds, cumin, curry powder, fennel seeds, ginger, juniper berries, mace, nutmeg, paprika, pepper, peppercorns, saffron, Sichuan pepper, star anise, sumac, and turmeric.

Superfine Sugar

Granulated sugar that has been ground into extra-fine granules. Superfine sugar melts easily in liquid and works well in most baking recipes.

Table Salt

A fine-grained salt that contains additives that prevent caking, which allows the salt to flow freely. It is also available with iodine added. Table salt is used as an "at the table" seasoning that is added to food when it is eaten at a meal but is also used as an ingredient when baking and cooking. It should not be used in canning and pickling because the additives in it can cause the water to turn cloudy and pickles to darken in colour.

Unflavoured Gelatin

Unflavoured gelatin is made from the collagen protein found in the bone, skin, and cartilage of animals. It is added to sweet and savory foods to cause the liquid in the dishes to jell, which thickens or gives shape to the dish. One tablespoon of gelatin is generally enough to jell two cups of liquid.

Wheat Germ

Refers to the embryo of the wheat kernel, which is removed for the production of refined white flour, but remains as part of whole-wheat flour. The wheat germ is a good source of protein, vitamins, and minerals. It is used to add fiber and flavour, and can be substituted for up to 1/3 of the flour called for in a recipe.

Yeast

Tiny microorganisms that grow and multiply when activated by the addition of warm water. As the microorganisms increase in size and number, they give off carbon dioxide, which causes the dough to rise and produce a light and airy loaf of bread. The addition or removal of other ingredients, such as sugar and salt, affect the action of the yeast, and if less yeast is used than called for, it will increase the amount of time it takes the dough to reach the proper volume. There are three types of yeast available, which include active dry yeast sold in granule form; compressed fresh yeast sold in cake form, which is found in the refrigerator section of a food store; and quick-rising yeast, which decreases the rising time by approximately 1/3 in comparison to active dry yeast.

Solid Ingredients

Almond Paste

A paste made from blanched almonds, sugar and glycerine. The paste is used as a flavouring agent for pastries. Almond extract is sometimes added to the paste to bring out the almond flavour. The paste is also used for decorating baked goods. Almond paste is similar to marzipan but they are not interchangeable in recipes.

Baking or Bitter Chocolate

Unsweetened chocolate that contains no other ingredients other than chocolate liqueur and 50 to 58% cocoa butter. Do not substitute any of the sweetened chocolates in a recipe calling for unsweetened chocolate.

Caramel

Sugar that has been slowly heated until it melts and becomes slightly burned. Once the sugar has melted, it takes on varying degrees of colour and develops a distinct flavour. If it is cooked too long it will become bitter and quite dark in colour. It is used in candies, desserts and savory dishes to add colour and flavour.

Caramel Candies

Candies made form butter, sugar and cream. They are generally sold as small square candies that are individually wrapped. These squares are melted and used as a filling or topping for desserts or baked goods. They are also melted and. used to coat apples to make caramel apples.

Chocolate

Cocoa beans are ground and then processed to separate the cocoa butter from the chocolate liqueur. The chocolate liqueur is then further processed and mix with other ingredients to create different varieties of chocolate. Some of the different varieties are dark chocolate, milk chocolate, white chocolate, unsweetened, bittersweet, and semi-sweet chocolate.

Cream Cheese

A smooth white cheese that is made from cream and milk. Cream cheese is a fresh cheese so it does not keep for a long period of time. It has a sweet tangy flavour, and is available in several varieties: regular, which contains about 33% milkfat; light, which is softer and contains less calories and fat than regular; nonfat, which is made from skim milk and contains no fat; and whipped, which is regular cream cheese that has been whipped to make it fluffy and easier to spread. It is also available in several flavours. Cream cheese is used as a spread but is also used to make dips, desserts and frostings.

Dark Chocolate

Dark chocolate includes sweet, semisweet and bittersweet chocolate. They are made up of chocolate liqueur, sugar and vanilla. Bittersweet contains more chocolate liqueur than sweet and semisweet chocolate.

Fruits

There are many different types of fruit that are used in baking and cooking, such as apples, bananas, oranges, lemons, limes, pineapple, strawberries, peaches, pears, apricots, and berries. They are used fresh, cooked, and dried. Check the recipe for the type of fruit needed and how it needs to be prepared.

Raisins

Raisins are dried grapes, which can be eaten plain or used as an ingredient in both sweet and savory dishes. They are available in two varieties, dark and golden. The dark raisin is dark in colour, has a drier, more shriveled texture, and has a sweet flavour. The golden raisin is a light golden colour, is more moist and plump, and has a sweet, tangy flavour. Raisins add flavour and texture to salads, baked goods, and cooked dishes.

Sour Cream

Sour cream is a dairy product produced from sweet pasteurised cream. It has a thick consistency and a flavour that is slightly tangy. It is fairly acidic, which activates the leavening action of baking soda. It is used as a topping and for making dips. It is also used as an ingredient in both sweet and savory dishes. Sour cream is also available in low-fat and nonfat varieties.

Vegetables

There are many different types of vegetables that can be used when cooking, such as potatoes, beans, peas, carrots, corn, onions, broccoli, cauliflower, and many more. They are used fresh, cooked, and dried. Check the recipe for the type of vegetables needed and to see how they need to be prepared. Vegetables are used on their own to create a vegetable dish or with other ingredients to create a one-dish meal.

White Chocolate

White chocolate is not actually a true chocolate because it

does not contain any chocolate liqueur. It contains pure cocoa butter, sugar, milk solids, lecithin, and vanilla. It is can be eaten on its own or it can be used in cookies, cakes, bars, and desserts. It is also used as a coating on snacks, such as pretzels and nuts.

Liquid Ingredients

Buttermilk

Traditionally buttermilk was the liquid that was left after whole milk has been churned into butter, but today commercial buttermilk is produced by adding lactic-acid bacteria to low-fat or nonfat milk. Buttermilk has a thick consistency and adds a tangy flavour to baked goods, sauces, and dressings. It can be used in many recipes to replace yogurt and sour milk. Buttermilk is also available in powdered form.

Corn Syrup

A thick, sweet syrup extracted from corn. It is available in a light and dark variety. The light syrup is clear in colour and sweet but does not have much flavour. The dark syrup is brown in colour and has a sweet molasses or caramel-like flavour. Corn syrup works well in frostings, candies and jams because it hinders crystallisation. It produces a denser, chewier dough when used in baked goods. Corn syrup can also be used in place of honey or maple syrup but it is not as sweet so it may have a slight affect on the finished product.

Eggs

Eggs can be cooked and eaten as a food themselves but they also serve several purposes as an ingredient. They give cooked dishes and baked goods structure. They also add flavour, colour, liquid, protein, and fat. The egg yolks add to the tenderness and provide consistent flavour and texture to the product. Egg whites add volume to the recipe. Two egg whites can be substituted for one whole egg if concerned about cholesterol. Grade A large eggs are the best size to use for most recipes calling for eggs.

Evaporated Milk

Whole, low-fat, or nonfat milk that has had approximately 60% of the water removed. It has been heat-treated to sterilize it in the can. This allows the milk to be stored at room temperature. Evaporated milk is used undiluted in sauces, soups and custards to give them a rich creamy texture. It is also used in baked goods and other dishes. Do not interchange with sweetened condensed milk, which is very sweet and sticky. Evaporated milk can also be reconstituted by adding water and it can then be added to recipes calling for milk.

Extracts

Extracts are produced by extracting the oils from fruits, nuts, and plants and then dissolving the in an alcohol base. Extracts are used to add flavouring to baked goods, candies, desserts, sweet fillings, and frostings. There are imitation flavourings also available that are used in the same manner as extracts but to provide the best flavour to your foods use pure extracts. Some of the common extracts available are vanilla, almond, maple, anise, lemon, orange, and peppermint.

Food Colouring

A colouring solution used to add colour to foods. Food colouring is generally added to frostings or batters for decorating purposes but can also be added to other foods to enhance their colour. Food colouring adds colour but does not affect flavour. It is generally available in the primary colours and they can be mixed to create additional colours. Start with a small amount and add more to darken to the desired colour. Food colouring is also available in a paste form.

Heavy Cream

A dairy product that has a butterfat content of at least 36%. It is also known as whipping cream and double cream. Heavy cream provides a rich, creamy texture to the foods it is added to. It is used in sweet and savory sauces, baked goods, desserts and dessert toppings. It is also used as an ingredient in cocktail drinks.

Honey

Honey is the nectar from flowers and other plants that is collected by bees. Honey is used as a sweetener and has a distinctive flavour that is influenced by the type of flowers and plants that the nectar is taken from. A product containing honey is likely to be fairly moist because it contains fructose, which absorbs moisture from the air around it. When using honey in a recipe in place of sugar, use 3/4 cup plus 1 tablespoon of honey per cup of sugar being replace. The liquid in the recipe should also be decreased by 2 tablespoons to help offset the additional moisture that will be created by the honey. If too much honey is used in a recipe, excessive browning may occur. Honey is also used as a spread similar to jam or jelly. It is available in three basic forms—liquid honey (liquid containing none of the comb), chunk-style honey (liquid with pieces of the comb), and comb honey (a square or round piece of the honeycomb containing the honey inside).

Juices

Juices are liquids extracted from food items that are used to make beverages and sauces. The fruit juices are also used as liquid ingredients in recipes for some baked goods.

Fruit juices are acidic, so when combined with baking soda in a recipe, they cause the chemical reaction that results in the baking soda acting as a leavening agent.

Light Cream

A dairy product containing 18 to 30% milkfat, also referred to as table cream. It is used in making soups, sauces, desserts and baked goods. When used in place of heavy cream, the foods texture will not be as creamy. Light cream will separate or curdle easier than heavy cream so when using in soups and sauces, use a lower heat, heat slowly, and do not let it boil.

Low-fat Milk

Milk that has had most of the fat removed. It is available in varieties containing 1% or 2% milkfat. It can be used in recipes as a substitution for whole milk or fat-free milk.

Milk

When called for in a recipe it is referring to cow's milk. It is available as whole milk, low-fat milk, and skim (fat-free) milk. Also available powdered and condensed. Most often they are interchangeable in a recipe. The milk adds nutrition and browning capabilities. When heating milk, heat slowly and watch carefully to prevent it from scorching.

Molasses

A thick, strong flavoured syrup, produced as a byproduct of sugar refining. Molasses is used as a sweetener but is not as sweet as sugar. It is available in three varieties: light, which is from the first boiling and the sweetest of the three; dark, which is from the second boiling and is a little less sweet but has a deeper flavour; and blackstrap, which is from the third boiling and is very dark in colour with a bitter flavour. Blackstrap is rarely used in baking. Light and dark molasses are interchangeable in recipes, resulting in the finished product having a slightly deeper flavour when the dark molasses is used.

Skim Milk

A fat-free variety of milk that contains no more than .5% of milkfat. Skim milk can be interchanged with low-fat or whole milk in a recipe without a noticeable difference in the end product. Depending on the amount of milk called for in the recipe, you may notice slightly less flavour and richness when skim milk is substituted whole milk.

Soy Milk

A milk substitute made from pressed, cooked soybeans. Plain soy milk can be used in place of cow's milk in puddings, sauces and soups. Using soy milk in place of cow's milk will affect the taste of the end product. You may want to start by only replacing half of the cow's milk with soy milk. In addition to plain soy milk, there are flavoured varieties, and low-fat, fat-free, and fortified versions. Soy milk is high in protein, low in saturated fats, and cholesterol free. People who are lactose intolerant can use soy milk as a replacement for milk in some of their recipes. Soy milk has a tendency to curdle so you have to be careful when adding to acidic foods.

Sweetened Condensed Milk

Whole milk that has had 60% of the water removed and then sugar added. The amount of sugar added makes up 40% of the sweetened condensed milk's volume. It is very sweet and sticky, and adds a richness to the foods it is added to. It is used to make candies, bars, pies, and puddings. Sweetened condensed milk turns a golden colour and takes on a caramel like flavour when heated. It also thickens as it is heated.

Vinegar

An acidic solution resulting from allowing wine or an alcoholic liquid to ferment a second time. Vinegar adds a sour, pungent taste to the foods it is added to. It has a tendency to lose its pungency when heated so if you desire a stronger flavour from the vinegar when adding it to a heated dish, you should add it after the dish is removed from the heat. The two most common types of vinegar are apple cider vinegar, which has a tart fruity flavour and distilled white vinegar, which has a more pungent flavour that is too harsh for regular cooking. Apple cider vinegar is most often used in recipes for foods such as salads, dressings, sauces, marinades and condiments. The distilled white is used most often for pickling and cleaning purposes. Other varieties include balsamic vinegar, malt vinegar, wine vinegar, and rice vinegar.

Sanitation and Hygience in Baking

Bakery personnel should maintain extreme cleanliness and sanitation in the bakery to protect the health of the consumer of bakery foods. It is the responsibility of the bakery production manager or the person in charge to make daily inspections of the bakery and personnel. It is advisable to set up a cleaning frequency chart to provide for the daily cleaning of every area of baking equipment that actually touches the baked bread or pastry. Cream-filled pies and whipped cream products have been involved in food poisoning outbreaks. Protection against Staphyloccus poisoning can be controlled by good sanitation practices and by holding of prepared foods under refrigeration until they are served. At a temperature of 42 degrees F. or lower, the growth of staphylocci is completely inhibited. This temperature is merely a safeguard, but it is not completely reliable, since the bacteria merely becomes dormant at the low temperature and resume their active growth as soon the temperature is raised to a suitable level.

Breeding of insects and animal pests such as rats and mice will cause unsanitary conditions. Rodents not only eat costly ingredients and manufactured products, but they also create a potential danger to consumers of bakery foods. Rodents are dangerous transmitters of Yellow Jaundice, Typhus, Food Poisoning, and Tapeworms or other internal parasites. To prevent the entrance of rodents, seal the bakery tightly. When preventive measures fail, and rodents get inside the bakery, use traps or call a Pest Control Agency. Clean all flour bins, conveyors and flour sifters. All dead flour which is flour that collects at the bottom, sides, and inside of the flour handling equipment should be removed to prevent insect eggs from hatching.

Salmonella has been known to be present in eggs, dried milk, and cocoa. Any of these ingredients, when incorporated in foods could be a source of infection. Baking usually inactivate these organisms, however, if infected marerials exist in the bakery, re-infecting the baked product is possible. When Staphylococci infects an individual, it may be dead, but the poison produced by this bacterium can still make one sick. The poison is not destroyed by heat. However, Salmonella does not produce any poison and must be alive to make one sick.

All bakery personnel should observe and practice rules of cleanliness such as keeping the body clean. The bakery should provide hot showers for bakery personnel. Clean white uniforms including headgear should be worn while on duty. Arm pits should always be covered. Hands should be washed with soap and hot water when returning from work after any absence, particularly after using the toilet. Personnel having skin eruptions or infectious cuts should never be allowed to work with food. Clean bakery equipment should be mandatory in bakery production, because unsanitary bakery equipment may cause the two most dreaded deseases in bakery foods-mold and rope.

Food inspectors, state health department inspectors, and city health department inspectors are authorised to perform inspections. Also inspectors from the American institute of baking which developed the consolidated sanitation standards are recognised by the government and are authorised to make legal inspections. These inspections are authorised to be made at reasonable working hours. When inspectors arrive at the bakery, he or she presents credentials before presenting the notice of inspection form to the plant manager.

2

Wheat Flour: The Elementary Ingredient of Baking

Wheat flours do one thing extremely well that the flours of other grains cannot: create a gluten network. Gluten is the substance formed when two proteins present in flour, glutenin and gliadin, are mixed with water. Gluten is both plastic and elastic. It can stretch and expand without easily breaking. A gluten structure allows dough to hold steam or expanding air bubbles, so that yeasted dough can rise and puff pastry can puff.

As with many discoveries, the domestication of wheat and the making of risen bread was as much accident as intent. A truly remarkable series of fortuitous, mutually beneficial interactions between wheat and humankind helped to guarantee the success of both species.

Domestication

Today's wheat is descended from wild grasses. Our hunter-gatherer ancestors certainly supplemented their diets with large-seeded wild wheat grasses for thousands of years, perhaps even cultivating the stands sporadically. Necessity, however, seems to have been the impetus for domestication of these wild grasses. A climatic shift about 10,000 years ago in the southern Levant (modern Jordan and Israel) brought warm, dry summers. Heat-resistant adaptive grasses thrived as other vegetable food sources diminished. Humans harvested the grasses more frequently, especially favoring the large-seeded, nutrient-packed wild wheats like einkorn and emmer.

Wild wheats are self-sowing. That is, the upper portion of the grass stem that bears the seeds, the rachis, becomes brittle upon maturity. It breaks apart easily in a good breeze or upon contact, scattering the seeds that will become next year's plants. Archeologists and agricultural scientists theorise that when humans gathered the wheat, most of the seeds fell to the ground. The seeds that made it home, attached by an unusually tough rachis, were mutants.

Inadvertently, humans selected wheat that would not have survived natural selection: If the stem and kernels remain stubbornly intact, the grass is no longer self-sowing. Perhaps this new wheat was easier to transport back to camp in quantity, meaning a bit of leftover grain could then be planted conveniently close by. In a span of what archeologists estimate to be less than thirty years, humans and this now co-dependent strain of wheat set up housekeeping. Hunter-gatherers became farmers.

Transformation

Selection continued to occur not only for obvious boons like bigger kernels and greater yields but also for ease of processing. The advent of a free-threshing wheat, where the seed or kernel separates relatively easily from the husk by mere agitation, was a critical step in the evolution toward bread wheat. Previously, parching—or heating the grain on a hot stone—was a favored method for removing the tightly attached husk from the kernel.

The more palatable naked kernels were then softened in boiling water and the resulting gruel was eaten plain or baked later into flatbreads. And flat was most likely the name of the game: Parching at least partially denatures or cooks the gluten-forming proteins in wheat, as well as destroys critical enzymes that help yeast convert sugar into starch. With free-threshing wheat, raw wheat kernels sans husk could be dried and ground, and the resulting "flour" had the potential to consistently produce risen loaves.

Wild yeasts had probably colonised grain pastes on occasion, but it was the availability of a wheat flour that could form a gluten network which made leavened bread feasible. The baker could replicate yesterday's loaf by saving a bit of the old risen dough to use as leavening for the next day's batch. The risen loaves had an appealing texture and aroma, as well as providing a more easily digestible form of nutrients.

The Egyptians were using baked loaves of risen bread to start the fermentation process in beer by 5000 B.C.E. The brewery's use of malted grain (usually barley or wheat, sprouted and then lightly toasted) in the beer ferment (wort) attracted the species of yeasts and their symbiotic bacteria that produce bread humans find most appealing.

The yeasty dregs of the beer provided bakers with a reliable, predictable yeast variety that is the ancestor of commercial yeast used today. During the Dark Ages and up until the nineteenth century, wheat waned a bit, perhaps because it required more effort and time than its more self-sufficient cousins like rye and oats. Wheat returned to preeminent stature early in the twentieth century.

Modern Wheat

Wheat is the second largest cereal crop in the United States; corn, with its myriad uses in industrial food and even nonfood applications, ranks first. Worldwide, however, wheat or rice, depending on the region, is the dominant food grain. It is wheat's gluten-forming proteins, so inextricably linked with the development of baking, that, when combined with a willingness to adapt to new environments and new demands, help to explain its enormous popularity.

It grows well over a wide range of moderate temperatures. It is relatively easy to cultivate and consistently produces high crop yields. The wheat kernel has high nutritional value and good keeping qualities. Wheat can be processed with very little waste; what is not sold as flour is used for animal feed.

Genetically, wheat carries seven chromosomes to a cell. In diploid wheats like einkorn, there are two sets of chromosomes per cell. In tetraploid wheats—durum wheat being the best known example—there are four sets of chromosomes per cell. Hexaploid wheats have six sets of chromosomes and include bread wheat (*Triticum aestivum*), club wheats, and spelt wheats. *Triticum aestivum* accounts for 92 percent of the American wheat crop.

Of the remaining percentage, about 5 percent is *Triticum durum*, or durum wheat, and 3 percent is *Triticum compactum* (red and white club wheats). Durum wheat is used almost exclusively in pasta making, and the club wheats are used in crackers and other products requiring flour with a low protein content.

Classes of Bread Wheat

Of the types of bread wheat grown here in the United States, 5 primary classifications are of major importance:

hard red spring wheat, hard red winter wheat, soft red winter wheat, hard white wheat, and soft white wheat. Hardness, growing season, and color are the three criteria used to draw the distinctions among these classes. *Hard* and *soft* refer not only to the actual hardness of kernel of wheat (i.e., how hard it is to chew) but more specifically to the kernel's protein content: The hardest wheats genetically contain more protein and fewer starch granules. Hard wheats contain a layer of water-soluble protein around the starch granules; in soft wheats this trait is far less prominent.

For the baker, this means that hard wheat flours produce doughs capable of the greatest gluten development. These hard or "strong" flours are ideal for bread. Hard wheats are grown where rainfall is low and the soil is more fertile, generally west of the Mississippi River and east of the Rocky Mountains up into Canada. Hard wheats account for about 75 percent of the American crop, but only a tiny amount of the Western European crop. This factor requires some juggling of flours when, for instance, adapting a classic French baguette recipe for American flour.

Generally, soft wheats have a high starch yield on milling and a low protein content. They are grown in areas of high rainfall and lower soil fertility, primarily east of the Mississippi River. Low-protein southern flours are deployed to their best advantage in their growing region's specialties—biscuits, pies, and cakes where tenderness is prized over strength. Beyond wheat's given genetic quotient of hardness or softness, environmental conditions determine the hardness of any given crop. Not only the overall protein content but also the quality and specific amounts of each protein present can be affected by seasonal variations.

Winter and *spring* refer to the two growing seasons for wheat. Winter wheats are planted in the fall. They grow for a very short period of time, become dormant during winter, resume growing in the spring, and are harvested in early summer. They are usually grown in areas that have relatively dry, mild winters, like Kansas. Winter wheat is generally higher in minerals. Spring wheats are planted in the spring and harvested in late summer. They are usually grown in areas with severe winters, such as Minnesota and Montana. Spring wheat usually contains more gluten than winter wheat of the same variety. Color is the final determining criterion in classifying wheat.

A slightly bitter red pigment is present in the seed coat of red wheats, similar to the tannins in tea; this trait has been bred out of white wheats. Hard white wheats are used primarily in whole wheat products where the bitter taste is undesirable, but a relatively strong flour is desired. Tortillas and bulgur are examples. Hard white wheat flour is also becoming popular with artisan bread bakers. Its higher mineral (ash) content makes it ideal for long fermentation periods, and it has a slight natural sweetness. Red wheat generally has more gluten than white wheat.

Components of the Wheat Kernel

A wheat kernel consists of three basic parts: the bran, the germ, and the endosperm. The bran consists of several layers of protective outer coverings. The aleurone layer of starch-free protein that surrounds the endosperm is not truly a part of the bran, but usually comes off with it during the milling process. The bran, comprising 13 to 17 percent of the weight of the wheat kernel, contains relatively high amounts of celluloses (fiber), protein, and minerals. The endosperm, the part of the kernel beneath the bran covering, acts as a food reservoir for the growing plant. It composes 80 to 85 percent of the grain's weight, including the aleurone layer removed with the bran. The endosperm consists of starch granules embedded in a matrix made up of gluten-forming proteins. In its center, near one end, is the germ. The germ, composing 2 to 3 percent of the kernel's weight, is the embryonic wheat plant. It contains high levels of proteins, lipids, sugars, and minerals.

Grist milling

Milling is the mechanical process in which wheat kernels are ground into a powder or flour. Beginning with simple crushing in a mortar and pestle, humans rapidly devised more and more efficient ways to accomplish this feat. The ancient Egyptians advanced to grinding the grain (grist) between two large flat stones (grooved or dressed to let the fine flour particles escape), moving in opposite directions and driven by animal power. Grist mills soon employed the power of running water to drive wheels. Stone-ground flour is de facto whole-grain flour; only when the flour is bolted or sifted will it become white stoneground flour. The finer the sieve, the whiter the flour will be; it will, however, always contain some of the finely crushed wheat germ. Flour was usually produced in just one session of grinding—only with the advent of new harder wheat varieties was it necessary to pass the grist through again, this time with the stones set closer together.

Stoneground flour is generally produced without generating excessive heat, which is thought to be beneficial to both flavor and performance of the flour in breads. Also, the presence of small amounts of finely ground wheat bran (with its relatively high amounts of pentosans) is believed to increase moisture content in breads and helps prevent staling. Wheat germ provides a nutty, pleasant taste and aroma to the baked loaf. Flour must be oxidised before it is ready to use. This can be done by adding a chemical to the flour or it can be done naturally by letting the flour age.

Natural aging, or oxidising, takes three to six weeks. In whole-grain or stone-ground white flours, natural aging of flour can be problematic since both the thiol groups and the fats (wheat germ oils) oxidise. When fats oxidise, they become rancid; therefore, the aging must be done at a cool temperature. Once purchased, naturally aged whole-grain flours must be stored in the refrigerator if they are not used in a timely fashion. Use freshly milled whole-grain flours promptly—or, even better, grind the grain as needed if you work on a very small scale—to prevent off flavors from developing.

Roller milling

For the past hundred years, roller milling has been used to produce the majority of flours. It is especially suited for producing white flours. Roller milling, in addition, creates the capability to produce hundreds of "streams" of flour from one single grain stock. Flour producers can combine various streams to produce flours of a desired protein content or particular makeup.

In either grist or roller milling, the kernel is first cleaned in a series of operations designed to remove dust and any foreign particles. In roller milling, the wheat kernel is then dried and rehydrated to a specific moisture content designed to optimise the separation and grinding processes that follow. At this point, different strains of wheat can be blended to produce a stock with the desired characteristics. The first pass between heavy ridged metal rollers revolving toward one another serves to break the kernel into its component pieces; this first break roll produces some flour, chunks of endosperm (termed variously "shorts," "overtails," or "overs"), bran, and germ.

The process is repeated another four or so times, using rollers with successively smaller grooves that are set closer and closer to one another. These are all break rolls, designed to separate the endosperm from the bran. The germ is quite plastic owing to its high oil content and is easily flattened into a single plug on the first couple of passes. It is usually removed by the third break roll (despite its high nutritive content of lipids or fats) because it easily becomes rancid and will cause spoilage in the resulting flours.

The bran is somewhat flexible and progressively detaches from the endosperm in large flakes. After each break roll, the stock is sifted or bolted to remove the flour, the smaller and smaller pieces of endosperm (or middlings), and bran pieces. After about the sixth break, practically all that remains is bran. Bran is removed from white flours since its particles have sharp edges that can disrupt gluten formation.

Flour grades

At this point all the middlings (endosperm fragments) plus minute amounts of germ and bran are sifted and then ground into flour between smooth rollers in a series of seven to nine reduction rolls. Flour, middlings, and bran are again produced every pass, separated out by bolting, with the middlings continuing through further rolls. Different streams of flour may be separated out at any point to be sold. All flour streams contain individual starch grains, small chunks of the protein matrix in which the starch is embedded, and bigger chunks of the protein matrix with some of the starch granule still attached.

Different streams of flour will have different ratios of starch to protein, however, and may be kept and packaged separately for this feature. The first flour streams separated out in the breaking process contain the least bran and germ; they are more "refined." These are sold as patent flours. Within this class are further grades ranging in refinement (or absence of bran and germ) from fancy to short to medium to long. Subsequent streams of refined middlings produce flours known as clear flours. These also have grades from fancy clear to first clear to second clear. Lower grades of flour are usually quite dark and are most frequently used in combination with other flours, particularly in rye bread baking.

Extraction rate

From a given batch of 100 pounds of grain, only 72 pounds of straight flour result. A straight flour is one in which all the various streams of flours are combined. Of the remaining 28 pounds, the separated bran or germ may be added back in varying percentages to make "whole wheat" flour. The final shorts—a mixture of bran bits, plus some pulverised endosperm and germ—is sold as animal feed. The 72 pounds of flour from 100 pounds of grain is referred to as a 72 percent extraction rate, meaning there is little or no bran or germ in the finished flour.

European flours generally have a slightly higher extraction rate—between 75 and 78 percent. The inclusion of more bran and germ, along with the fact that European wheat is softer, means that French bread flour has about 2 percent less protein than American bread flour. Many artisan bread bakers making hearth breads prefer a higher extraction flour (one with more residual bran and germ) for its flavor and baking quality. Home bakers can achieve roughly the same substance by adding a small percentage of sifted whole wheat to their bread flour.

Fractionation

Since the 1950s a technique has existed called fractionation that can produce flours that are significantly higher or lower in protein content than the parent stock. Flours with different ash contents, particle size, or amylase activity than the parent stock can also be produced. It's a complicated process involving air streams and centrifugal force, but it basically uses particle size and density to sort for the desired characteristics.

Flour and oxidation

Flour that is freshly milled, or green, does not make great bread. The dough is lacking in extensibility, and is slack and difficult to handle. The resulting baked loaves tend to have coarse crumb and poor volume. Aging the flour over a period of several months with repeated stirring so that fresh flour is continually exposed to air corrects this problem.

The process of oxidation thus occurs naturally; as the flour sits and is repeatedly exposed to air, many of the thiol groups on the protein molecules oxidise, or give up their free sulfur to an oxygen molecule. If not oxidised, these thiol groups can disrupt the sulfur-to-sulfur protein bonds that help give a dough elasticity as gluten is developed; these are the bonds that allow a dough to snap back into shape after being stretched. In unaged flour, thiol groups grab onto the free sulfur when the dough is stressed, the original sulfur-to-sulfur bond is broken, and the dough becomes slack.

Bromation and alternate methods of oxidising

As in any business, a period of waiting such as for oxidation is viewed as a hindrance to profit. And natural oxidation results are not always completely uniform. Large milling operations since the early 1900s have been sidestepping this process by the addition of inexpensive chemical oxidants. A few parts per million of potassium bromate was generally thought to strengthen the dough throughout the handling process as well as allow for shorter fermentation times, reduced mixing times, and faster processing. Any flour that has potassium bromate added is known as bromated flour.

However, since the early 1990s, potassium bromate has been suspected as a possible carcinogen; in 1991, California began mandatory labeling of all products containing potassium bromate. Although potassium bromate is still legal, the following substances have also been FDA approved as alternate oxidising agents in flour: ascorbic acid (vitamin C), azodicarbonamide (ADA), iodate of calcium, and iodate of potassium. In Germany and France, the only oxidising agent for flours allowed by law is L-ascorbic acid. Ascorbic acid is frequently used in the United States along with other oxidising agents to improve gluten quality.

Bleaching

Bleaching flour with one of several agents removes the xanthophyll, a carotenoid pigment that causes the flour to be slightly yellow in color. Some, but not all, bleaching agents can also perform the function of aging or oxidising the flour. Chlorine dioxide, chlorine, and acetone peroxide are used to both bleach and age flour. When bread flour is bleached it is usually done for color purposes alone: The bleaching agent, usually benzoyl peroxide, does not oxidise the flour. All-purpose flours are available bleached or unbleached, and cake flour is always bleached with chlorine. Bleaching with chlorine oxidises both the starches and protein present in flour at the relatively low levels employed in cake flour.

This oxidation improves dough strength, which seems antithetical to the idea of soft cake flour. Chemically bromated and/or bleached flours are designed to perform particularly well in industrial-scale breadmaking where their abilities to minimise fermentation and mixing times and make the dough withstand high-speed mixing are viewed as a bonus. Artisan breadmaking, with its long fermentation periods and relatively gentle handling of the dough, usually does not employ bromated or bleached flours.

The bleach residues may also adversely affect the balances of yeast and bacterial cultures in wild yeast starters. Bleaching affects the behavior of starch in flour much more advantageously than it affects the behavior of protein. Cake flour, milled from soft red winter wheat with a low-protein, high-starch content, profits from a certain degree of bleaching in several aspects. Chlorination makes the wheat starches in cake flour able to absorb more water, resulting in moister baked goods. (In bread flours, on the other hand, protein rather than starch is primarily responsible for flour hydration. The high protein content [needed to build gluten structure] of bread flour ensures adequately hydrated dough. Bleaching bread flour would be superfluous and counterproductive.)

Cake flour is traditionally bleached with chlorine gas and is left a bit acidic. Fat will stick to chlorinated wheat starch, but not to unchlorinated starch. Air bubbles in creamed cake batters are dispersed primarily in fat; distribution of bubbles is thus more regular and a finer texture is produced when bleached (cake) flour is used. The acidity will cause the structure of cakes to set faster as the starch gelatinises sooner in the oven, reducing baking time and keeping the cake moister. Acidity also discourages the development of gluten, important in making tender cakes.

Other additives

Some flours can be deficient in enzymes, particularly beta amylase, that convert starch into sugars. Since yeast feeds on sugar, not starch, this can be a problem. To correct an enzymatically unbalanced flour, either malted barley flour (from germinated grain) or fungal amylase is added at the flour mill. To perform this correction on your own, add ½ teaspoon of enzymatically active (diastatic) malted barley flour per 1 cup of flour. If bread doughs are fermenting sluggishly or have poor volume, the flour may not be enzymatically balanced. Too many enzymes produce a slack, sticky dough that results in gummy bread. Calcium phosphate may be added to bolster the leavening action of baking powder in doughs or batters that contain significant amounts of acidic ingredients like buttermilk.

Mold inhibitors like vinegar or other acids can discourage microbial action. Certain bacteria form thick-walled spores that are not killed by baking; they form sticky, yellowish patches in the bread that pull apart into ropelike strands. The addition of propionates (salts of propionic acid) inhibits the growth of both mold and rope-forming bacteria. Most of the vitamins present in wheat (particularly B-vitamins and vitamin E) are concentrated in the bran, the germ, and the aleurone layer of the endosperm that is removed with bran during milling. Whole-grain flours, flours with higher extraction rates, and the end streams of flours will contain more vitamins. Cake flour, with its lower extraction rate, contains the fewest vitamins. To offset the loss of these vital nutrients, the government dictates that flour be enriched with iron, B-complex vitamins, thiamin, riboflavin, niacin, and folic acid. Vitamin E is volatile, subject to oxidation and rancidity, and so it is not added to the flour. Flour is usually fortified by the miller.

Components of Flour

The wheat grain is characterised by a high carbohydrate content (about 70 percent), relatively low protein content (9 to 13 percent), low moisture content (11 to 13 percent), small amounts of lipids, a number of enzymes, and fiber, minerals, and vitamins. The carbohydrates are primarily starch and cellulose. The proteins include, of course, glutenin and gliadin, the gluten formers, as well as minute amounts of other proteins.

Lipids are present primarily in the germ and bran of the wheat kernel and are not a significant factor in white flours. Minerals make up what is known as the ash content of the flour. The ash refers to the amount of mineral residue left behind in a controlled burn of a flour sample. Vitamins, predominantly the B-complexes and vitamin E, are again present most significantly in the bran and germ, but are removed during milling and may be added afterwards.

Carbohydrates

Starch, dextrins, cellulose, pentosans, and various free sugars make up the carbohydrate content of wheat. Milling removes almost all the cellulose as well as most of the pentosans. Most fiber in wheat is in the cellulose.

Damaged starch granules (altered during the process of milling) play an invaluable role in structural development in leavened breads and batters. In yeast doughs, the amylase enzymes attack damaged starch first, producing sufficient simple sugars (carbohydrates) to feed the yeast during fermentation. Damaged starch also affects the formation of dextrins during baking and the moisture level of the finished product.

Ratios exist for the optimum level of damaged starch found to be beneficial in flour, directly correlating with the protein content of the flour. Flour contains a small amount of sugar; melbiose is converted by an enzyme in yeast, melbiase, to produce simple sugars directly available to the yeast as food. The pentosans in flour may amount to 2 to 3 percent, primarily in the tailings or end runs in milling. Pentosans can aid in producing bread with a higher moisture content and reduced staling.

Protein

Flour is produced from the endosperm of the wheat. The endosperm contains about 80 percent of the total amount of protein in the whole kernel. Gliadin and glutenin make up most of this and are usually present in almost equal proportions. Variations in their relative proportions may significantly affect gluten formation. Gliadin seems to be a key player in the volume attained in breadmaking, imparting viscosity and extensibility. Glutenin provides elasticity and strength to the dough. Both of these proteins are directly affected by both environment and genetics.

Environmental conditions influence protein quantity while genetics seem to determine protein quality. In other words, even low-quality wheat can produce some high-protein flours. The quality of wheat is determined, rather tautologically, by how well it performs in the task it has been given. Good cake flour will rely upon the same factors to produce lovely tender cakes that would produce horrible, flat, gummy bread. American hard wheat flours, with their high protein content and ability to absorb large amounts of water, may make it difficult to produce a European hearth bread with crisp, brittle crust and open crumb. Quality flours perform well over a broad range of protein contents.

Glutenformation

When wheat flour is mixed with water and stirred or kneaded, the glutenin and gliadin proteins not only bond with the water but also link and crosslink with one another to eventually form sheets of a flexible, resilient film called gluten. Gluten can trap air and gases formed by yeast, causing bread to rise. As the yeasts feed on the sugars, they produce a liquid containing both alcohol and carbon dioxide. The carbon dioxide is released upon contact into the air bubbles, enlarging them. In baking, the alcohol converts to gas, enlarging the bubble even more—producing ovenspring. Flexible starch granules held in place by the gluten network also bend around the air bubble.

The gluten protein eventually cooks, releases its water into the starch, and begins to firm. This provides the structural framework for the loaf of bread. As the starch gelatinises, it also becomes semi-rigid, giving even more support. In cakes or quick breads, however, too much gluten can be detrimental. The efficacy of chemical leaveners can be compromised when gluten prevents them from bubbling through a batter. Protein content determines how much water a flour can absorb—the greater the amount of protein, the more hydration is possible.

Enzymes

Enzymes are biochemical proteins that act as catalysts, meaning they have the ability to instigate chemical changes without themselves being changed. Flour naturally contains small amounts of enzymes called amylases and diastases that can break down starch into simple sugars needed by yeast. Wheat flour does not contain sufficient sugar for optimal yeast growth and gas production, but the enzymes break down damaged starch into maltose and glucose. Frequently wheat flour is deficient in these enzymes. As a corrective measure, additional enzymes are introduced. The resulting flour is enzymatically balanced.

The first source of these enzymes was malted wheat flour, then malted barley flour, and most recently fungal amylase. Sprouted, or malted, grain increases the presence of diastase enzymes and is particularly beneficial to naturally leavened doughs. Enzyme activity confers a number of boons. Crust color improves from Maillard reactions (browning reactions) enhanced by increased amount of sugars. Flavor is improved by the same Maillard reactions.

Reactions induced by the addition of small amounts of certain heat-stable amylases present, for instance, in rye flour or in fungal amylase can continue well into baking, producing sweetness without the detrimental effects of added sugar on yeast fermentation and gluten structure of a dough. An excess of these enzymes, however, will cause too much of the starch to be converted to sugar and result in a flat loaf. One other class of enzymes, the proteases, is significant. An excess of protease enzymes, which prefer to digest gluten proteins, will result in slack, sticky dough.

Lipids

Only 1 to 2 percent of lipids make it past milling into flour. The glycolipids seem to aid the gluten-forming proteins in retaining the carbon dioxide gas produced in fermentation. In effect, they seem to be sealing the burst gas cells as the proteins denature during baking, preserving volume. Lipids can also bind glutenin to starch to gliadin; this very thin lipid layer increases plasticity and ovenspring. They may also help in preserving freshness in the baked bread for the same reason. Other lipids—free fatty acids such as lineoleic and linolenic acids and the monoglycerides—are oxidated by the enzyme lipoxygenase, naturally present in wheat, during the process of dough mixing. This causes a natural bleaching of the carotenoids, brightening the crumb, imparting a pleasantly nutty flavor, and binding those troublesome thiol groups that cause poor dough performance.

Mineralcontent

Minerals are the inorganic substances present in wheat that are derived from the soil. Wheat flour contains anywhere from 1 to 2 percent minerals. Ash content is affected by the soil itself, rainfall, type and amount of fertiliser, and so on. Once again, during milling most of the wheat kernel that contains significant proportions of minerals is removed with the bran and germ.

The minerals that remain in white flour are actually in excess of what minerals occur in the endosperm. Thus, the ash content of the flour is directly related to the amount of bran particles in the flour. High-extraction flours generally have a high ash content. A level of at least .44 to .48 percent of ash in bread flour is viewed as favorable, and many artisan bread bakers prefer higher values. High ash content ensures the presence of minerals that cause the gluten formed to be more tensile.

Flour Varieties

Flour performs a number of functions in baked goods: It provides structure; it binds and absorbs; it affects keeping qualities; it affects flavor; it imparts nutritional value. Not every flour is going to do the same job well, so over the years "flour" has become many, many "flours." Pastry chefs today are presented with a bewildering array of flours tailored to meet specific requirements in different products. The big variable at the heart of this proliferation is protein content (and quality) and its consequences for gluten development. Modern milling practices can further modify the inherent ability of a specific wheat through choices in blending, milling, and processing.

Flour should be stored in a cool, dry, well-ventilated area free of odors. Flour can readily absorb odors that spoil the taste of the finished baked product. A storage temperature somewhere between 60 to 70°F is ideal. Wheat germ, wheat bran, or flours that contain significant amounts of them should be refrigerated as they quickly become rancid.

Non-wheat flours ryeflour

Rye is another member of the wild grass family whose cultivation stretches back into antiquity. Rye is hardier than wheat in challenging climates and is frequently grown either side by side or in rotation with wheat to ensure some sort of grain crop. More rye than wheat was grown during the Middle Ages, and it is still a favored grain in the colder European climates, especially the Scandinavian countries. Whole rye flour does not have enough of or the right kinds of gluten-forming proteins to make light bread by itself.

Rye does contain a roughly similar amount of protein, even both of the gluten-forming proteins, glutenin and gliadin, but in proportions smaller than in wheat. The gliadin in rye, however, doesn't interact with the glutenin in the same way as wheat gliadin does in forming gluten. Most of the structure provided by rye flour in bread comes from the interaction of its proteins with pentosans (gumlike substances) and the gelatinisation of its starch.

Rye doughs containing more than 20 percent rye flour rely on the viscosity of starches and pentosans to trap carbon dioxide gas and provide structure. Any air trapped in the dough is not enclosed in gluten cells that can expand, but in an unstable foam. As the loaf of rye bread enters the oven, in the absence of gluten, the gelatinised starch on the outside of the loaf forms a sort of skin that aids in gas retention. Wheat flour is added in varying amounts to compensate for the gluten deficiency in rye.

Another problem in making light, well-shaped rye loaves arises in the heat-stable nature of an enzyme, amylase, that breaks down starch. During baking, the starch granules in both wheat and rye uncoil from their crystalline structure and are basically dissolved in the water. This process creates a kind of gel that sets as it cooks, providing structure to the baked bread.

In wheat breads, the amylase enzyme is denatured or made inactive before starch gelatinisation takes place. In rye bread, however, this enzyme is far more heat-stable. This means the amylase is free to attack not just the initially available damaged starch, but the starch made available by gelatinisation. The result is that way too much starch is converted to sugar and the bread flattens, sags, and becomes heavy as the loaf undergoes hydrolysis. The action of rye amylase is inhibited, however, in an acid environment, especially in conjunction with salt. Traditional rye breads are made with sour starters; the low pH slows down enzyme action and protects the starch until the rye amylase is finally denatured during baking. Long fermentation also makes the rye more digestible.

Rye flour comes in a wide variety of styles and sizes. Commercial rye flour is usually not made from the whole grain; instead, different parts of the endosperm are separated out during the milling process. Most of the mineral content, and hence the ash percentage, of rye is contained in the outermost layer of the endosperm, just inside the bran coat. Ash content is significant in breadmaking as it can appreciably affect the vigorousness of natural fermentation. White rye flour is milled from the center of the endosperm.

Cream or light rye flour is from the next layer of the endosperm. Dark rye flour comes primarily from the outer portion of the endosperm. Rye is also available as a meal: ground from the whole kernel. Rye meal is available in various particle sizes, ranging to fine, medium, or coarse. The coarse grade of rye meal is what is commonly referred to as pumpernickel flour. Rye chops are the equivalent of cracked wheat. Rye bread is traditionally strongly flavored with caraway seeds. Its baking quality is dependent on its enzyme content, which can vary widely from one batch of grain to another. Wholegrain rye flours are particularly sensitive to deterioration in storage; not only do they smell rancid but their performance in doughs is compromised as well.

Rye flour is extremely hygroscopic, meaning that it will absorb moisture from the environment. For this reason, rye breads have an extremely high moisture content that translates to very good keeping qualities. It also means that the baking breads take longer to set. Occasionally rye breads are not sold until the following day.

Riceflour

Rice flour is produced by grinding uncoated rice. It is used like pastry flour and is a good substitute for wheat flour in food allergy cases as long as the appropriate changes are made in the recipe to accommodate the lack of gluten. Rice flour is traditionally used in some shortbread recipes owing to the fine, sandy texture it produces.

Cornmeal and cornflour

Cornmeal is available in two colors, yellow and white. Yellow cornmeal is a good source of vitamin A; white cornmeal is not. Either color of cornmeal is available in either a fine or coarse grind. Old-process cornmeal is prepared by grinding the whole corn kernel with the exception of the outer bran coat. New process, or degerminated cornmeal, has the germ and all the bran removed. Degerminated cornmeal keeps better, as the fats in the germ do become rancid quickly. Old-process cornmeal, however, has superior flavor and food value. Cornmeal is used in some hearty breads, in muffins, and, of course, in cornbread. Corn flour is very finely ground degerminated cornmeal. It is used in crepes, cakes, muffins, and breads in combination with wheat flour.

Triticale

An extremely hardy and nutritious hybrid of wheat and rye cereal grasses, triticale is used primarily for animal feed in the United States. Triticale flour does not make good bread unless it is used in combination with wheat flour; it performs similarly to rye. Bread made from triticale alone will have poor volume and a gummy texture. The gluten formed by triticale is of poor quality; doughs are more extensible, but less elastic.

Soy flour

Soy flour is made from soybeans, a member of the legume family. Soybeans are cultivated worldwide, but only as a primary food crop in Asia. Elsewhere, soybeans are more frequently used to produce oils, both edible and industrial, and as animal feed. Since soybeans contain high levels of easily digestible protein and oils and are an excellent source of amino acids, their popularity and use in other forms are beginning to increase in Western culture.

Soy flour is frequently used in creating baked goods for those people who have allergies to wheat protein. Soy flour is usually defatted to prevent spoilage and heat-treated to remove the beany taste. When added to wheat bread in a percentage below 3 percent, defatted soy flour does not have any appreciable effect on the dough's performance or taste, other than a slight increase in water absorption.

Beyond this rate, it begins to disrupt gluten formation and good structure; soy flour has no elastic properties whatsoever. It is used in small quantities as a replacement for milk in breadmaking to improve texture and decrease staling. In doughnut making, up to 15 percent soy flour can be used to reduce oil absorption and improve shelf life. It can be added to chemically leavened baked goods in a higher proportion than to yeasted products.

Barley

Barley cultivation most likely began at the same time as wheat. Barley has two advantages over wheat: a short growing season and an extremely hardy nature. Flatbreads made from barley, a grain that has no gluten-forming proteins, were popular until the Roman era, when wheat was favored. During the Middle Ages, especially in the Scandinavian countries, barley was a staple food of the lower classes. In Middle Eastern countries today, barley is still widely used. Western countries use barley primarily as animal feed and to make malt—pulverised, sprouted grain.

Malted grain contains more of an enzyme that converts starch to sugar and is used to supplement wheat flour to ensure a good fermentation rate in yeasted breads. Malt is also used, of course, to transform grain mashes into beer or liquor. Barley is available in a number of forms for use in soups, pilafs, and breads. Hulled barley has been husked, but retains most of its bran; it is the most nutritious form of barley. Scotch or pot barley is triplepolished to remove the bran (and many of its nutrients). Pearled barley is polished even more and in the process loses not only its bran but its germ as well. Most of the vitamins, minerals, and fiber are also removed by this point. Barley flakes are made from the flattened whole seed and used like rolled oats. Barley flour is available in a range of whole-grain composition; whole-grain barley flour has a darker color and pronounced nutty flavor.

Oats

Oat products are available in a number of forms for the baker: rolled oats, quick oats, steelcut oats, and oat flour. Oats are processed differently from wheat and rye; an adherent husk must be removed from the grain before it can receive further processing. Once the oat berries or groats are hulled, they are heat-treated to both soften the groats and to inactivate the enzymes that would eventually cause the fats to become rancid. Rolled oats are groats that have been flattened by passage between two rollers. They are used primarily in cookies, whole-grain breads, streusels, and granola.

For quick oats, the groats are cut into pieces before being flattened; they require shorter cooking than rolled oats, but are used almost interchangeably in baking. Steelcut oats are quick oats that have not been flattened; they are used in specialty breads for their nutty flavor and nubby texture. Oat flour is either a by-product of the above processes or is milled intentionally as an end product from the whole groat. Oat flour is most frequently employed in chemically leavened products such as pancakes, waffles, and muffins. Since it has almost no gluten, it is not a primary bread ingredient.

Millet

Millet is an umbrella term for several unrelated cereal grains, including common millet, pearl millet, sorghum or milo, and teff. All of these grains have been cultivated for many thousands of years, throughout the world. Generally, all millets are small in size, but are very high in protein, around 16 to 22 percent. Millet grows well in hot, arid climates and even thrives in poor soils. In parts of Asia it is an important food source, usually consumed as a porridge, unleavened bread, or beer. Western cultures tend to use cooked millet as an ingredient in healthy, high-nutrition wheat breads.

Potato flour

Potato flour (ground dried potatoes) or dehydrated potato

flakes can be added to wheat flour in low percentages (typically around 3 percent). It can aid in moisture retention, act as an extender, and help to keep bread soft as it ages. Potato flour contains 8 percent protein and is higher in thiamin, riboflavin, and niacin than wheat flour.

Buckwheat

Buckwheat is not a cereal grain at all, not even a grass. It is a member of the same family as rhubarb and sorrel. Its kernels are actually achenes, or dry fruits, similar to the "seeds" in strawberries. Buckwheat grows well in cold climates and in poor soils. Eastern European cultures (especially Russian) and the Japanese use buckwheat most frequently. Buckwheat flour is used in a number of breads and pancakes, or blinis, as well as noodles. The whole buckwheat grain may be cooked in the same way as rice and is most familiar in the preparation known as kasha, a type of pilaf.

Miscellaneous seeds/ legumes

Peanut flour and cottonseed flour are high in protein with good amounts of vitamins, particularly the B-complexes. They are added in small percentages (under 5 percent) to increase the nutritive content of bread produced on a large commercial scale without changing the texture or flavor greatly.

Spelt

Spelt wheat is one of the ancestors of modern bread wheat. It is not free-threshing wheat; its hull requires considerable effort to remove. Hulled spelt wheat can be prepared like rice. It has a mellow, nutty flavor and a higher overall protein content than common bread wheat.

Spelt protein, however, is seemingly tolerated better by people with wheat allergies. Spelt flour can be substituted for wheat flour in recipes.

Quinoa

Quinoa is an annual plant of a family that includes beets, chard, and spinach. It is native to South America and has been grown in the Andes for over 5,000 years. It is very hardy, resistant to both cold and drought. Quinoa's many tiny seeds resemble a cross between millet and sesame seeds. Quinoa provides more nutrients than cereal grains; it is high in protein, magnesium, iron, and potassium. Quinoa can be used whole, cooked or soaked, in wheat health breads. Ground quinoa can be substituted for a small portion of the wheat flour in breads, cookies, and muffins. It is usually not used alone since it does not form gluten.

Amaranth

Amaranth is an herbaceous plant native to the Americas. It was farmed extensively in Mexico before the Spanish conquest. The seeds are rich in nutrients with a distinctive, slightly spicy flavor. Amaranth can be used whole, cooked or soaked, in health breads and is also available as a flour. Amaranth has no gluten-forming proteins; it could conceivably be used alone only in waffles, pancakes, or perhaps cookies. Any instance when some gluten formation is needed for structure, however, as in breads and cakes, it should be used in combination with wheat flour.

3

Fruits and Vegetables in Baking

Spring and summer are the seasons when stone fruits are at their finest. Cherries appear first in May, followed by apricots, peaches, plums, and nectarines. Because commerce can move agricultural goods all over the world fairly rapidly, it is possible to get fresh stone fruit from anywhere in the world no matter what the season.

When selecting stone fruits, choose those that look good, with even colour and only minor blemishes. Watch out for mold and decay, which is often on the underside of the fruit. Also, check for any tears or cracks in the skin. When choosing stone fruits, it's important to feel them. Generally they shouldn't be too hard or too soft. Softness means the meat of the fruit is less juicy and possibly even dried out and mealy.

Stone fruits should have a pronounced sweet aroma. Watch out for odd and sometimes chemical aromas, which mean there may still be a residue of sprays that were used on the fruit. One of my mottos when I'm selecting stone fruit is, "If it doesn't smell good, it won't taste good." If you can taste-test the stone fruit before you buy it, you will be able to see inside, smell the flesh, get some good mouthfeel, and most important, see if it tastes like it should.

Sometimes you must buy fruit before it is fully ripe because that is the only way you can get it. A big problem with underripe fruit is that it may have been picked too early and/or kept in cold storage too long. This means that it may not ripen fully. If you have this problem, my advice is not to buy from that purveyor again, if possible.

However, to ripen stone fruits, simply leave them out in the open at room temperature, away from direct sunlight, until they are fragrant and give slightly when touched. Once a day, turn the fruit around so all sides get exposed to the light and air evenly. Make sure to handle stone fruits with great care. They are easy to bruise, dent, tear, and poke holes into. All stone fruits must be thoroughly washed in cold water with very mild soap or a specified produce wash (so there won't be any soapy taste) before using to remove any pesticide residue. Don't wash them until you are ready to use them, or they may become moldy.

Apricots, nectarines, plums, and cherries don't need to be peeled for use. For apricots, nectarines, and plums, simply wash and dry them, then cut them in half around the center, gently twist the two sides against each other until they separate, and remove the stone. For cherries, remove their stems and use a cherry pitter or a small sharp knife to remove the center stone. Often it's necessary to remove the skin from peaches using a technique called blanching. To do this, bring water to a boil in a large saucepan or stockpot over high heat.

Using a sharp knife, score a small X in the bottom of each peach. Add the peaches to the hot water and let them boil for 1 or 2 minutes. Use a slotted spoon or skimmer to remove the peaches from the boiling water. Then, starting at the X, use a small sharp knife to gently peel the skin off of the peaches. It should slip off easily. If the peaches are too hot, peel them under cold running water.

Apricot Frangipane Tart

Frangipane is a classic French almond cream that is used as the filling for tarts and other pastries. This tart is a medley of complementary flavours. Almond pastry dough holds the frangipane filling, then apricot halves are fanned out over the top of the frangipane, which bakes up around them, leaving them nestled in a golden blanket. The top of the warm tart is brushed with apricot glaze, making it glisten. Makes one 9½-inch round tart, 8 to 12 servings.

Almond Pastry Dough

In the work bowl of a food processor fitted with the steel blade, combine the flour, almonds, sugar, and salt. Pulse until the almonds are very finely ground, about 1 minute.

Cut the butter into small pieces and add to the almond mixture. Pulse until the butter is cut into very tiny pieces, about 30 seconds.

The texture should be sandy with very tiny lumps throughout. In a small bowl, combine the lemon juice, 2 tablespoons of water, and the lemon zest. With the food processor running, pour this mixture through the feed tube. Process until the dough wraps itself around the blade, 30 seconds to 1 minute. If the dough seems dry, add the remaining tablespoon of water and process until the dough comes together.

Turn the pastry dough onto a large piece of plastic wrap. Shape into a flat disk and wrap tightly in a double layer of plastic wrap. Chill in the refrigerator until firm before using, about 2 hours. Chilling the dough relaxes the gluten in the flour so it won't be too elastic and will roll out easily. It also firms up the butter in the dough so it will need less flour when rolled out. If the dough is too firm, it will splinter and break when rolled out. Let it stand at room temperature for 10 to 15 minutes before rolling to become more pliable.

On a smooth, flat surface, roll out the pastry dough between sheets of lightly floured waxed or parchment paper to a large circle about 11 inches in diameter. Carefully peel the paper off the top of the dough. Brush excess flour off the dough, then loosely roll the pastry dough around the rolling pin without the other piece of paper. Place the tart pan directly underneath the rolling pin and carefully unroll the pastry dough onto it.

Gently lift up the sides and ease the pastry dough into the bottom and sides of the tart pan, pushing it lightly into the fluted edges. Trim off the excess pastry dough by running the rolling pin over the top of the pan. Or use your fingers to press against the top of the pan to trim the excess pastry dough.

Place the tart pan on a jelly-roll pan and chill while preparing the filling.

Center a rack in the oven and preheat it to 375°F.

Frangipane Filling

In the work bowl of a food processor fitted with the steel blade, combine the almonds and sugar. Pulse until the almonds are very finely ground, about 1 minute.

Add the egg, vanilla, and almond extract and pulse several times to blend together well.

Cut the butter into small pieces and add to the almond mixture.

Pulse several times to blend.

Add the flour and pulse until the mixture is smooth, about 15 seconds.

Transfer the frangipane mixture to the chilled pastry shell and spread it out evenly with a rubber spatula.

Assembly

Using a sharp knife, slice the fruit in half along the seam and remove the stones. Rounded sides up, cut each half horizontally into ½-inchthick slices, leaving them attached at one side. Place the halves around the outer edge of the tart, leaving about 2 inches of space between them. Gently press on the halves and they will fan out. Continue slicing and fanning the apricot halves, filling the center of the tart.

Bake the tart for 40 to 45 minutes, until the filling is puffed and light golden. Remove the tart from the oven and place on a cooling rack.

Apricot Glaze

Stir together the apricot preserves and liquid in a small saucepan. Bring to a boil over medium heat. Remove the pan from the heat and strain the glaze into a small bowl, pushing through as much of the pulp as possible.

Use a goose-feather pastry brush to lightly brush the top of the tart with the glaze. Don't apply a thick layer, which looks unappetizing. The purpose of the glaze is to keep the apricots from drying out and to make the top of the tart glisten.

Remove the sides of the tart pan (see page 42) before serving. Serve the tart warm or at room temperature.

Apricot Galette

Galette is a rustic, free-form fruit tart, baked directly on a lined baking sheet rather than in a tart pan. Some galettes are made with puff pastry, others with yeast dough, and yet others with sweet tart or pastry dough. This galette is made with pastry dough and is chock full of sweet, fresh apricots. It's a perfect summertime dessert. Makes one 9-inch tart, 8 to 10 servings

Pastry Dough

In the work bowl of a food processor fitted with the steel blade, combine the flour, sugar, and salt. Pulse briefly to blend.

Cut the butter into small pieces and add to the flour mixture. Pulse until the butter is cut into very tiny pieces, about 30 seconds. The texture should be sandy with very tiny lumps throughout. In a small bowl, combine the lemon juice, 2 tablespoons of water, and the lemon zest. With the food processor running, pour this mixture through the feed tube. Process until the dough begins to hold together. Turn off the food processor, remove the top, and feel the dough. If it holds together, it is done. If it is still crumbly, add the remaining tablespoon of ice water and process briefly, then check again.

Turn the pastry dough onto a large piece of plastic wrap. Shape into a flat disk and wrap tightly in a double layer of plastic wrap. Chill in the refrigerator until firm before using, about 2 hours. Chilling the dough relaxes the gluten in the flour so it won't be too elastic and will roll out easily. It also firms up the butter in the dough so it will need less flour when rolled out. If the dough is too firm, it will splinter and break when rolled out. Let it stand at room temperature for 10 to 15 minutes before rolling to become more pliable.

Apricot Filling

Using a sharp knife, slice the fruit in half along the seam. Remove the stone and cut the fruit into ½-inch-thick slices. You should have approximately 3 cups of sliced fruit.

Place the sliced apricots in a mixing bowl. Add the sugar and toss together to distribute evenly. Taste the fruit to see if it needs any more sugar.

Assembly

Center a rack in the oven and preheat it to 375°F. On a smooth, flat surface, roll out the pastry dough between sheets of lightly floured waxed or parchment paper to a large circle 11 to 12 inches in diameter. Carefully peel the paper off the top of the dough. Brush excess flour off the dough, then loosely roll the pastry dough around the rolling pin without the bottom piece of paper. Place the lined baking sheet directly underneath the rolling pin and carefully unroll the pastry dough onto the baking sheet. Mound the sliced apricots in the center of the dough circle, leaving a 21/2- to 3-inch border all around.

Cut the butter into small pieces and distribute evenly over the sliced apricots.

Fold the border up so that it partially covers the apricots. It will naturally form pleats as it is folded.

Brush the dough border with the cream, being careful that it doesn't run down the sides and under the galette. If it does, wipe it up because it can cause the bottom of the galette to burn. Gently lift up the folds of the dough and brush under those areas with cream, then replace the folds. Evenly sprinkle the sugar over the dough border. Bake the galette for 35 to 40 minutes, until light golden. Remove the pan from the oven and transfer to a rack to cool. Cut the galette into pie-shaped wedges to serve.

Apricot Streusel Pie

Fresh Apricots nestled in a classic pie dough shell are topped with a crumbly, crunchy topping full of toasted walnuts, light brown sugar, nutmeg, and chilled butter. This pie is perfect to bring to a picnic gathering. Makes one 9-inch round pie, 12 to 14 servings

Pie Dough

In the work bowl of a food processor fitted with the steel blade, combine the flour, sugar, and salt. Pulse briefly to blend.

Cut the butter into small pieces and freeze for 20 minutes. Add the butter to the flour mixture. Pulse until the butter is cut into pea-sized pieces, 30 to 45 seconds. The texture should be sandy with very tiny lumps throughout.

Remove the top of the food processor and sprinkle on 2 tablespoons of the ice water. Replace the top and pulse for 10 seconds. Squeeze a small amount of the dough in your hand. If it holds together, don't add any more water. If the dough is still very crumbly, add another tablespoon of water, pulse to blend, then check the dough again. It won't hold together unless you squeeze it, but that's the texture you want.

Turn the dough onto a smooth, flat work surface. Use the heel of your hand to push the dough a few times for a final blend. Don't mush all the butter into the dough, however. For a flaky crust, you want to see thin flicks of butter in the dough.

Shape the dough into a flat disk and wrap tightly in a double layer of plastic wrap. Chill in the refrigerator until firm before using, at least 2 hours. Chilling the dough relaxes the gluten in the flour so it won't be too elastic and will roll out easily. It also firms up the butter in the dough so it will need less flour when rolled out. If the dough is too firm, it will splinter and break when rolled out. Let it stand at room temperature for 10 to 15 minutes before rolling to become more pliable.

On a smooth, flat surface, roll out the pie dough between sheets of lightly floured waxed or parchment paper to a large circle about 12 inches in diameter. To tell if the dough will fit the pie pan, invert the pan over the dough. If there are 2 to 3 inches of dough that protrude beyond the sides of the pan, it will fit.

Carefully peel the paper off the top of the dough. Brush excess flour off the dough, then loosely roll the pastry dough around the rolling pin without the bottom piece of paper. Place the pie pan directly underneath the rolling pin and carefully unroll the pastry dough into the pan. Or loosely fold the dough in half. Carefully place it in half of the pie pan and gently unfold the dough. Gently lift up the sides and ease the pie dough into the bottom and sides of the pie pan. Trim off the excess pie dough at the top of the pan and crimp the sides.

Transfer the pie pan to a baking sheet and chill in the freezer for 15 to 20 minutes. This helps prevent the pie dough from shrinking as it bakes and sets the butter in the dough to ensure flakiness. Center a rack in the oven and preheat it to 350°F.

Egg Glaze

Using a fork, lightly beat the egg with the water in a small bowl.

Using a pastry brush, brush the glaze over the inside of the pie shell. This will help prevent the shell from becoming soggy from the apricot juice.

Apricot Filling

Using a sharp knife, slice the apricots in half along the seam. Remove the stone and cut the fruit into ½-inch-thick slices. Place the sliced apricots in a large bowl.

Add the sugar and toss together lightly to distribute evenly. Transfer the apricots to the pie shell. Cut the butter into small pieces and distribute evenly over the sliced apricots. Refrigerate the pie while preparing the topping.

Streusel Topping

Place the walnuts in a single layer in a cake or pie pan. Toast in the oven for 4 minutes. Shake the pan to stir the walnuts and toast for another 4 to 6 minutes, until lightly colored. Remove from the oven and cool.

In the work bowl of a food processor fitted with the steel blade, combine the flour, sugar, nutmeg, and salt. Add the toasted walnuts and pulse until the walnuts are coarsely chopped, 20 to 30 seconds. Cut the butter into small pieces and add to the dry ingredients. Pulse until the butter is cut into very small pieces, 30 seconds to 1 minute.

Evenly sprinkle the topping over the apricots in the baking pan.

Bake the pie for 35 to 40 minutes, until the topping is light golden.

Remove the pan from the oven and transfer to a rack to cool.

Cherry and Apricot Crisp

This is an easy dessert to make and to eat. A crumbly topping of toasted oats is scattered over fresh cherries and apricots, mixed together in a square pan, and then baked. It's excellent eaten either warm or at room temperature. Be sure to use fresh, sweet fruit for the best flavour. The final garnish for this delicious dessert is a scoop of lightly whipped cream. To make it even better, add a scoop of vanilla ice cream to each serving. Makes one 8-inch square crisp, 8 to 10 servings

Cherry and Apricot Filling

Use a cherry pitter or a small sharp knife to remove the pits from the cherries. Place the cherries in the baking pan.

Using a sharp knife, slice the fruit in half along the seam. Remove the stone and cut each half into quarters. Place the cut apricots in the baking pan. Toss the cherries and apricots together lightly to mix evenly.

Topping

Center a rack in the oven and preheat it to 350°F. Place the oats in a single layer in a cake or pie pan. Toast in the oven for 15 minutes, until light golden. Remove from the oven and cool slightly.

In the work bowl of a food processor fitted with the steel blade, combine the oats, sugar, cinnamon, nutmeg, and salt and pulse briefly to blend.

Cut the butter into small pieces and add to the dry ingredients. Pulse until the butter is cut into very small pieces, 30 seconds to 1 minute. Evenly sprinkle the topping over the fruit in the baking pan.

Bake the crisp for 25 to 30 minutes, until the topping is light golden.

Remove the pan from the oven and transfer to a rack to cool.

Garnish

Place the cream in the bowl of an electric stand mixer or in a large mixing bowl. Use the wire whip attachment or a hand-held mixer to whip on medium speed until frothy.

Add the confectioners' sugar and continue whipping the cream until it holds soft peaks.

Cut the crisp into squares, scooping up the fruit. Serve each square with a large dollop of whipped cream.

Cherry Clafouti

A Clafouti is a classic, rustic dessert that originated in the Limousin region of France. It is a cross between a tart and a custard dessert, traditionally made with unpitted black cherries that are native to the region. This version uses pitted cherries, which makes the dessert much easier to eat. The cherries are placed in a deep pie dish and covered with a thick pancake-type batter that puffs up around the cherries as it bakes. Makes one 10-inch clafouti, 8 to 10 servings.

Center a rack in the oven and preheat it to 375°F. Use your fingertips or a paper towel to butter the bottom and sides of the pie dish. Sprinkle the inside of the pan with sugar. Tilt and shake the dish so the sugar sticks to the butter. Turn the dish over and shake out any excess sugar over the sink.

Cherry Filling

Use a cherry pitter or a small sharp knife to remove the pits from the cherries. Place the cherries in the pie dish.

Batter

In a large mixing bowl, combine the eggs, milk, cream, butter, kirsch, and vanilla. Stir together to blend.

Add the flour and salt and whisk together until smooth.

Push the batter through a fine-mesh strainer to remove any lumps.

Pour the batter evenly over the cherries in the pie dish. Bake the clafouti for 40 to 45 minutes, until it is puffed and light golden. Remove the pan from the oven and transfer to a rack to cool.

Garnish

Dust the top of the clafouti evenly with confectioners' sugar. Cut into pie-shaped wedges and serve warm or at room temperature.

Cherry Pie

Fresh Cherries have a short season and this pie is one of the best ways to enjoy them. Sour cherries are the classic type used in this pie, but they can be hard to find. Bing cherries work equally well. The pie dough is made with a combination of unsalted butter and cream cheese, which gives it both a luscious flavour and a fiaky texture.

Makes One 10-inch round pie, 12 to 14 servings

Pie Dough

In the work bowl of a food processor fitted with the steel blade, combine the flour, sugar, and salt. Pulse briefly to blend.

Cut the butter into small pieces and freeze for 20 minutes. Cut the cream cheese into small pieces and add to the dry ingredients in the food processor. Pulse to cut the cream cheese into very tiny pieces. The texture should be sandy with very tiny lumps throughout.

Add the butter to the flour mixture in the food processor. Pulse until the butter is cut into pea-sized pieces, 30 to 45 seconds. Remove the top of the food processor and sprinkle on 3 tablespoons of the cream. Replace the top and pulse for 10 seconds. Squeeze a small amount of the dough in your hand. If it holds together, don't add any more cream. If the dough is still very crumbly, add another tablespoon of cream, pulse to blend, then check the dough again. It won't hold together unless you squeeze it, but that's the texture you want.

Divide the dough in two equal pieces and shape each piece into a flat disk. Wrap each disk tightly in a double layer of plastic wrap. Chill in the refrigerator until firm before using, at least 2 hours. Chilling the dough relaxes the gluten in the flour so it won't be too elastic and will roll out easily. It also firms up the butter in the dough so it will need less flour when rolled out. If the dough is too firm it will splinter and break when rolled out.

Let it stand at room temperature for 10 to 15 minutes before rolling to become more pliable. On a smooth, flat surface, roll out one of the disks of pie dough between sheets of lightly floured waxed or parchment paper to a large circle about 12 inches in diameter. To tell if the dough will fit the pie pan, invert the pan over the dough. If there are 2 to 3 inches of dough that protrude beyond the sides of the pan, it will fit.

Carefully peel the paper off the top of the dough. Brush excess flour off the dough, then loosely roll the pastry dough around the rolling pin without the other piece of paper. Place the pie pan directly underneath the rolling pin and carefully unroll the pastry dough into the pan. Or loosely fold the dough in half. Carefully place it in half of the pie pan and gently unfold the dough. Gently lift up the sides and ease the pie dough into the bottom and sides of the pie pan. Trim off the excess pie dough at the top of the pan and crimp the sides.

Transfer the pie pan to a baking sheet and chill in the freezer for 15 to 20 minutes. This helps prevent the pie dough from shrinking as it bakes and sets the butter in the dough to ensure flakiness.

Cherry Filling

Use a cherry pitter or a small sharp knife to remove the pits from the cherries. Place the cherries in a large bowl. Add the sugar, cornstarch, lemon juice, almond extract, and salt and stir together to coat the cherries completely. Cover the bowl with plastic wrap and let the mixture stand for at least 15 minutes or up to 2 hours in the refrigerator.

Transfer the cherry filling to the pie shell.

Adjust an oven rack to the lower third and preheat the oven to 425°F.

Use a fork to lightly beat the egg yolk and cream together in a small bowl. Use a pastry brush to brush the mixture on the edges of the bottom pastry shell to help the pastry and lattice topping stick together.

Roll out the remaining disk of pie dough on a smooth, flat surface between sheets of lightly floured waxed or parchment paper to a large circle about 12 inches in diameter. Peel off the top piece of paper. Use a ruler and a plain or fluted-edge pastry wheel to cut ½-inch-wide strips of dough. Form the strips into a lattice on top of the cherries. Trim off the edges of both the lattice and the bottom pie shell evenly, leaving a ¾-inch overhang.

Fold the edges of the lattice over the bottom crust and press them to seal together. Crimp or flute the edges. Brush the top of the lattice with the egg yolk/milk mixture and sprinkle sugar over the top of the dough.

Bake the pie for 40 to 45 minutes, until the crust is light golden and the filling is thickly bubbling inside. Remove the pie from the oven and cool on a rack. Serve warm or at room temperature.

CHERRY-RHUBARB LATTICE PIE

Sour Cherries and naturally tart rhubarb create a delectable flyover combination in this pie. The leaves of rhubarb are not edible and are slightly toxic, so be sure to remove them completely before using the stalks. The top of this pie has a lattice, it allows the fruit to show through. Makes one 10-inch round pie, 12 to 14 servings

Pie Dough

In the work bowl of a food processor fitted with the steel blade, combine the flour, sugar, and salt. Pulse briefly to blend.

Cut the butter into small pieces and freeze for 20 minutes. Cut the cream cheese into small pieces and add to the dry ingredients in the food processor. Pulse to cut the cream cheese into very tiny pieces. The texture should be sandy with very tiny lumps throughout.

Add the butter to the flour mixture in the food processor. Pulse until the butter is cut into pea-sized pieces, 30 to 45 seconds. Remove the top of the food processor and sprinkle on 3 tablespoons of the cream. Replace the top and pulse for 10 seconds. Squeeze a small amount of the dough in your hand. If it holds together, don't add any more cream. If the dough is still very crumbly, add another tablespoon of cream, pulse to blend, then check the dough again. It won't hold together unless you squeeze it, but that's the texture you want.

Divide the dough in two equal pieces and shape each piece into a flat disk. Wrap the disks tightly in a double layer of plastic wrap. Chill in the refrigerator until firm before using, at least 2 hours. Chilling the dough relaxes the gluten in the flour so it won't be too elastic and will roll out easily. It also firms up the butter in the dough so it will need less flour when rolled out. If the dough is too firm it will splinter and break when rolled out. Let it stand at room temperature for 10 to 15 minutes before rolling to become more pliable.

On a smooth, flat surface, roll out one of the disks of pie dough between sheets of lightly floured waxed or parchment paper to a large circle about 12 inches in diameter. To tell if the dough will fit the pie pan, invert the pan over the dough. If there are 2 to 3 inches of dough that protrude beyond the sides of the pan, it will fit. Carefully peel the paper off the top of the dough. Brush excess flour off the dough, then loosely roll the pastry dough around the rolling pin without the bottom piece of paper.

Place the pie pan directly underneath the rolling pin and carefully unroll the pastry dough into the pan. Or loosely fold the dough in half. Carefully place it in half of the pie pan and gently unfold the dough. Gently lift up the sides and ease the pie dough into the bottom and sides of the pie pan. Trim off the excess pie dough at the top of the pan and crimp the sides. Transfer the pie pan to a baking sheet and chill in the freezer for 15 to 20 minutes. This helps prevent the pie dough from shrinking as it bakes and sets the butter in the dough to ensure flakiness.

Cherry-Rhubarb Filling

Place the cherries and rhubarb in a large bowl. Add the granulated sugar and brown sugar and toss to coat the fruit. Add the cornstarch and lemon zest and gently toss the fruit to coat with the ingredients. Transfer this mixture to the chilled pie shell and spread it out evenly. Use a pastry brush to apply water to the edges of the bottom pastry shell to help the pastry and lattice topping stick together.

Roll out the remaining disk of pie dough on a smooth, flat surface between sheets of lightly floured waxed or parchment paper to a large circle about 12 inches in diameter. Peel off the top piece of paper. Use a ruler and a plain or fluted-edge pastry wheel to cut ½-inch-wide strips of dough. Form the strips into a lattice on top of the filling. Trim off the edges of both the lattice and the bottom pie shell evenly, leaving a ¾-inch overhang. Fold the edges of the lattice over the bottom crust and press them to seal together. Crimp or flute the edges.

Bake the pie for 15 minutes, then reduce the oven temperature to 350°F. Bake the pie another 40 to 50 minutes, until the crust is light golden and the fruit is thickly bubbling inside. Remove the pie from the oven and cool on a rack. Serve warm or at room temperature.

Cherry-Almond Cake

This is a rustic-style cake that is baked in a glass pie plate and cut into pie-shaped wedges for serving. Fresh cherries are baked into a rich, buttery almond batter. A light dusting of confectioners' sugar is all this cake needs for decoration, but a scoop of vanilla ice cream or freshly whipped cream makes it a standout. If you use canned cherries, be sure to drain off the liquid. Makes one 9-inch cake, 8 to 10 servings.

Center a rack in the oven and preheat it to 400°F.

Use your fingertips or a paper towel to butter the bottom and sides of the pan.

Use a cherry pitter or a small sharp knife to remove the pits from the cherries. Place the cherries in a small bowl.

Add the liqueur, stir to coat all the cherries, and let them marinate while you prepare the cake batter.

Place the almonds and sugar in the work bowl of a food processor fitted with the steel blade. Pulse until finely ground, about 2 minutes. Place the butter in the bowl of an electric stand mixer or in a large mixing bowl. Use the flat beater attachment or a hand-held mixer to beat the butter on medium speed until it's fluffy, about 2 minutes. Add the sugar, and cream together well. Stop occasionally and scrape down the sides and bottom of the bowl with a spatula. One at a time, add the eggs to the butter mixture, stopping to scrape down the bottom and sides of the bowl after each addition. At first the mixture may look curdled as the eggs are added, but as you stop and scrape down the bowl, the mixture will smooth out. Add the vanilla and mix well.

Sift the flour and mix with the salt and the finely ground almonds. Add this mixture to the butter mixture.

Blend together on low speed briefly until the ingredients are combined.

Remove the mixing bowl from the mixer and use a rubber spatula to fold in the cherries and liquid.

Transfer the mixture to the pie pan. Use the rubber spatula to spread the mixture evenly in the pan.

Bake the cake for 20 to 23 minutes, until it is set and light golden.

Remove the pan from the oven and transfer to a rack to cool.

Garnish

Dust the top of the cake evenly with confectioners' sugar. Cut into pie-shaped wedges and serve warm or at room temperature.

Fresh Peach Buttercream Layer Cake

This is one of my all-time favourite cakes because it is a symphony of flavours that work perfectly together. The cake layers are rich and dense, with the slight tangy flavour of sour cream. The buttercream is flavored with fresh peach puree and the cake is decorated with fresh peach slices and toasted sliced almonds. Although there are several steps involved in making this cake, most can be done in advance, making it easy to fit into your schedule.

Assemble the cake a few hours before serving so the flavours and textures have time to marry together. Makes one 9-inch round cake, 12 to 14 servings.

Cake

Center a rack in the oven and preheat it to 325°F.

Using a paper towel or your fingertips, generously butter the inside of the cake pans, coating them thoroughly.

Dust the inside of each pan with some of the flour. Shake and tilt the pans to evenly distribute the flour, then turn the pans over and shake out the excess over the sink.

Cut a round of parchment paper to fit the bottom of each pan. Butter each parchment paper round and place in each pan, butter-side up.

Place the butter in the bowl of an electric stand mixer or in a large mixing bowl. Use the flat beater attachment or hand-held mixer to beat the butter on medium speed until it's fluffy, about 2 minutes.

Gradually add the sugar to the butter and cream together well. Stop occasionally and scrape down the bottom and sides of the bowl with a rubber spatula.

One at a time, add the eggs, stopping to scrape down the bottom and sides of the bowl after each addition. At first the mixture may look curdled as the eggs are added, but as you scrape down the bowl, the mixture will smooth out.

Add the sour cream and vanilla to the butter mixture and blend together well.

Over a large piece of waxed or parchment paper or a bowl, sift together the flour, baking powder, and baking soda. Add the salt and toss to blend well.

With the mixer on low speed, add the dry ingredients to the batter in 4 stages. Blend well after each addition and stop often to scrape down the bottom and sides of the bowl with a rubber spatula. Divide the batter evenly between the two cake pans. Smooth the top of each pan with a rubber spatula.

Bake the cakes for 45 minutes, until they are golden and a cake tester inserted in the center comes out with no crumbs clinging to it. Remove the cake pans from the oven and cool completely on racks. Invert the pans to remove the layers, then peel the parchment paper off the back of each layer. Re-invert the layers onto plates or cardboard cake circles.

Peach Buttercream

Bring water to a boil in a large saucepan or stockpot over high heat. Using a sharp knife, score a small X in the bottom of each peach. Add the peaches to the water and let them boil for 1 to 2 minutes. Use a slotted spoon or skimmer to remove the peaches from the boiling water. Place them in a bowl of cold water, which will stop them from further cooking.

Starting at the X, use a small sharp knife to gently peel the skin off the peaches. It should slip off easily. If the peaches are too hot, peel them under cold running water.

Cut 2 of the peaches in half and remove the pits. Place the peach halves in the work bowl of a food processor fitted with the steel blade or into the blender. Pulse until the peaches are pureed. You should have 1/3 to ½ cup peach puree.

Slice the remaining two peaches into ½-inch-thick slices. Place the slices on a plate and cover them with waxed paper to keep them from turning brown while you are assembling the cake.

Place the eggs, egg yolks, and sugar in the bowl of an electric stand mixer or in a large mixing bowl. Use the wire whip attachment or a hand-held mixer and whip on medium speed until the mixture is very pale colored and holds a slowly dissolving ribbon as the beater is lifted, about 5 minutes.

While the eggs are whipping, place the sugar, water, and cream of tartar in a 2-quart heavy-bottomed saucepan. Bring the mixture to a boil, without stirring. Place a wet pastry brush at the point where the sugar syrup meets the sides of the pan and sweep it around completely. Do this two times. Brushing down the sides of the pan while the sugar is cooking prevents sugar crystals from coming out of the mixture, which causes crystallization. This is a condition that creates a crust around the side of the pan. Once crystallization occurs, the sugar syrup won't come up to temperature correctly and has to be thrown away. Don't brush around the pan more than a few times. If you do, you're adding extra water to the sugar syrup, which takes more time to cook off and reach the desired temperature.

Cook over high heat until the mixture registers 242°F on a sugar thermometer (soft-ball stage). Immediately remove the thermometer and place it in a glass of warm water, then remove the pan from the heat so it won't continue to cook.

Adjust the mixer speed to low and pour the sugar syrup into the whipped eggs in a slow, steady stream. Aim the sugar syrup between the beater and the side of the bowl, so it doesn't get caught up in the beater or thrown against the sides of the bowl. Turn the mixer speed up to medium-high and whip until the bowl is cool to the touch, about 8 minutes.

Once the cooked sugar syrup is added to the whipped eggs, the mixture must whip until the bowl is completely cool to the touch before the butter is added, or the butter will melt. If this happens, the texture and consistency of the buttercream will be too soft and more butter needs to be added to bring it to the right point. Adjust the mixer speed to medium and add the butter, 2 tablespoons at a time. Continue to beat until the buttercream is thoroughly blended and fluffy.

Add the peach puree and beat until it is completely blended. With your fingertips, gently peel the skin off the top of each cake layer. Using a serrated knife, cut each cake layer in half horizontally (see page 34). Place the bottom of one cake layer on a serving plate. Use the flexible-blade spatula to spread the layer evenly with the peach preserves.

Place strips of waxed paper around the bottom edges of the cake to protect the plate while assembling the cake. With a clean, flexibleblade spatula, evenly spread some of the buttercream over the cake layer.

Position the second cake layer evenly over the buttercream and spread some of the buttercream over the layer. Repeat with the remaining 2 cake layers and buttercream.

Spread the remaining buttercream over the sides and top of the cake. Press the toasted sliced almonds onto the sides of the cake just up to, but not over, the top edge.

Arrange the sliced peaches in a circle over the top outer edge of the cake. Arrange a second circle of sliced peaches inside of the outer circle and use any remaining slices to fill in the center of the top of the cake.

Peach Glaze

Combine the peach preserves and liquid in a small saucepan. Bring to a boil over medium heat. Remove the pan from the heat and strain the glaze into a small bowl, pushing through as much of the pulp as possible. Use a goose-feather pastry brush to lightly brush the top of the sliced peaches with the glaze. Don't apply a thick glaze, which looks unappetizing. The purpose of the glaze is to keep the peaches from drying out and to make the top of the cake glisten.

Fresh Peach Coffee Cake

There's no coffee in this cake, but it does taste great with a cup of coffee or tea. It's baked in a quiche pan with fluted edges that give the cake an attractive design. A batter accented with lemon and orange zest and a little ground cinnamon bakes up to enclose fresh peach halves. For dessert, try serving this yummy cake with vanilla ice cream or whipped cream. You can eat this cake any time of day, even for breakfast. Makes one 91/2-inch cake, 8 to 10 servings.

Center a rack in the oven and preheat it to 400°F.

Bring water to a boil in a large saucepan or stockpot over high heat.

Using a sharp knife, score a small X in the bottom of each peach.

Add the peaches to the water and let them boil for 1 to 2 minutes. Use a slotted spoon or skimmer to remove the peaches from the boiling water. Place them in a bowl of cold water, which will stop them from further cooking.

Starting at the X, use a small sharp knife to gently peel the skin off the peaches. It should slip off easily. If the peaches are too hot, peel them under cold running water.

Cut the peaches in half and remove the pits. Place the peach halves on a plate and cover with waxed paper while preparing the cake. Place the flour, granulated sugar, brown sugar, baking powder, cinnamon, and salt in a medium mixing bowl. Use a rubber spatula or wooden spoon to stir together.

Use a fork to lightly beat the eggs in a small mixing bowl. Add the butter, cream, vanilla, lemon zest, and orange zest and stir together until combined.

Add this mixture to the dry ingredients. Use a rubber spatula or wooden spoon to stir together until evenly blended. Turn the mixture out into the quiche pan and spread it evenly.

Press the peach halves into the dough around the top of the cake.

Place the quiche pan on a jelly-roll pan.

Bake the cake for 25 to 30 minutes, until puffed and golden colored, and a toothpick inserted into the center comes out clean. Remove the pan from the oven and cool on a rack for 15 minutes. Carefully remove the sides of the quiche pan. Cut the cake into slices and serve warm.

Peach Shortcakes with Honey Whipped Cream

Peaches and cream are a natural combination. When honey is added into the equation, the result is a subtle yet compelling flavor combination. Try using different types of honey to change the overall flavor of this dessert, but don't use a strongly flavored honey that will overpower the peaches and cream.

These scrumptious shortcake biscuits are the perfect foil for peaches and honey whipped cream. Makes ten 31/4-inch round shortcakes.

Center a rack in the oven and preheat it to 400°F. Line a baking sheet with parchment paper or a non-stick liner.

In the work bowl of a food processor fitted with the steel blade, combine the flour, sugar, baking powder, nutmeg, and salt and pulse a few times to blend.

Cut the butter into small pieces and chill in the freezer for 15 minutes. Add to the food processor and pulse until the butter is cut into pea-sized pieces, 30 to 45 seconds. The mixture should be crumbly. Don't cut the butter too small or the shortcakes will lose their flaky quality.

With the food processor running, pour the cream through the feed tube and process until all the ingredients are combined and the dough is moist, about 30 seconds.

Turn the dough out onto a large piece of waxed or parchment paper lightly dusted with flour. Dust your hands with flour and shape the dough into a circle or rectangle about ¾ inch thick. Use the biscuit cutter to cut out shortcakes. Cut straight down through the dough without twisting the cutter, which seals the edges of the dough and keeps the biscuits from rising in the oven. Place them on the lined baking sheet, leaving at least 2 inches of space between them so they have room to expand as they bake. Gather the scraps together and knead slightly. Pat them into a ¾-inch-thick circle or rectangle and proceed as above to get 10 shortcakes. Brush any excess flour off the shortcakes.

Garnish

Brush the top of the shortcakes with cream, being careful that it doesn't run down the sides and underneath. If it does, wipe it up because it can cause the bottom of the shortcakes to burn. Lightly sprinkle the top of the shortcakes with sugar. Using these types of sugar adds extra texture to the shortcakes. Bake the shortcakes for 12 to 15 minutes, until light golden. Remove the baking sheets from the oven and cool completely on racks.

Assembly

Bring water to a boil in a large saucepan or stockpot over high heat. Using a sharp knife, score a small X in the bottom of each peach. Add the peaches to the water and let them boil for 1 to 2 minutes. Use a slotted spoon or skimmer to remove the peaches from the boiling water. Place them in a bowl of cold water, which will stop them from cooking. Starting at the X, use a small sharp knife to gently peel the skin off the peaches. It should slip off easily. If the peaches are too hot, peel them under cold running water.

Slice the blanched peaches into ½-inch-thick slices. Place the slices in a medium bowl. Add the sugar and amaretto, if using. Toss the peaches lightly to coat them completely. Cover the bowl tightly with plastic wrap and let the peaches marinate for 15 to 30 minutes. Place the cream in the chilled bowl of an electric stand mixer or a medium mixing bowl. Using the wire whip attachment or a handheld mixer, whip the cream on medium speed until it is frothy. Add the honey and continue to whip the cream on medium speed until it holds soft peaks.

Slice each shortcake in half horizontally. Place the bottom of a shortcake on a serving plate and cover with a scoop of whipped cream. Place about 3 tablespoons of sliced peaches on top of the cream and cover the peaches with another small scoop of whipped cream. Lightly place the top of the shortcake on top of the peaches or arrange it at an angle to the bottom of the shortcake. Top with a dollop of whipped cream and scatter a few slices of peaches around the plate. Repeat with the remaining shortcakes. Serve immediately.

Spiced Fresh Peach Pie

A blend of cinnamon, ginger, and nutmeg brings out the

best in fresh, ripe peaches nestled in a classic pie crust and covered with a lattice topping. This pie says "summer" to me.

Makes one 10-inch round pie, 12 to 14 servings

Pie Dough

In the work bowl of a food processor fitted with the steel blade, combine the flour, sugar, and salt. Pulse briefly to blend.

Cut the butter into small pieces and freeze for 20 minutes. Cut the cream cheese into small pieces and add to the dry ingredients in the food processor. Pulse to cut the cream cheese into very tiny pieces. The texture should be sandy with very tiny lumps throughout.

Add the butter to the food processor. Pulse until the butter is cut into pea-sized pieces, 30 to 45 seconds.

Remove the top of the food processor and sprinkle on 3 tablespoons of the cream. Replace the top and pulse for 10 seconds. Squeeze a small amount of the dough in your hand. If it holds together, don't add any more cream. If the dough is still very crumbly, add another tablespoon of cream, pulse to blend, then check the dough again. It won't hold together unless you squeeze it, but that's the texture you want.

Divide the dough in 2 equal pieces and shape each piece into a flat disk. Wrap the disks tightly in a double layer of plastic wrap. Chill in the refrigerator until firm before using, at least 2 hours. Chilling the dough relaxes the gluten in the flour so it won't be too elastic and will roll out easily. It also firms up the butter in the dough so it will need less flour when rolled out. If the dough is too firm it will splinter and break when rolled out. Let it stand at room temperature for 10 to 15 minutes before rolling to become more pliable.

On a smooth, flat surface, roll out one of the disks of pie dough between sheets of lightly floured waxed or parchment paper to a large circle about 12 inches in diameter. To tell if the dough will fit the pie pan, invert the pan over the dough. If there are 2 to 3 inches of dough that protrude beyond the sides of the pan, it will fit.

Carefully peel the paper off the top of the dough. Brush excess flour off the dough, then loosely roll the pastry dough around the rolling pin without the bottom piece of paper. Place the pie pan directly underneath the rolling pin and carefully unroll the pastry dough into the pan. Or loosely fold the dough in half. Carefully place it in half of the pie pan and gently unfold the dough. Gently lift up the sides and ease the pie dough into the bottom and sides of the pie pan.

Transfer the pie pan to a baking sheet and chill in the freezer for 15 to 20 minutes. This helps prevent the pie dough from shrinking as it bakes and sets the butter in the dough to ensure flakiness.

Spiced Peach Filling

Cut the peaches in half and remove the stones. Cut each peach half into 4 slices. Place the sliced peaches in a 2-quart bowl.

Sprinkle the brown sugar, flour, cinnamon, ginger, nutmeg, and salt over the peaches. Using a rubber spatula, gently toss and stir to evenly distribute the dry ingredients and coat the peaches completely. Transfer the peach filling to the pie shell.

Cut the butter into small pieces and place evenly over the top of the peaches.

Adjust an oven rack to the lower third and preheat the oven to 400°F.

Use a fork to lightly beat the egg yolk and cream together in a small bowl. Use a pastry brush to brush the edges of the bottom pastry shell to help the shell and lattice topping stick together.

Roll out the remaining disk of pie dough on a smooth, flat surface between sheets of lightly floured waxed or parchment paper to a large circle about 12 inches in diameter. Peel off the top piece of paper. Use a ruler and a plain or fluted-edge pastry wheel to cut ½-inch-wide strips of dough. Form the strips into a lattice on top of the sliced peaches. Trim off the edges of both the lattice and the bottom pie shell evenly, leaving a ¾-inch overhang. Fold the edges of the lattice over the bottom crust and press them to seal together. Crimp or flute the edges. Brush the top of the lattice with the egg mixture and sprinkle sugar over the top of the dough.

Bake the pie for 50 to 60 minutes, until the crust is light golden and the filling is thickly bubbling inside.

Remove the pie from the oven and cool on a rack. Serve warm or at room temperature.

Nectarine and Almond Galette

This is a Free-form tart made with almond pastry dough that encloses a creamy frangipane filling and fresh nectarines. It's one of my very favourite summer fruit desserts. Be sure to use perfectly ripe fruit for the best flavor. Makes one 9-inch tart, 8 to 10 servings.

Pastry Dough

In the work bowl of a food processor, combine the flour, almonds, sugar, and salt. Pulse until the almonds are very finely ground, about 1 minute.

Cut the butter into small pieces and add to the flour mixture. Pulse until the butter is cut into very tiny pieces, about 30 seconds. The texture should be sandy with very tiny lumps throughout.

In a small bowl, combine the lemon juice, 2 tablespoons of water, and the lemon zest. Seconds to 1 minute. If the dough seems dry, add the remaining tablespoon of water and process until the dough comes together.

Turn the pastry dough onto a large piece of plastic wrap. Shape into a flat disk and wrap tightly in a double layer of plastic wrap. Chill in the refrigerator until firm before using, about 2 hours. Chilling the dough relaxes the gluten in the flour so it won't be too elastic and will roll out easily. It also firms up the butter in the dough so it will need less flour when rolled out. If the dough is too firm it will splinter and break when rolled out. Let it stand at room temperature for 10 to 15 minutes before rolling to become more pliable.

Nectarine Filling

Using a sharp knife, slice the fruit in half along the seam. Remove the stone and cut the fruit into ½-inch-thick slices. You should have approximately 3 cups of sliced fruit.

Place the sliced nectarines in a mixing bowl. Add the sugar and toss together to distribute evenly. Taste the fruit to see if it needs any more sugar.

Assembly

Center a rack in the oven and preheat it to 375°F. Line a baking sheet with parchment paper.

On a smooth, flat surface, roll out the pastry dough between sheets of lightly floured waxed or parchment paper to a large circle 11 to 12 inches in diameter. Carefully peel the paper off the top of the dough. Brush excess flour off the dough, then loosely roll the pastry dough around the rolling pin, without the bottom piece of paper. Place the lined baking sheet directly underneath the rolling pin and carefully unroll the pastry dough onto the baking sheet. Spread the filling over the center of the pastry dough, leaving a 3-inch border all around.

Mound the sliced nectarines in the center of the dough circle, leaving a 21/2- to 3-inch border all around.

Cut the butter into small pieces and distribute evenly over the sliced nectarines.

Fold the border up so that it partially covers the nectarines. It will naturally form pleats as it is folded.

With a pastry brush, apply cream to the dough border, being careful that it doesn't run down the sides and under the galette. If it does, wipe it up because it can cause the bottom of the galette to burn. Gently lift up the folds of the dough and brush under those areas with cream, then replace the folds. Evenly sprinkle the sugar over the dough border.

Bake the galette for 35 to 40 minutes, until light golden. Remove the pan from the oven and transfer to a rack to cool. Cut the galette into pie-shaped wedges to serve.

Nectarine Cobbler

Sweet, Fresh Nectarines mixed with cinnamon are topped with a biscuit crust and baked to make this delectable cobbler. The name "cobbler" comes from the look of the biscuit topping of this dessert, which has a cobbled or broken appearance. This is a rustic dessert that's super easy to prepare and even easier to eat. Makes one 8-inch square cobbler, 8 to 10 servings.

Center a rack in the oven and preheat it to 375°F.

Nectarine Filling

Using a chef's knife, cut the nectarines in half and remove the stones. Cut each half into ½-inch-thick slices. You should have about 6 cups of sliced nectarines. Place the slices in the baking pan. Add the sugar, flour, cinnamon, lemon zest, and lemon juice to the sliced nectarines and toss together to coat them completely.

Biscuit Dough Topping

In the work bowl of a food processor fitted with the steel blade, combine the flour, sugar, cinnamon, baking powder, salt, and baking soda. Pulse briefly to blend.

Cut the butter into small pieces and add to the dry ingredients. Pulse until the butter is cut into very tiny pieces, about 1 minute. The texture should feel sandy with tiny lumps throughout.

Combine the buttermilk and vanilla in a liquid measuring cup. With the food processor running, pour this mixture through the feed tube. Process until the dough wraps itself around the blade, about 30 seconds.

Drop about 8 large spoonfuls of the dough over the top of the sliced nectarines, spacing them evenly.

Use a pastry brush to brush the top of the dough with cream, then sprinkle the top of the dough with the sugar.

Bake for 30 to 35 minutes, until the biscuit topping is set and a toothpick inserted into it comes out clean. Remove the pan from the oven and transfer to a rack to cool.

Garnish

Place the cream in the bowl of an electric stand mixer or in a large mixing bowl. Use the wire whip attachment or a hand-held mixer to whip on medium speed until frothy.

Add the confectioners' sugar and continue whipping the cream until it holds soft peaks.

Cut squares of the cobbler, scooping up the fruit. Serve each square with a large dollop of whipped cream.

Fresh Nectarine Pandowdy

A pandowdy is a classic American deep-dish fruit dessert that traces its heritage as far back as the Colonial period. It's a rustic dessert that is composed of fruit tossed with spices and topped with a biscuit-like crust. Part way through baking, the crust is broken up and pressed down into the fruit so it can absorb the juices. This technique is called "dowdying" and is where the dessert gets its name. After the crust is broken and baked, it becomes crispy. A pandowdy is traditionally served warm with heavy cream.

Makes one 9-inch square pandowdy, 8 to 10 servings

Pastry Crust

In the work bowl of a food processor fitted with the steel blade, combine the flour, sugar, and salt. Pulse briefly to blend.

Cut the butter into small pieces and add to the dry ingredients. Pulse until the butter is cut into very tiny pieces, about 30 seconds. The mixture should be sandy with very tiny lumps throughout.

Combine the ice water and lemon juice in a liquid measuring cup. With the food processor running, pour this mixture through the feed tube. Process just until the dough begins to hold together.

Form the dough into a flat square and wrap tightly in plastic wrap. Chill in the refrigerator until firm before using, at least 1 hour. Chilling the dough relaxes the gluten in the flour so it won't be too elastic and will roll out easily.

Line a baking sheet with a sheet of parchment paper.

On a smooth, flat surface, roll out the dough between sheets of lightly floured waxed or parchment paper to a 10-inch square. While rolling the dough, give it a quarter turn often so it is always in a comfortable position for you to roll. Check to make sure that the waxed or parchment paper is not sticking to the dough by lifting it up often. Occasionally turn the dough package over and check the bottom piece of waxed or parchment paper to make sure it is not sticking. Sprinkle more flour on the dough as needed, to keep it from sticking.

Peel off the top piece of paper and brush off any excess flour. Holding the bottom piece of paper by the sides, turn the dough over and place it on the lined baking pan. Remove the paper and brush off any excess flour. Cover the dough with plastic wrap and chill 30 minutes.

Center a rack in the oven and preheat it to 400°F.

Use a fork to lightly beat the egg yolk and cream together in a small bowl.

Use a pastry brush to brush the top of the pastry crust with the mixture. Evenly sprinkle the almonds over the top of the crust. Bake the pastry crust for 15 minutes, until it is set and lightly colored.

Remove the baking pan from the oven and cool on a rack.

Nectarine Filling

Using a paper towel or your fingertips, generously butter the inside of the pan.

Using a chef's knife, cut the nectarines in half and remove the pits. Cut each nectarine half into ½-inch-thick slices. Place the slices in a 2-quart mixing bowl.

Add the brown sugar, cornstarch, lemon juice, salt, ginger, nutmeg, and allspice to the nectarines and toss together with a rubber spatula or wooden spoon to coat them completely.

Transfer the nectarine mixture to the prepared baking pan. Bake the pandowdy for 30 minutes. Lower the oven temperature to 350°F and bake for another 15 minutes. Remove the baking pan from the oven.

Using a large, flat spatula, transfer the pastry crust to the top of the fruit.

Return the baking pan to the oven and bake for 10 minutes. Use the back of a large spoon to gently press down on the pastry crust, break it into pieces, and press the pieces into the fruit. Bake for another 10 to 15 minutes, until the fruit is bubbling and the pastry crust is golden brown.

Remove the baking pan from the oven and cool on a rack.

Garnish

Place the cream in the bowl of an electric stand mixer or in a large mixing bowl. Use the wire whip attachment or a hand-held mixer to whip on medium speed until frothy.

Add the confectioners' sugar and continue whipping the cream until it holds soft peaks.

Cut squares of the pandowdy, scooping up the fruit. Serve each square with a large dollop of whipped cream.

Plum and Almond Cake

This Cake is rich and satisfying without being too sweet. Almond paste adds flavor, texture, and moisture to the cake mixture. Fresh plums are cut in half and arranged over the top of the batter and sink to the bottom of the cake as it bakes. When the cake is cool, it's turned upside down and the plums adorn the top. Although it sounds like an upside-down cake, this is much richer and denser than the classic version. It is perfect served with afternoon coffee or tea, but is equally good for dessert or warmed up for breakfast. Makes one 9-inch round cake, 12 to 14 servings.

Cake

Position a rack in the center of the oven and preheat it to 325°F. Using a paper towel or your fingertips, generously butter the inside of the cake pan, coating it thoroughly.

Dust the inside of the pan with some of the flour. Shake and tilt the pan to evenly distribute the flour, then turn the pan over and shake out the excess over the sink.

Cut a round of parchment paper to fit the bottom of the pan. Butter the parchment paper round and place in the pan, butter-side up. Place the almond paste and butter in the bowl of an electric stand mixer or in a large mixing bowl. Use the flat beater attachment or hand-held mixer to beat on medium speed until the mixture is fluffy, about 2 minutes.

Gradually add the sugar to the butter mixture and cream together well. Stop occasionally and scrape down the bottom and sides of the bowl with a rubber spatula.

One at a time, add the eggs, stopping to scrape down the bottom and sides of the bowl after each addition. At first the mixture may look curdled as the eggs are added, but as you stop and scrape down the bowl, the mixture will smooth out.

Combine the milk and vanilla in a liquid measuring cup or a small bowl and add to the butter mixture. Blend together well.

Over a large piece of waxed or parchment paper or a bowl, sift together the flour and baking powder. Add the salt and toss to blend well.

With the mixer on low speed, add the dry ingredients in 4 stages. Blend well after each addition and stop often to scrape down the bottom and sides of the bowl with a rubber spatula.

Transfer the batter to the prepared cake pan. Smooth the top of the batter with a rubber spatula.

Cut the plums in half and remove the stones. Place the plum halves around the outside edge of the cake, cut-side down, leaving about ½ inch of space between them. Arrange 2 plum halves in the center of the cake.

Scatter the chopped walnuts over the top of the cake batter and in between the plums.

Bake the cake for 1 hour, until golden and a cake tester inserted in the center comes out with no crumbs clinging to it.

Remove the cake pan from the oven and cool on a rack for 15 minutes. Place a serving plate or 9-inch cardboard cake circle over the top of the cake pan. Invert the pan to remove the cake, then peel the parchment paper off the back of the cake. Let the cake cool to room temperature.

Garnish

Dust the top of the cake with confectioners' sugar. Cut the cake into wedges to serve.

Fresh Plum Cobbler

Ripe, Juicy Plums, accented with cinnamon and nutmeg, are topped with a delectable biscuit crust. The biscuit topping has a cobbled or broken appearance, which is what gives this dessert its name. This is a very quick and easy dessert to prepare and it's so scrumptious that it's even easier to eat. Makes one 8-inch square cobbler, 8 to 10 servings.

Center a rack in the oven and preheat it to 400°F.

Plum Filling

Using a chef's knife, cut the plums in half and remove the stones. Cut each plum half into ½-inch-thick slices. Place the sliced plums in the baking pan.

Add the brown sugar, granulated sugar, cornstarch, vanilla, cinnamon, and nutmeg to the sliced plums and toss together to coat them completely.

Biscuit Dough Topping

In the work bowl of a food processor fitted with the steel blade, combine the flour, granulated sugar, brown sugar, baking powder, salt, and nutmeg. Pulse briefly to blend.

Cut the butter into small pieces and add to the dry ingredients. Pulse until the butter is cut into very tiny pieces, about 1 minute. The texture should feel sandy with tiny lumps throughout.

Combine the cream and egg yolk in a liquid measuring cup and use a fork to lightly blend the two together. With the food processor running, pour this mixture through the feed tube. Process until the dough wraps itself around the blade, about 30 seconds.

Remove the baking pan from the oven. Stir the plum mixture, then drop about 8 large spoonfuls of the dough over the top of the mixture, spacing them evenly.

Use a pastry brush to brush the top of the dough with cream, then sprinkle the top of the dough with the sugar.

Bake for 30 minutes, until the biscuit topping is set and the fruit is bubbling. Remove the pan from the oven and transfer to a rack to cool.

Garnish

Place the cream in the bowl of an electric stand mixer or in a large mixing bowl. Use the wire whip attachment or a hand-held mixer to whip on medium speed until frothy.

Add the confectioners' sugar and continue whipping the cream until it holds soft peaks.

Cut squares of the cobbler, scooping up the fruit. Serve each square with a large dollop of whipped cream.

4

Exclusive Cookies

A cookie is a small, round, flat cake. In most English-speaking countries outside North America, the most common word for this is biscuit; in many regions both terms are used, while in others the two words have different meanings—a cookie is a plain bun in Scotland, while in the United States a biscuit is a kind of quick bread not unlike a scone.

The earliest cookie-style is thought to date back to 5th century Persia (now Iran), one of the first regions to cultivate sugar (luxurious Biscuits and pastries in large and small versions were well known in the Persian Empire). According to historians, sugar originated either in the lowlands of Bengal or elsewhere in Southeast Asia. Sugar spread to Persia and then to the Eastern Mediterranean. With the Muslim invasion of Spain, and the Crusades and the developing spice trade, the cooking techniques and ingredients of Arabia spread into Northern Europe and eventually present day America.

Its name derives from the Dutch word koekje or (informal) koekie which means little cake, and arrived in the English language through the Dutch in North America. It spread from American English to British English where biscuit is still the more general term.

Cookies can be baked until crisp or just long enough that they remain soft. Depending on the type of cookie, some cookies are not cooked at all. Cookies are made in a wide variety of styles, using an array of ingredients including sugars, spices, chocolate, butter, peanut butter, nuts or dried fruits. The softness of the cookie may depend on how long it is baked.

A chocolate chip cookie

A general theory of cookies may be formulated this way. Despite their descent from cakes and other sweetened breads, the cookie in almost all its forms has abandoned water as a medium for cohesion. Water in cakes serves to make the base as thin as possible, which allows the bubbles – responsible for a cake's fluffiness – to form better. In the cookie, the agent of cohesion has become some form of oil. Oils, whether they be in the form of butter, egg yolks, vegetable oils or lard are much more viscous than water and evaporate freely at a much higher temperature than water. Thus a cake made with butter or eggs instead of water is far denser after removal from the oven.

Oils in baked cakes do not behave as soda in the finished result. Rather than evaporating and thickening the mixture, they remain, saturating the bubbles of escaped gases from what little water there might have been in the eggs, if added, and the carbon dioxide released by heating the baking powder. This saturation produces the most texturally attractive feature of the cookie, and indeed all fried foods: crispness saturated with a moisture (namely oil) that does not sink into it.

Classification of Cookies

Cookies are broadly classified according to how they are formed, including at least these categories:

— *Drop cookies* are made from a relatively soft dough that is dropped by spoonfuls onto the baking sheet. During baking, the mounds of dough spread and flatten. Chocolate chip cookies are an example of drop cookies.

— *Refrigerator cookies* are made from a stiff dough that is refrigerated to become even stiffer. The dough is typically shaped into cylinders which are sliced into round cookies before baking.

— *Molded cookies* are also made from a stiffer dough that is molded into balls or cookie shapes by hand before baking. Snickerdoodles are an example of molded cookies.

— *Rolled cookies* are made from a stiffer dough that is rolled out and cut into shapes with a cookie cutter. Gingerbread men are an example.

— *Pressed cookies* are made from a soft dough that is extruded from a cookie press into various decorative shapes before baking. Spritzgebäck are an example of a pressed cookie.

— *Bar cookies* consist of batter or other ingredients that are poured or pressed into a pan (sometimes in multiple layers), and cut into cookie-sized pieces after baking. Brownies are an example of a batter-type bar cookie, while Rice Krispie treats are a bar cookie that doesn't require baking, perhaps similar to a cereal bar. In British English, bar cookies are known as "tray bakes".

— *Sandwich cookies* are rolled or pressed cookies that are assembled as a sandwich with a sweet filling. Fillings may be with marshmallow, jam, or icing. The Oreo cookie, made of two chocolate cookies with a vanilla icing filling is an example.

— *Fried cookies* including traditional cookies such as the krusczyki, rosettes and fattigmann as well as a newer American trend of deep-frying ordinary drop cookie dough.

Cookies also may be decorated with an icing, especially chocolate, and closely resemble a type of confectionery.

Preparation of Different Types of Cookies

Cashew Cookies

Ingredients:

— 400 gms. plain flour

— 400 gms. wheat flour

— 200 gms. cashews, powdered coarsely

— 500 gms. sugar powdered

— 500 gms. solidified ghee dalda

— 1/4 tsp. baking powder

— 1/2 cups broken bits of cashews or halved cashews

— 1-2 tbsp. warm milk if required

Directions:

— If ghee if not solidified, then refrigerate for some time.
— Take in a large deep plate, run in circular direction with a flat palm.
— Rub enough to make ghee white, fluffy and light.
— Sieve baking powder with flours.
— Add sugar to ghee and mix till light.
— Fold in sieved flours, cashew powder till well mixed.
— Sprinkle some milk if dough seems too dry to hold.
— Mix with a light hand.
— Do not knead too much or make dough gooey.
— Coarse dough will make better and lighter cookies.
— Shape in small rounds, arrange on baking sheet.
— Preheat oven to 200°C, before putting in cookies.
— Press on cashew bit on each cookie in centre.
— Bake at 180°C for 7-8 minutes or till very light golden.
— Remove, cool on a wire mesh or rack till completely cooled.
— Store in airtight container, in dry place.
— One may even add milk when rubbing ghee and sugar.

Walnut Cookies

Ingredients:

— 400 gms. plain flour
— 400 gms. rice flour
— 200 gms. walnuts, powdered coarsely
— 500 gms. sugar powdered
— 500 gms. solidified ghee dalda
— 1/4 tsp. baking powder
— 1-2 tbsp. warm milk if required

Directions:

— If ghee if not solidified, then refrigerate for some time.
— Take in a large deep plate, run in circular direction with a flat palm.
— Rub enough to make ghee white, fluffy and light.
— Sieve baking powder with flours.
— Add sugar to ghee and mix till light.
— Fold in sieved flours, walnut powder till well mixed.
— Sprinkle some milk if dough seems too dry to hold.
— Mix with a light hand.
— Do not knead too much or make dough gooey.
— Coarse dough will make better and lighter cookies.
— Shape in small rounds, arrange on baking sheet.
— Preheat oven to 200°C, before putting in cookies.
— Bake at 180°C for 7-8 minutes or till very light golden.
— Remove, cool on a wire mesh or rack till completely cooled.
— Store in airtight container, in dry place.
— One may even add milk when rubbing ghee and sugar.

Chocolate Cookies

Ingredients:

— 1 packet glucose biscuits
— 1 tbsp. cocoa powder
— 1 tbsp. walnuts crushed
— 1/2 tin condensed milk
— 1 tsp. cornflour
— 1 tbsp. butter, softened

— 4-5 drops vanilla essence
— 1/2 cup milk
— 1/2 cup coconut fine white flakes

Directions:

— Put glucose biscuits in a plastic bag, crushed coarsely with rolling pin
— Make a paste of cornflour, cocoa and half the milk.
— Heat remaining milk to a boil, pour into cocoa paste, mix till well blended.
— Empty condensed milk, butter, essence into a large bowl
— Beat till light and blended.
— Add cocoa milk mixture, mix again.
— Add crushed biscuits and walnuts, mix well.
— On a clean dusted surface, press out mixture into a square.
— Mark out square piece with a knife.
— Allow to cool completely. Cut pieces fully.
— Place in a tray on greaseproof paper and chill till well set.
— Serve chilled. Store in refrigerator till required.

Walnut-Chocolate Cookies

Ingredients:

— 800 gms. plain flour
— 200 gms. walnuts, powdered coarsely
— 2 tbsp cocoa powder
— 500 gms. sugar powdered
— 500 gms. solidified ghee dalda

— 1/4 tsp. baking powder
— 1-2 tbsp. warm milk if required
— 1/2 cups broken bits of chocolates

Directions:

— If ghee if not solidified, then refrigerate for some time.
— Take in a large deep plate, run in circular direction with a flat palm.
— Rub enough to make ghee white, fluffy and light.
— Sieve baking powder, cocoa powder with flour.
— Add sugar to ghee and mix till light.
— Fold in sieved flours, walnut powder till well mixed.
— Sprinkle some milk if dough seems too dry to hold.
— Mix with a light hand.
— Do not knead too much or make dough gooey.
— Coarse dough will make better and lighter cookies.
— Shape in small rounds, arrange on baking sheet.
— Preheat oven to 200°C, before putting in cookies.
— Press on chocolate bit on each cookie in centre.
— Bake at 180°C for 7-8 minutes or till very light golden.
— Remove, cool on a wire mesh or rack till completely cooled.
— Store in airtight container, in dry place.
— One may even add milk when rubbing ghee and sugar.

Butter Coockies

Ingredients:

— 1 c. butter
— 1 c. sugar

- 1/4 c. orange juice
- 1/2 t. orange extract
- 3 c. sifted flour
- 1/2 t. baking soda
- 1 t baking powder
- 1/2 t salt

Directions:

- Cream butter until very light. Add sugar gradually and continue creaming until light and fluffy.
- Add orange juice and extract.
- Sift together flour, salt, soda and powder. Add to creamed mixture bit by bit.
- When well mixed, cover bowl with plastic wrap and chill at least 1 hour (or overnight) in the refrigerator.
- Roll out on floured surface and cut with cookie cutters. Brush lightly with water and add colored sprinkles if desired.
- Place on ungreased cookie sheets or use baking parchment (easiest) and bake at 350 degrees F for about 13 minutes or until delicately brown. Cool before storing.

Otameal Wafers

Ingredients :

- 1/2 cup butter
- 3/4 cup sugar
- 2 tablespoons flour
- 1 teaspoon cinnamon
- 1 teaspoon baking powder
- 1 egg

- 1 cup oatmeal
- Aluminum foil
- 3 or 4 cardboard tubes, like from paper towels, gift wrap

Directions:

- Preheat oven to 375 degrees. Butter cookies sheets well AND flour them. Wrap the cardboard tubes in aluminum foil and set aside.
- Melt the butter. Stir in remaining ingredients. and mix until well blended. Drop the batter from a teaspoon approx. 3 inches apart on the cookie sheet.
- Bake for 6-8 minutes.. just til cookie looks "set" It is going to be very thin looking.
- After removing sheet from oven. let sit for a couple of minutes. Remove each cookie and drape over the foil covered tubes (this gives them a neat curl). The cookies are very delicate when they are hot, so work quickly and carefully. (Draping over foil tubes is not necessary)

Dreamz Coockies

Ingredients:

- 3 cubes of butter - 3/4 pound
- 3 cups flour, unsifted, sifted.. I never bothered
- 3/4 cup sugar
- 1 teaspoon ammonium carbonate - this is really important. You can get this at a good delicatessan..
- in a pinch, can substitute baking soda, but results won't be the same
- 1 teaspoon vanilla
- Blanched almonds - halves or slivers

Directions:

— Pre heat oven to 350 degrees.. get out baking sheet.. no need to grease it

— Brown butter over medium heat. I mean really get it brown. The butter will get all foamy: don't be alarmed. Keep stirring occasionally.. don't want it to burn.

— Stir in rest of ingredients, except slivered almonds.. and add everything right into the same pan you used to brown butter.

— You might want to let this mixture cool a bit first to handle; Roll the dough into balls the size of walnuts. Place on your cookie sheet. Top with almonds. Press the almonds into the cookie a bit so it will stay, but don't flatten the cookie like a pancake.

— Bake for 12 - 15 minutes. Let these cool on a sheet for a few minutes; hot cookies are pretty fragile most of the time.

— Transfer to wire racks to cool the cookies completely before you store them.

Oatmeal Apple Coockies

Ingredients:

— Quantity/Servings:

— Makes 2 1/2 dozen

— 3/4 cup Crisco shortening

— 1 1/4 cups firmly packed brown sugar

— 1 egg

— 1/4 cup milk

— 1 1/2 tsp. vanilla

— 1 cup all-purpose flour

— 1 1/4 tsp. ground cinnamon

— 1/2 tsp salt

— 1/4 tsp. baking soda

— 1/4 tsp. ground nutmeg

— 3 cups quick oats (not instasnt or old-fashioned)

— 1 cup peeled, diced apples

— 3/4 cup raisins (optional)

— 3/4 cup coarsely chopped walnuts (optional)

Directions:

— Preheat oven to 375 F. Grease cookie sheet.

— Combine shortening, sugar, egg, milk and vanilla in large bowl. Beat at medium speed with electric mixer until well blended.

— Combine flour, cinnamon, salt, baking soda and nutmeg in small bowl. Mix into creamed mixture at low speed until just blended. Stir in, one at a time, oats, apples, raisins and nuts with spoon.

— Drop rounded tablespoonfuls of dough 2 inches apart onto cookie sheet.

— Cool 2 minutes on cookie sheet. Remove to wire rack. Cool completely.

— Bake:

— Bake at 375 F for 13 minutes or until set.

Pecan Crescent Coockeis

Ingredients:

— Quantity/Servings:

— (makes 64 cookies)

— I cup butter (at room temp)

— 1/2 cup confectioners' sugar

— 2 tsp. vanilla extract

— 1 cup pecans (finely chopped)

— 1 3/4 cups all purpose flour (for decoration) confectioner's sugar

Directions:

— Mix butter, sugar and vanilla until fluffy. Stir in flour and pecans.

— Shape into crescents. Place on ungreased baking sheets.

— Bake in oven for 10 minutes or until firm but not brown.

— Gently roll each cookie in powdered sugar; cool on wire racks.

— Bake:

— 350 F oven for 10 minutes

— Drizzle cookies with melted chocolate. Let stand on waxed paper until chocolate is firm.

Lemon Bar Coockies

Ingredients:

— Quantity/Servings: Makes 36 bars

— 1 18oz. pkg. refrigerated sugar cookie dough

— 4 eggs (slightly beaten)

— 1 1/2 cups sugar

— 1/4 cup all-purpose flour

— 1 tsp baking powder

— 1/4 cup lemon juice

— 1 to 2 tsp powdered sugar

Directions:

— Heat oven to 350 F. Slice cookie dough as directed on pkg.

— Arrange slices in bottom of ungreased 13X9-inch pan. With lightly floured fingers, press dough evenly in pan. Bake at 350 F for 15 to 20 minutes or until light brown.

— In large bowl, combine eggs, sugar, flour and baking powder; blend well. Stir in lemon juice. Pour mixture over warm crust.

— Bake at 350 F for an additional 20 to 30 minutes or until top is light golden brown. Cool completely. Sprinkle with powdered sugar; cut into bars.

— Bake:

— Bake twice (read instructions) at 350 F.

— For best lemon flavor, use fresh lemons.

Grandmas's Gigerbread Coockies

Ingredients:

— 2 sticks butter

— 1 cup sugar

— 1 cup molasses

— 2 eggs

— 4 cups flour

— 2 teaspoons baking soda

— 1/2 teaspoon salt

— 2 teaspoon ginger

— 2 teaspoon cinnamon

— 1/4 teaspoon ground cloves

Directions:

— Beat butter with sugar and molasses Mix in eggs

— Sift dry ingredients and add to wet mixture. Mix well.

— Freeze for 1 hour or refrigerate for 2 hours.

— Roll out a portion of the dough to 1/4 inch thick on lightly floured board keeping balance of dough refrigerated.

— Cut with cookie cutter and place on lightly greased cookie sheet.

— Bake 8-10 minutes at 350 degrees. Cool , and decorate as desired.

Cake Mix Coockies

— Very Easy to do. Baking. Adult supervision is needed. Makes 15 pieces.

Ingredients:

— 1 box 2 layer cake mix any flavor

— 2 large eggs

— 1/2 cup oil

Directions:

— Mix them together in large bowl until well blended.

— Add 1 cup of chocolate chips, nuts, candies and mix them in

— Drop by teaspoon on cookie sheet.

— Bake at 350 until done approx. 7-9 minutes.

— Cool for a few minutes.

Gingerbread Men:

Ingredients :

— 3/4 cup light or dark brown sugar

— 1/2 cup butter or margarine (softened)

— 2 eggs

— 1/4 cup molasses

— 3 1/4 cups self-rising flour
— 2 tsp. ginger
— 1/2 tsp. allspice
— 1/2 tsp. cinnamon
— 1/2 tsp. nutmeg
— 1/2 tsp. salt

Directions:

— In large bowl, beat sugar & butter until well blended. Add eggs and molasses. Stir in remaining ingredients. Cover and chill 1 hour. Roll dough on well-floured board or countertop until 1/8-inch thick. Cut into shapes. Place on greased backing sheet. Bake for 10 minutes at 350 degrees. Cool on rack. You can decorate with frosting if desired. This recipe makes 24 cookies.

Ultimate Coockies

— Easy to do. Cooking necessary. Very colorful and delicious. Makes about 3 dozens cookies.

Ingredients :

— 1 cup (2 sticks) butter, softened
— 1/2 cup granulated sugar
— 1/2 cup firmly packed light brown sugar
— 1 large egg
— 1 teaspoon vanilla extract
— 2 cups all-purpose flour
— 1/2 teaspoon baking soda
— 1/8 teaspoon salt
— 3/4 cup chopped nuts (optional)
— 1 12 oz pkg. M&M's Semi-Sweet ..OR..
— (1 12 oz pkg. Milk Chocolate Mini Baking Bits)

Directions:

— Preheat oven to 350 F.

— In large bowl, cream butter and sugars until light and fluffy.

— Beat in egg and vanilla.

— In medium bowl, combine flour, baking soda and salt.

— Blend in creamed mixture.

— Stir in M&M's and nuts.

— Drop by heaping tablespoonfuls about 2 inches apart onto un greased cookie sheet.

— Bake 10-13 minutes.

— Bake 10-13 minutes. Do not over bake.

— Cool one minute on cookie sheet; cool completely on wire racks.

— Store in tightly covered container.

Sugar Coockies

Ingredients :

— 1 1/8 qts. self-rising flour

— 1 1/2 cup butter

— 2 1/4 cup of sugar

— 4 large eggs

— 1 tsp. vanilla

— Green sugar & Red sugar (optional but, recommended)

Directions:

— Blend the dry ingredients except sugar. Cream butter and sugar; add eggs. Then add the dry ingredients. Blend. Form into a big ball & separate into 4 medium sized balls. Roll out each and use Christmas cookie cutters to cut out the cookies. Place on a greased baking pan and cook at 350 degrees. This recipe can make a lot of cookies but, it's according to what size your cookie cutters are.

Cream Wafers

Ingredients:

— 1 cup butter, softened
— 1/3 cup whipping cream
— 2 cups all purpose flour
— Granulated sugar

Filling:

— 1/2 cup softened butter
— 1 1/2 cups confectioners sugar
— 1 teaspoon vanilla

Directions:

— Peanut butter mixture:
— red or green food coloring With electric mixer, thoroughly mix butter, cream, and flour. Cover; refrigerate dough for 1 hour. Divide into 3 pieces. Work with one piece at a time, keeping remaining pieces refrigerated until needed. Roll out dough 1/8 inch thick on floured surface. Cut into 1 1/2 inch circles. Transfer circles to a sheet of waxed paper that has been heavily coated with granulated sugar. Coat both sides with sugar. Place on un greased baking sheet. Prick each circle with a fork about 4 times. bake in preheated 350 degree oven 7 to 9 minutes, or just until set but not brown. Let cool on wire racks. For creamy filling. With electric mixer, cream butter,

confectioners sugar and vanilla until smooth and fluffy. Tint with few drops of food coloring. A few drops of water may be added for proper spreading consistency. Spread one side of half the circles with filling. Top with remaining circles. Store in air tight container or freeze until needed. Makes about 5 dozen cookies.

German Anise Drops

Ingredients :

— 2 eggs
— 1 cup sugar
— 2 teaspoons anise extract
— 1 1/4 cups all purpose flour

Directions:

— Beat eggs and sugar together for 20 minutes(either by hand or with electric mixer on low speed.) Add anise and stir in flour gradually. Drop by half teaspoon on greased cookie sheets. Let these stand over night or at least 8 hours before baking. Bake at 325 degrees until cookies are a pale yellow color on the bottom (about 12 minutes.) If these get to hard in the storing process, store in tin with a couple of slices of white bread. This will soften them some what. One recipe makes 45 cookies.

Peanut Blossoms

Ingredients :

— 1/2 cup shortening
— 3/4 cup creamy peanut butter
— 1/3 cup granulated sugar

— 1/3 cup brown sugar
— 1 egg
— 2 tablespoons milk
— 1 teaspoon vanilla
— 1 teaspoon baking soda
— 1/2 teaspoon salt
— 1 1/2 cups flour
— 10 ounce pkg of chocolate mini kisses

Directions:

— Beat shortening and peanut butter together, add sugars and beat until fluffy. Add egg, milk, and vanilla beat until well blended. Mix all dry ingredients, gradually until all is blended in. Shape dough into 1 inch balls, roll each ball in granulated sugar. Bake on un greased cookie sheet at 375 degrees for 8 to 10 minutes. Immediately after removing from oven, place 3 mini kisses on each one pressing down slightly. Makes about 4 dozen cookies.

Snowball Coockies

— Cooking necessary. Very easy to make. A tasty treat!
— Ingredients :
— 2 sticks margarine (or butter)
— 1/2 cup powdered sugar
— 2 cups all purpose flour
— 1/2 teaspoon vanilla
— 1 cup pecans (chopped fine)

Directions:

— Cream margarine and sugar together.

— Add other ingredients.
— Mix well and form into balls.
— Place on ungreased baking sheet and (with an adult supervision) bake at 350 degrees for 20 minutes.
— Let cool and then roll in powdered sugar.

Toffe-topped Bards

Ingredients :

— 2 cups firmly packed brown sugar
— 2 cups flour
— 1/2 cup butter, softened
— 1 teaspoon baking powder
— 1/2 teaspoon salt
— 1 teaspoon vanilla
— 1 cup milk
— 1 egg
— 1 cup semi-sweet chocolate chips
— 1/2 cup walnuts
— 1/4 cup flaked unsweetened coconut

Directions:

— Mix the brown sugar and flour together. Using a pastry cutter or two knifes cut in the butter until mixture resembles coarse crumbs. Remove one cup of mixture and set aside. To the rest of mixture add baking powder and salt. Using a fork, lightly beat in vanilla, milk and egg. Continue beating until smooth. Pour batter in greased 13x9 baking pan. Gently mix chocolate chips, nuts, and coconut together. Sprinkle reserved crumbs over top of batter. Then sprinkle chocolate chip mixture over top of crumbs. Spread evenly over top of batter. Bake at 350 degrees for 35 minutes. Cools bars completely before cutting. Cut into 24 bars. Store in air tight container for up to 5 days.

Almond Nankathai

Ingredients:

— 800 gms. plain flour

— 200 gms. almonds, powdered coarsely

— 500 gms. sugar powdered

— 500 gms. solidified ghee dalda

— 1/4 tsp. baking powder

— 1/2 cups broken bits of almonds or halved almonds

— 1-2 tbsp. warm milk if required

Directions:

— If ghee if not solidified, then refrigerate for some time.

— Take in a large deep plate, run in circular direction with a flat palm.

— Rub enough to make ghee white, fluffy and light.

— Sieve baking powder with flour.

— Add sugar to ghee and mix till light.

— Fold in sieved flour, almond powder till well mixed.

— Sprinkle some milk if dough seems too dry to hold.

— Mix with a light hand.

— Do not knead too much or make dough gooey.

— Coarse dough will make better and lighter cookies.

— Shape in small rounds, arrange on baking sheet.

— Preheat oven to 200°C, before putting in cookies.

— Press on almond bit on each cookie in centre.

— Bake at 180C for 7-8 minutes or till very light golden.

— Remove, cool on a wire mesh or rack till completely cooled.

— Store in airtight container, in dry place.

— One may even add milk when rubbing ghee and sugar.

5

Types of Icings

Icing (also frosting) is a sweet glaze made of sugar, that often also contains butter, water, egg whites, milk, or flavorings and is used to cover or decorate baked goods, such as cakes or biscuits.

Icing can be formed into shapes such as flowers and leaves using a pastry bag. Such decorations commonly grace birthday and wedding cakes. Chef's color dye (food coloring) is commonly added to icing mixtures to achieve the desired color. Sprinkles, coloring mist, or other decorations are often used on top of icing.

The simplest icing is a glacé icing, containing icing sugar and water. This can be flavored and colored as needed, for example by using lemon juice in place of the water. More complicated icings can be made by beating fat into icing sugar (as in butter cream), by melting fat and sugar together, by using egg whites (as in royal icing), and by adding other ingredients such as glycerin (as in fondant). Some icings can be made from combinations of sugar and cream cheeses, or by using ground almonds (as in marzipan).

Icing can be applied with a utensil such as a knife or spatula, or it can be applied by drizzling or dipping (see glaze) or by rolling the icing out and draping it over the cake. Icing may be used between layers in a cake as a filling, or it may be used to completely or partially cover the outside of a cake or other baked product.

There are different types of icings: some types are cooked, such as meringue-based frostings and chocolate glazes. Others, such as Royal Icings and certain Buttercream frostings, are simply mixed together without any cooking on the stove.

Cake icings

The basic frosting recipe contains butter, sugar, and a liquid such as water or milk. More liquid is added for a glaze. Flavorings such as extracts, fruit zest or juice, and chocolate are often added. Sugar is the most important ingredient in all types of frostings, providing sweetness, flavor, bulk and structure. For richer flavor, unsalted grade A butter is used instead of margarine or shortening, but icings made with shortening hold up better in a warm room. Eggs are used in cooked frostings. For safety, frostings containing raw eggs should be heated to kill any bacteria. Frostings containing egg whites should be whipped with oil-free utensils. Any oil on utensils or in the mixing bowl will prevent the egg whites from whipping into peaks. Many types of cake, cookie, cupcake and dessert are covered with icing. Icing can be used to decorate a variety of pastries and baked goods. Icing adds flavor and texture, as well as enabling a chef to decorate her creation so that it is a treat for the eyes as well as the palate. There are seven basic types of icing: buttercream, flat icings, foam icings, fondant, fudge icings, royal icing, and glazes.

Buttercream Icing

Buttercream icing is one of the most popular icings for cakes. It is easy to spread, has a sweet flavor and a soft, smooth texture and is simple to make. Buttercream icing is made with a type of fat, often butter, and sugar. It can also contain eggs or milk to change the texture and thickness. Most icing found in the supermarket in the cake mix section is basic buttercream icing.

Buttercream Icing Recipe

Ingredients:

— 1/2 cup solid vegetable shortening

— 1/2 cup butter or margarine, softened

— 1 teaspoon Clear Vanilla Extract

— 4 cups sifted confectioners' sugar (approx. 1 lb.)

— 2 tablespoons milk

In large bowl, cream shortening and butter with electric mixer. Add vanilla. Gradually add sugar, one cup at a time, beating well on medium speed. Scrape sides and bottom of bowl often. When all sugar has been mixed in, icing will appear dry. Add milk and beat at medium speed until light and fluffy. Keep bowl covered with a damp cloth until ready to use. For best results, keep icing bowl in refrigerator when not in use. Refrigerated in an airtight container, this icing can be stored 2 weeks. Rewhip before using.

Yield: Makes about 3 cups.

For thin (spreading) consistency icing, add 2 tablespoons light corn syrup, water or milk.

For Pure White Icing (stiff consistency), omit butter; substitute an additional 1/2 cup shortening for butter and 1/2 teaspoon No-Color Butter Flavor. Add up to 4 tablespoons light corn syrup, water or milk to thin for icing cakes.

Vanilla Butter Icing

For coating, filling or piping, but does not have a sheen)

Ingredients:

— 3 tbsp. butter, softened

— 2 cups icing sugar, sifted

— 2-3 drops vanilla essence

— 1 pinch salt

— 4-5 drops lemon juice

Directions:

— Put butter in a deep bowl.

— Add flavouring and beat till smooth.

— Add sugar, beat with a wooden spoon till well blended.

— Add salt and lemon juice, beat again till light, white and smooth.

- When spoon is lifted the icing lifted in a peak should hold.
- Spoon into an icing bag, fit nozzle as required.
- Pipe carefully over prepared cake.
- Refrigerate if required to be used later.

Pineapple Butter Icing

Ingredients:

- 3 tbsp. butter, softened
- 2 cups icing sugar, sifted
- 2-3 drops pineapple essence
- 4 drops of yellow colour
- 1 pinch salt
- 4-5 drops lemon juice

Directions:

- Put butter in a deep bowl.
- Add flavouring and beat till smooth.
- Add sugar, beat with a wooden spoon till well blended.
- Add salt and lemon juice, beat again till light, white and smooth.
- When spoon is lifted the icing lifted in a peak should hold.
- Spoon into an icing bag, fit nozzle as required.
- Pipe carefully over prepared cake.
- Refrigerate if required to be used later.
- Food colour and essence can be replaced with different flavour: For orange use orange, strawberry for pink, icecream for blue, etc.

Foam Icing

Foam icing comes in a variety of flavors and has a soft, fluffy appearance. A meringue is made of whipped egg whites with a flavored syrup added. Marshmallow foam is a common foam icing, but other flavors such as chocolate or vanilla can also be added to the meringue.

Sea Foam Recipe

Ingredients:

— 1 1/2 c. brown sugar

— 1/2 c. water

— Boil soft ball or threads on spoon.

— 1/4 tsp. salt

— 3 eggs

— 1/8 tsp. cream of tartar

Directions:

Beat until stiff. Pour slowly into egg white topping.

Fondant Icing

Fondant icing gives a cake or pastry an elegant appearance and is popular for wedding cakes and other show pieces. Fondant icing is simply sugar and water, with either glucose or cream of tartar used to produce the proper crystallization to give it a smooth, almost porcelain look.

Easy Fondant Icing Recipe

Ingredients:

— 2 pounds confectioner's sugar, sifted

— 1/4 cup cold water

— 1 tablespoon unflavored gelatin

— 1/2 cup glucose (found in cake decorating stores) or white corn syrup

— 1 1/2 tablespoons glycerine (found in cake decorating stores)

— 1 teaspoon desired flavoring (vanilla will give the fondant an off-white color)

— Cornstarch

Directions:

— In a large bowl (do not use metal), sift the sugar and make a well in the center. In a small saucepan, add the water and sprinkle the gelatin on top to soften for about 5 minutes. Begin to heat the gelatin and stir until the gelatin is dissolved and clear. Do not boil. Turn off the heat and add the glucose and glycerine, stirring until well blended. Add the flavoring. Pour into the well of sugar, and mix until all of the sugar is blended. Use hands to knead icing until it becomes stiff. Add small amounts of confectioner's sugar if the mixture is sticky.

— Form the mixture into a ball and wrap tightly in plastic wrap. Place in an airtight container. This icing works best if allowed to rest at room temperature for about eight hours before using, particularly if the weather is humid. Do not refrigerate.

— To cover a cake with fondant: Dust a clean pastry cloth, or a smooth, clean surface, with cornstarch and roll the fondant with a rolling pin until it is approximately 1/4 inch thick. Make sure that the fondant is large enough to fit over the top and sides of the cake. Slide both hands under the fondant and carefully center it on top of a cake that has been freshly iced with buttercream.

— Dust your hands with cornstarch and smooth the fondant, starting at the top and working down the sides until the entire surface is even and flat. Cut off the excess icing around the bottom of the cake with a pizza cutter or sharp knife. Decorate the cake with buttercream or royal icing. This fondant keeps a cake fresh for two days at room temperature. Do not refrigerate a cake with fondant icing.

FUDGE ICING

Fudge icing is thick and rich with a strong chocolate flavor. Other flavors, such as almond, peanut butter or mint, are often added. Using both butter and shortening, corn syrup, sugar and a variety of other ingredients, fudge icing can be somewhat time consuming to prepare, but the finished product is stable and can be refrigerated and used at a later time.

Chocolate Fudge Icing Recipe

Ingredients:

— 1 c. firmly packed brown sugar

— 3 tbsp. cocoa

— 3 tbsp. Crisco

— 1 tbsp. butter

— Dash of salt

— 1/4 c. milk

— 1 1/2 c. sifted powdered sugar

— 1 tsp. vanilla

Directions:

— Combine brown sugar, cocoa, Crisco, butter, salt and milk in saucepan. Bring to a boil stirring constantly. Then remove from heat.

— Cool to lukewarm. Add powdered sugar and vanilla. Beat with electric beater until thick enough to spread.

Royal Icing

Royal icing is similar to flat icing, but adds egg whites to produce a thicker icing which hardens to a brittle texture. Royal icing can be used to make beautiful, artistic decorations because it hardens when dried, but the same property makes it less enjoyable to eat. Royal icing is used primarily for decorative additions to cakes and for show work such as sugar sculptures.

Royal Icing Recipe

Ingredients:

— 3 large egg whites

— 3 tsp cream of tartar

— 4 cups of confectioners sugar, sifted

— If using icing to frost cookies, 1/4 to 1/2 c water will be needed

Directions:

— Place egg whites, cream of tartar and half of the confectioners sugar into a bowl.

— With an electric mixer at low speed, slowly add remaining sugar

— Beat on low speed for at least 2 minutes to assure even mixing

— Beat on highest speed for 8 - 10 minutes

— A knife drawn through the icing should leave a clear path

— Icing must be kept covered with a damp cloth or paper towel

— To COLOR icing, use paste or powdered colors
— Add water a little bit at a time
— Icing will flow slowly in an even stream like heavy cream when ready
— Color icing in the same way as Royal Icing

Glazes

Glazes are thin, watery icings which form a hard, crisp shell when poured or brushed over cakes and pastries. Glazes are usually made with a fruit flavor, although other flavors, such as chocolate or coffee, are sometimes popular as well. Like flat icing, glazes can be used on sweet breakfast pastries like coffee cakes. They add flavor, and also help keep the pastry moist and improve its shelf life.

With seven basic types of icing to choose from, and myriad possibilities within each type, pastry chefs have a great variety of options when topping their creations. Using buttercream, flat icing, foam icing, fondant, fudge icing, royal icing and glazes, an experienced chef can produce countless delicious creations.

Brown Sugar Glaze Recipe

Ingredients:

— 4 Tbsps. brown sugar
— 6 Tbsps. milk
— 2 Tbsps. butter
— 1 cup powdered sugar

Directions:

— In a saucepan, over low heat, combine brown sugar, milk, butter, heat only until sugar is dissolved stirring

constantly. Remove from heat and stir in the powdered sugar, blend until smooth. Use while hot.
Return to Menu

Chocolate Glaze

Ingredients:

— 1 square unsweetened chocolate

— 2 Tbsps. butter

— 1 cup powdered sugar

— 1/2 tsp. vanilla

— 3 to 5 Tbsps. milk

Directions:

— In a saucepan, over low heat, melt chocolate and butter, stirring until smooth. Remove from heat and blend in vanilla, powdered sugar and enough milk for desired glaze consistency. Use while hot.

Butterscotch Glaze

Ingredients:

— 1 cup brown sugar

— 1/2 cup buttermilk

— 1/4 cup butter

— 1/4 cup corn syrup

— 1/2 tsp. baking soda

— 1/2 tsp. vanilla

Directions:

— In a saucepan, combine all ingredients and boil for 10 mins. Use while hot.

Butter Glaze

Ingredients:

— 1/3 cup butter (softened)

— 1 cup sugar

— 1/2 cup condensed milk

Directions:

— Mix ingredients, bring to a boil and cook for 1 min. Then remove from heat and beat until thick and pour over the cake while it is still hot.

FRUITY GLACE ICING

Ingredients:

— 1 cup sugar

— 1/2 to 1 tbsp. fruit juice (for stiffer icing)

— 1 to 1-1/2 tbsp. fruit juice (for flowing icing)

— 2-3 drops food colour as desired

— 2-3 drops essence to match

Directions:

— Put icing sugar, cocoa powder in a bowl, no sifting required, unless very lumpy.

— Pour juice, either stir to mix in the basin, or over very gently heat.

— When fully dissolved add colour and flavour, mix till even.

— Pour all at once over cake.

— Quickly spread evenly, allowing to flow over sides.

— Run with a knife dipped in hot water to even top.

— When fully cooled, slash off side overruns if so desired.

— Allow to cool completely before touching it for further decorations.

— Add a tsp. of melted butter while mixing, to give a shiny gloss.

Light and Easy Fruit Icing

Not only is this recipe light and easy, it's quick too.

Ingredients:

— 1/2 cup fruit preserves or curds*

— 1/4 cup water

— 8 ounce container whipped topping, thawed

— 3/4 cup powdered sugar

Directions:

— In medium bowl, mix water with preserves and/or curd. Stir in whipped topping and powdered sugar. Makes enough for 2- 8 or 9-inch cake layers.

— Preserves like Strawberry, Seedless Raspberry.

— Curds such as Lemon or Lime. Marmalades may also work. If there's too much fruit in the preserves, you may wish to put it in the blender with the water to thin it out a little.

Decorator's Icing

This Decorator's Icing will work great on any cake.

Ingredients:

— 1/2 cup (4 ounces) butter, softened

— 2/3 cup shortening

— 1 pound box powdered sugar

— 1-1/2 teaspoons vanilla

— milk or water

Directions:

— Cream butter and shortening with electric mixer. Add powdered sugar and mix well. Add vanilla extract and continue to beat for several minutes until almost white. When ready to pipe through pastry tube, thin slightly with water or milk, added a tablespoon at a time.

— Mix in tint, as desired.

Caramel Icing

A good icing for coating, and piping if kept a little stiffer.

Ingredients:

— 3 cups icing sugar, sifted

— 2 tbsp. castor or granular sugar

— 5 tbsp. thin cream or wholefat milk

— 75 gms. white butter

Directions:

— Sift icing sugar into a bowl. Keep aside.

— Melt butter carefully in a pan.

— Add milk and bring to just below simmering point (71°C).

— Simultaneously, heat castor sugar in another pan.

— Pour into caramel, stir to dissolve.

— Pour over icing sugar, beat till thick and creamy.

— Spread over cake immediately.

Tips for Icing

— Use softened butter to make icings, but do not try melting hard butter for use. Just let it thaw to room temperature till soft.

— Use unsalted white table butter to make icings. But if you have mastered the art of extracting butter from top cream or malai of milk, then you may use this butter too. But before using, wash this lump of butter with lots of cold milk 3-4 times, and remove all water traces before proceeding with recipe.

— Whether or not a recipe mentions it, a pinch of salt make all the difference to the texture and keeping quality of the icing. Also, a few drops of lemon juice added towards the end, to white icing, will make it whiter.

— For icings which are used for spreading (not piping), a little milk added instead of only butter, will reduce the calories, the texture will be smoother, and handling will be easier.

— Invest in a good set of icing nozzles, preferably one which uses bags, and a basic screwnozzle attachment for easier handling. Icing guns can be messy if you want to change too many colours.

— Dip a knife in hot water, and run it flatly over icing of top and sides, to give a smooth even finish. The hot water will keep the icing from sticking back to the knife. Keep dipping the knife every now and then, till finished.

— If you are using a very stiff icing like fondant or pastillage, then, apply a thin layer of jam to the top and sides of the cake before spreading the icing. This will help to stick the icing firmly to the cake.

— Some setting icings may be made with milkmaid instead of icing sugar, as in the case of chocolate pourable topping. Make sure you follow instructions for these icings care fully, and attain proper thickness, before pouring. If it is too thin it will run down. If too thick it may set before you can pour it. The icing is done when it falls in a fat nonspreading drop when a drop is put in a plate.

— As a rule it is better to always sieve the icing sugar before using it, this will make it much easier to mix into the butter or other liquid. There will also be no lumps left, even the hard one can be broken while dry.

— You may use liquid, gel or powdered food colours, but make sure they are not ancient and are of the best quality. Do no go in for cheap hardly known brands, if you are not sure of its purity.

— Use setting agents like gelatine and chinagrass carefully where required. Mistakes in their use, may spoil the icing irreparably.

— Either use a dropper, or a small skewer to apply the colour to the icing, and add after the icing has been mixed halfway.

— Learn to choose the right type of icing for your cake. Glace and liquid icings may be alright for toppings but they cannot be piped. Butter icings are good for piping and topping. While fondants, pastillage, frostings are good not only for rolling, but also for moulding into shapes.

— If you are using a cooking theremometer: Just below simmering point is 160°F or 71°C. Boiling point of watery liquids is 212oF or 100°C. 'Soft ball' stage for cooked icings like fondant is 238°F-240°F. So just go ahead, use your imagination, and ice away, finding it more exciting and easy as you go.

— Spectacular effects can be got from simple items like silver balls (available in many sizes), multicoloured round sweet granules, coloured sugars(shown in next tip), chocolate sev, chocolate buttons big and small, gems or m&ms and even nuts like walnut halves, almonds, pistachios. Then glazed or canned cherries, strawberries, etc. may also be used.

— Put some sugar in a jar, add a few drops of desired food colour, shake jar well, and keep aside to allow the colour to permeate every grain.

— Fruit like cherries, strawberries, etc. may be dipped halfway in melted chocolate, allow to dry and used as a very attractive decoration for cakes, since the colour effect is spectacular, especially on a white cake topping.

— Powdered praline may be used to roll an iced cake in, to stud it all over and on the sides for a change. Coconut flakes may also be used similarly. Or a nice wide satin ribbon tied along the side of a round cake to end in a well shaped bow, will give a festive look to even the simplest cake.

6

Types of Tarts

A tart is a pastry dish, usually sweet, that is a type of pie with an open top that is not covered with pastry. The Tarte Tatin is a particular kind of "upside-down" tart, of apples, other fruit, or onions.

Bakewell Tart

A Bakewell tart is a traditional English baked dessert tart or cake. It is a distant cousin of the original "Bakewell Pudding".

Bakewell Cake

It consists of a shortcrust pastry shell, spread with jam and covered with a sponge-like filling enriched with ground almonds (known as Frangipane). They may also be covered with nuts such as almonds and peanuts. Alternative flavours, including blackcurrant, strawberry and apple are also produced. A Cherry Bakewell is a small cake, covered with a top layer of icing and a single central half-cherry, also known as a Bakewell Cake.

To some extent, the terms cake and tart are used interchangeably, though most insist the names are recipe specific. Recipes abound, for example those given by Ben Mathews, Eliza Acton, K Morgan, M Bates and Mrs Beeton, and modern commercial examples are to be found in most cake shops and on every supermarket shelf. The name only became common in the 20th Century; the dish was previously known as Bakewell Pudding.

Bakewell Pudding

The Derbyshire town of Bakewell claims to be the home of the authentic Bakewell Pudding and many believe it to originally come from the Rushbottom Lane district. A recipe still made there consists of a puff pastry shell with a layer of jam, covered with a filling of eggs, sugar, butter and almonds.

The tale told to tourists is that this dish is an accidental invention of the 1860s, which occurred when a nobleman visiting the White Horse Inn at Bakewell ordered strawberry tart. The cook, instead of stirring the egg mixture into the cake, spread it on top of the jam. However, this claim is almost certainly apocryphal, as the pudding was by then already well-known, and its antecedents can be traced back to medieval times.

Butter Tart

A butter tart is a type of pastry best known as a Canadian treat. It should not be confused with Butter pie a savoury pie from the Preston area of Lancashire, England or bread and butter pudding. The English Canadian tart consists of butter, sugar and eggs in a pastry shell, similar to the base of the U. S. pecan pie without the nut topping, and similar to the French-Canadian sugar pie. Additional ingredients can include raisins, pecans, walnuts, coconut, dates, butterscotch, chocolate chips or peanut butter.

Butter tarts were a staple of pioneer Canadian cooking, and they remain a characteristic pastry of Canada, considered one of only a few recipes of genuinely Canadian origin. One of the earliest known Canadian recipes is from northern Ontario and dates back to 1915. Yet similar tarts are made in Scotland, where they are often referred to as Ecclefechan butter tarts from the town of Ecclefechan; and in France, though they are uncommon. There, they are related to the much more common tarte à la frangipane, that differs from the basic Canadian recipe only by the addition of ground almonds. The origin thus appears to be unknown.

Egg Tart

Egg Tarts are a kind of pastry that is popular in Hong Kong, Macau, surrounding areas in southern China and overseas Chinese communities. It consists of a flaky outer crust, with a middle filled with egg custard, which is then baked. It is related to the English-style custard tart, a pastry commonly enjoyed in the British Isles, Australia, and New Zealand. Egg tarts are typically marketed at Chinese, Hong Kong, and Macau bakeries, cha chaan tengs, and some dim sum restaurants.

The earliest record of Egg tart in the east is in a royal banquet for the Kangxi Emperor as part of the Manchu Han Imperial Feast. Custard tarts were introduced in Hong Kong in the 1940s by cha chaan tengs and western cafes and bakeries to compete with dim sum restaurants particularly for yum cha. It later evolved to become egg tarts today. At the time, egg tarts were twice the size of today's tarts. During the 1950s and 1960s when the economy started taking off, Luk Jyu took the lead with the mini-egg tart.

One theory suggests Chinese egg tarts are a Chinese adaption of English tarts with custard filling. Guangdong had long been the region in China with most frequent contact with the West, in particular Britain. As a former British colony, British food naturally assimilated to local Hong Kong tastes. Custard tarts made of shortcrust pastry, eggs, sugar, milk or cream, vanilla, and nutmeg have long been a favourite pastry in the British Isles, Australia, and New Zealand.

According to Laura Mason and Catherine Bell's Traditional Foods of Britain: An Inventory a version of custard tart has been made in England since the Middle Ages. The medieval recipe was a shortcrust pastry case filled with a mixture of milk or cream, eggs, sweetening agents, and other spices. Gary Rhodes's New British Classics states the recipe of making the modern version of English custard tart has been more or less set since the Tudor times.

Variety

Hong Kong-style

Today egg tarts come in many variations within Hong Kong cuisine. These include egg white tarts, milk tarts, honey-egg tarts, ginger-flavoured egg tarts (the two aforementioned variations were a take upon traditional milk custard and egg custard, which was usually served in cha chaan tengs, chocolate tarts, green-tea-flavoured tarts and even bird's nest tarts.

Overall, Hong Kong-style egg tarts have two main varieties, divided according to the type of the outermost layer or crust:

— Butter-flavoured shortcrust pastry: made with shortcrust pastry. It is named "butter skin" in Chinese since it possesses a cookie-like flavour with a rich butter aroma.

— Puff pastry: made with puff pastry and with an extremely crisp texture. Lard is typically used in making the base rather than butter or shortening. This type is regarded as the most traditional and correct form of egg tart by food critics.

Other varieties becoming more popular in the ever increasing focus on health are:

— Milk-centered egg tarts. It is composed of a smooth milky egg-white center and is considered by some to be somewhat healthier than traditional egg tarts.

— Bird's nest egg tarts. Bird's nest pieces are added to the egg center.

Compared with the original English custard tarts, milk is normally not added to the egg custard, and the tart is not sprinkled with grounded nutmeg or cinnamon before serving. It is also sometimes (though not always) served piping hot rather than at room temperature as per English custard tarts.

Portuguese-style

Portuguese-style egg tarts were evolved from "pastel de nata", a traditional Portuguese custard pastry that consists of custard in a crème brûlée-like consistency caramelised fashion in a puff pastry case. It was created more than 200 years ago by Catholic Sisters at Jerónimos Monastery at Belém in Lisbon. Casa Pastéis de Belém was the first pastry shop outside of the convent to sell this pastry in 1837, and it is now a popular pastry in every pastry shop around the world owned by Portuguese descendants.

The Portuguese-style egg tarts known in Macau originated from Lord Stow's Café in Coloane, owned by a Briton named Andrew Stow. Stow modified the recipe of pastel de nata using techniques of making English custard tarts. It has since become available at numerous bakeries, as well as Macau-style restaurants and Chinese,

Hong Kong and Taiwan branches of the KFC restaurant chain. There was a craze in Singapore and Taiwan in the late 1990s.

Pop-Tarts

A Pop-Tart is a flat rectangular toaster pastry approximately 3 in (75 mm) by 5.5 in (115 mm), made by the Kellogg Company. Pop-Tarts have a sugary filling sealed inside two layers of rectangular, thin pastry crust; each layer of this crust is about 0.1 in (2 mm) thick. Most varieties have frosting, but some do not. They can be eaten without being warmed, but are often warmed inside a toaster. They are usually sold in pairs inside foil packages, and do not require refrigeration.

Popular flavours include blueberry, frosted strawberry, frosted brown sugar cinnamon, cherry, Hot Fudge Sundae, and s'mores. For a brief period in the 1990s, Kellogg's sold a strawberry and brown sugar cinnamon flavoured Pop-Tarts cold cereal, shaped like miniature frosted toaster pastries. Pop-Tarts are Kellogg's most popular brand to date, with more than two billion Pop-Tarts sold each year. They are distributed mainly in the United States, but also in the United Kingdom and Canada. Pop-Tarts were discontinued in Australia in 2005. To some extent, the brand name "Pop-Tart" has become a genericized trademark describing any toaster pastry.

Gypsy Tart

A gypsy tart is a type of pie made with evaporated milk, muscovado sugar (though some varieties include light brown sugar), and pie crust. It originates from East Kent((cn)) in England, and is little known outside that area. As would be expected, the tart is extremely sweet and is for many people associated with school dinners.

Although most will know the version of gypsy tart made with evaporated milk - as sold in shops in East Kent and served as part of school dinners - it can also be made with condensed milk in place of evaporated milk. This makes a firmer and even sweeter tart, with a darker colour.

Neenish Tart

A neenish tart, also in the past sometimes called a nienich tart, is a tart made with a pastry base, usually jam, sweet gelatine-set cream or mock cream paste filling, and icing on top in two colours, half one colour and half the other. They are almost exclusively sized as individual servings, 10-12 cm in diameter. This kind of tart (so far as is known) was created in Australia, and is still best known there. It is similar to a black and white cookie, although neenish tarts are filled with jam.

The origin of the name is uncertain. A Mrs Evans and her sister reported that it was named after a Ruby Neenish, a friend of their mother who lived in Grong Grong, New South Wales and was the first to make such a tart in about 1913. The two colour icing was because she ran out of cocoa to make it all chocolate. The name nienich suggests a German origin, except neenish was known before nienich.

Treacle Tart

A treacle tart is a traditional English dessert with a rich, treacle and breadcrumb filling in a pastry casing, traditionally with a lattice of pastry strips on top. Many recipes also add the juice and zest of a lemon to the filling. A treacle tart is normally eaten steaming hot, with custard, cream or ice cream.

Linzer Torte

The Linzer Torte (or Linzertorte) is an Austrian Tart or Pie made with a very short, crumbly pastry of flour, butter and ground nuts (usually almonds), in two thin layers, with a filling of jam (most often raspberry or red currant.) It has a round opening on the top revealing a layer of jam, or it may be covered by a lattice of dough strips.

Linzer Torte

It resembles a large cookie and indeed is often found made into small tarts or cookies in North American bakeries. The Linzer Torte, named for the city of Linz, Austria, is the oldest-known torte or cake in the world. For a long time a recipe from 1696 in the Vienna Stadt- and Landesbibliothek was the oldest one known.

Manchester Tart

A Manchester tart is a traditional English baked tart consisting of a shortcrust pastry shell, spread with jam, covered with a custard filling and topped with flakes of coconut and a Maraschino cherry. One variation includes slices of banana underneath the custard with the jam.

APPLE FRANGIPANE TART RECIPE

This tart is the perfect combination of pastry, almond cream, and fruit. It is quite similar to the Apple Galette recipe on the site, only we have changed the pastry crust and added some fresh blackberries for more flavour and color.

The pastry used here is called Pâte Brisee, which is a French short crust pastry dough made from a mixture of flour, sugar, salt, butter, and ice water. It is well suited for free form tarts as it has a high ratio of fat to flour which gives the pastry its crumbly texture and buttery flavour and is perfect with the sweet almond filling and sliced apples. The sweet almond filling (called Frangipane) is a pastry cream traditionally made with almond flour (meal) along with sugar, butter, and eggs.

Almond meal (flour) is blanched almonds that are finely ground and can be found at health food stores and many large grocery stores. If you cannot find it you can make your own by taking about 1/2 cup of blanched almonds (along with the flour in the recipe) and processing these two ingredients in your food processor until finely ground. Just make sure not to over process this mixture as it needs to be finely ground, not a paste. Once made, the frangipane is then spread over the unbaked pastry and is used not only for its wonderful flavour but it also acts as a shield to prevent the apple juices from penetrating into the crust.

Sliced apples and blackberries are then arranged over the cream and the edges of the pastry are folded up and over the filling. The assembled tart is then brushed with melted butter, and sprinkled with sugar, which only adds to this pastry's crisp and crumbly texture. You can serve this tart warm from the oven or at room temperature. Of course, a little whipped cream or vanilla ice cream finishes this tart off very nicely.

Apples are one of the more versatile fruits that are enjoyed both in baking and eating out of hand. Fortunately there is an apple for everyone as varieties number in the thousands and run the gamut from very sweet to very tart with textures from soft to firm.

In baking, it is important to use the right type of apple i.e. one that retains its shape when baked. Oftentimes recipes call for Granny Smith Apples and this is because they are readily available year round and their tart flavour and firm texture make them ideal in pies and tarts. But if you are fortunate enough to live near an apple orchard or can go to a farmer's market, your choice of suitable baking apples dramatically increases.

There are so many varieties with wonderful textures and flavours that are never sold at your local grocery stores. In my area Mutsu Golden, Rome, Stayman Winesap, Jonagold and Jonathan are available but try the varieties locally grown in your area. You won't be disappointed and even try mixing two or even three varieties for a more complex favoured tart.

Frangipane: In the bowl of your electric mixer, or with a hand mixer, cream the sugar and butter. Beat in the egg and vanilla extract until smooth. Add the almond meal and flour and beat until it forms a smooth paste. Transfer to a small bowl, cover and refrigerate.

Pate Brisee: In a food processor, place the flour, salt, and sugar and process until combined. Add the butter and process until the mixture resembles coarse meal (about 15 seconds). Pour 1/8 cup (30 ml) water in a slow, steady stream through the feed tube until the pastry just holds together when pinched. Add remaining water, if necessary. Do not process more than about 30 seconds. Turn the pastry out onto your work surface, gather it into a ball, cover with plastic wrap, and refrigerate for about one hour to chill the butter and allow the gluten in the flour to relax.

Once the pastry has chilled sufficiently, remove from refrigerator and place on a lightly floured surface. Roll the pastry into a 13 inch (33 cm) circle. Lift and turn the dough when rolling so it does not stick to the counter. If it gets too soft and starts to fall apart when rolling, put dough back in the refrigerator for 10 minutes to firm up. Transfer the circle to a baking sheet that has been lined with parchment paper, cover with plastic wrap, and return it to the refrigerator for about 15 minutes. Then remove the chilled pastry from the refrigerator and spread the frangipane evenly over the dough, leaving a 2 inch (5 cm) border. Cover and return to the refrigerator while you prepare the apples.

Assemble Tart

Preheat oven to 375 degrees F (190 degrees C) and place the rack in the center of the oven.

Arrange the apple slices evenly over the frangipane layer (concentrically or free form), again leaving a 2 inch (5 cm) border. Fold the 2 inch (5 cm) border of pastry up and over the apples (sealing any cracks) and brush the pastry crust with the melted butter. Pour any leftover butter over the apples. Sprinkle about 3 tablespoons (40 grams) of sugar over the crust and apples.

Bake the tart for 50 to 60 minutes or until the apples are cooked and the crust is golden brown. Remove from oven and place on a wire rack to cool. Serve warm or at room temperature with vanilla ice cream or softly whipped cream. Refrigerate any leftovers.

Apple Custard Tart

There are so many ways to use apples and this elegant tart not only presents apples beautifully but it also tastes delicious. This recipe is adapted from Bo Friberg's excellent book 'The Professional Pastry Crust' and it starts off with a pre baked sweet pastry crust made with butter which gives the crust a rich sweet buttery flavour with a crisp cookie-like texture.

We then glaze the baked and cooled tart shell with a thin layer of apricot preserves which not only adds flavour to the tart but it also acts as a shield to prevent the crust from becoming soft. Once the glaze has dried, lightly sweetened sautéed apples are artfully arranged on the tart shell. The important thing is to use a variety that holds its shape when cooked.

An apple brandy-laced custard is then poured over the apples and the tart is baked until the custard has set. The finishing touch is to broil the tart until the tips of the apple slices have nicely browned. Serve with softly whipped cream or vanilla ice cream.

Pastry Crust: Roll out the pastry and fit it into a 8 or 9 inch (20 to 23 cm) tart pan (instructions for how to roll out the pastry are given in the recipe for the Sweet Pastry Crust). Prick the bottom of the shell and chill for 20 minutes.

Preheat oven to 400 degrees F (205 degrees C) and place rack in center of oven. Line the unbaked pastry shell with parchment paper or aluminum foil. Fill tart pan with pie weights or beans, making sure the weights are to the top of the pan and evenly distributed over the entire surface. Bake crust for 20 to 25 minutes until crust is dry and lightly browned. Remove weights and cool crust on wire rack. When cool, spread a thin layer of warm apricot glaze over the bottom and sides of the tart to seal the crust and prevent it from getting soggy. Let the glaze dry between 20 - 30 minutes.

Apricot Glaze: In a small saucepan heat the apricot

preserves until boiling. Remove from heat and strain to get rid of lumps. Add the Cognac or water.

Brandy Custard: In a large bowl whisk the flour and sugar together. Mix in the eggs and stir with a wooden spoon to make a smooth paste. Do not let this mixture sit too long as it will form a crust.

Meanwhile, in a small saucepan over medium heat, heat the half-and-half with the vanilla bean until it just starts to boil and the cream foams up. Remove from heat, take out the vanilla bean, and gradually whisk into the egg mixture, stirring constantly. Whisk in the Apple Brandy. At this point, scrape out the seeds from the vanilla bean and add to egg mixture or, if using vanilla extract, add it now. Set this mixture aside while you prepare the apples.

Apples: Peel, core, and slice the apples into 1/4 inch thick slices. Melt the 2 tablespoons (26 grams) butter in a large skillet over medium heat and stir in the 2 - 4 tablespoons (25 - 50 grams) sugar. Add the apples and sauté until they begin to soften, approximately 5 - 10 minutes. Set the cooked apples aside.

Assemble Tart

Preheat oven to 350 degrees F (177 degrees C) and place rack in the middle of the oven. Arrange the apple wedges in concentric circles on top of the cooled and glazed tart shell. Carefully pour the custard over the apples to just below the top of the tart pan (do not fill all the way or the custard will drip between the crust and the pan). Sprinkle lightly with the Cinnamon Sugar.

Place tart pan on a larger baking sheet to make it easier to remove from oven and bake for about 25-30 minutes or until the custard has set. Let the tart cool on wire rack, then lightly sift powdered sugar over the top. Place the tart under the broiler in the oven just long enough to caramelize the sugar on the apples. To prevent the edges of the tart shell from over-browning, you can cover them with a thin piece of aluminum foil or pie shields. Be careful not to over brown.

To remove the tart from the fluted sides of the pan, place your hand under the pan, touching only the removable bottom not the sides. Gently push the tart straight up, away from the sides. The fluted tart ring will fall away and slide down your arm. If you want to remove the bottom of the pan, run a knife or thin metal spatula between the crust and metal bottom, then slide the tart onto a cardboard cake round or platter. Serve with softly whipped cream or vanilla ice cream.

Berry Tart

Once the pastry is made, in your food processor, and left to chill, it is then divided into four portions. Each portion is rolled into a 7 inch (18 cm) round and then a mixture of lightly sweetened berries and peaches are mounded in the center of each round of pastry. All that is left to do is to gently fold the pastry up and over the filling, making sure that the folds of pastry are sealed so that the pastry does not fall open during baking.

The important thing to remember is to bake the tarts until the crusts have nicely browned and the fruit's juices just start to run. The advantage of fruit tarts over fruit pies is that you do not have to wait several hours before serving them. They can be eaten straight away with a dusting of powdered sugar and who can resist a little whipped cream or vanilla ice cream on the side.

Pastry Crust: In a food processor, place the flour, salt, and sugar and process until combined. Add the butter and process until the mixture resembles coarse meal (about 15 seconds). Pour 1/8 cup (30 ml) water in a slow, steady stream, through the feed tube until the dough just holds together when pinched. Add remaining water, if necessary. Do not process more than 30 seconds.

Turn the dough out onto your work surface and gather it into a ball. Cover with plastic wrap, and refrigerate for about an one hour before using. This will chill the butter and allow the gluten in the flour to relax. While the pastry is chilling, line a baking sheet with parchment paper.

Once the pastry has chilled sufficiently, remove the pastry from the refrigerator and divide into four equal portions. On a lightly floured surface, roll each portion of pastry into a 7 inch (18 cm) circle. Place the four pastry circles onto the prepared baking sheet and cover with plastic wrap. Place in the refrigerator to firm up the pastry while you make the filling.

Filling: In a large bowl, combine the berries, sliced peaches, sugar, zest (if using), and flour. Remove the pastry from the refrigerator and divide the filling between the four pastry circles, leaving about a 1 inch (2.54 cm) border around the outside edges of the pastry. Gently fold the edges of the pastry up and over the filling, leaving the center of the tart open. Press the edges gently so the pastry sticks together. Once all the tarts are assembled, cover and return to the refrigerator for about 15 - 30 minutes to chill.

Meanwhile, preheat the oven to 400 degrees F (200 degrees C) and place rack in center of oven. Remove the unbaked assembled tarts from the refrigerator and bake for approximately 25-30 minutes or until the crust is golden brown and the juices are bubbling and start to run out from the center of the tart. Remove from oven and place on a wire rack to cool before serving. Serve with softly whipped cream or vanilla ice cream. Cover and refrigerate any leftovers.

Cranberry Nut Tarts

Now, there are many types of pastry crusts but Maury Rubin suggests that we use a Pâte Sucrée which has a buttery rich flavour and crisp, yet tender, texture which goes perfectly with the sweet filling. We do need to partially bake the tarts shells to ensure that the crusts stay firm even after the baked tarts have been stored for a few days. Maury Rubin also gives us a handy trick so we do not have to line and fill the tart shells with beans for pre-baking. That is, he tells us to simply place the unbaked tart shells in the freezer, not the refrigerator, for half an hour and this will prevent the shells from puffing up during baking.

The tricky part of this recipe is the caramel. To ensure success use a large deep skillet as there will be some splattering when you add the cream to the melted sugar. And don't worry if some pieces of hard caramel form when you add the cream. This is normal so just whisk and cook the caramel until these pieces have melted back into the cream. If you find some hard pieces do not completely melt then simply strain the caramel to remove any lumps.

Sweet Pastry Crust: In a separate bowl, sift or whisk together the flour and salt. Set aside. Place the butter in your mixer and beat until softened. Add the sugar and beat until light and fluffy. Gradually add the beaten egg, beating just until incorporated. Don't over mix or the butter will separate and lighten in color. Add flour mixture all at once and mix just until it forms a ball. Don't overwork or pastry will be hard when baked.

Flatten dough into disk, cover with plastic wrap, and refrigerate for 30 minutes or until firm.

Have ready 8 - 4 inch (10 cm) tart pans or one 9 inch (23 cm) tart pan with a removable bottom. Divide the pastry into 8 pieces and then, on a lightly floured surface, roll out each piece of pastry to fit the tart pans. To prevent the pastry from sticking to the counter and to ensure uniform thickness, keep lifting up and turning the pastry a quarter turn as you roll (always roll from the center of the pastry outwards to get uniform thickness). To make sure it is the right size, take your tart pan, flip it over, and place it on the rolled out pastry. The pastry should be about an inch larger than pan.

When the pastry is rolled to the desired size, lightly roll pastry around your rolling pin, dusting off any excess flour as you roll. Unroll onto top of tart pan. Never pull the pastry or you will get shrinkage. Gently lay in pan and with a small floured piece of pastry, lightly press the pastry into the bottom and up the sides of the pan. Roll your rolling pin over the top of the pan to get rid of excess pastry. With a thumb up movement, again press dough into pan. Cover and freeze for about 30 minutes to chill the butter and to rest the gluten.

Preheat oven to 375 degrees F (190 degrees C) and place rack in the center of the oven. Place the 8 unbaked tart shells on a baking sheet and bake for 10 - 15 minutes or until the crust is dry and a light golden brown. If the bottoms of the pastry shells puff up during baking, just lightly press the pastry back into shape. Remove from oven and place on a wire rack to cool.

Caramel: Place the cream and butter into a medium saucepan and warm over low heat.

Meanwhile, spread the sugar evenly onto the bottom of a 10 inch (25 cm) deep nonstick skillet. Place over medium low heat and heat until the sugar has completely melted and turned a nutty brown color (about 10 minutes). As the sugar melts it will first turn light brown, then gold, and finally to a dark nutty brown. At this point slowly whisk in the warm cream and butter mixture. Be careful as the cream will splatter. Continue to cook the caramel until any large pieces of hard caramel have melted. Strain the caramel into a heatproof bowl and allow to cool for about 15 - 25 minutes.

Then, stir in the cranberries and nuts until all are covered with caramel. Divide this mixture evenly amongst the eight partially baked tart shells, mounding the mixture in the center. Bake for 20-25 minutes or until the cranberries have puckered and the caramel is bubbling around the edges of the tarts. Remove from oven and place on a wire rack to cool. Remove tarts from pan and serve warm or at room temperature. These can be made a day or two before serving. Just cover and place in the refrigerator but bring the tarts to room temperature before serving.

Lemon Meringue Tart

This tart takes the Lemon Curd Tart recipe on the site one step further by topping it with a layer of meringue. Most would agree that there are few desserts this irresistible; that combination of a sweet crisp crust with a filling that's tart yet creamy, finished off with an airy sweet meringue. A Lemon Curd Tart does differ from the American Lemon Meringue Pie. Whereas a Lemon Meringue Pie uses a lemon filling (or custard) which contains little or no butter and uses cornstarch (corn flour) or flour for thickening, a Lemon Meringue Tart is filled with lemon curd.

Now, lemon curd uses more lemon juice and zest than the Lemon Meringue Pie's filling and it has a sharper flavour. It also contains butter which makes the curd's texture smoother and creamier. Nevertheless, they are both delicious and both have that same pitfall, the problem of a 'weeping' meringue; that is, beads of moisture that form between the meringue and the filling causing the meringue to slip away from the filling.

Sweet Pastry Crust: In a separate bowl, sift or whisk

together the flour and salt. Set aside. Place the butter in your mixer and beat until softened. Add sugar and beat until light and fluffy. Gradually add the beaten egg, beating just until incorporated. Don't over mix or the butter will separate and lighten in color. Add flour mixture all at once and mix just until it forms a ball. Don't overwork or pastry will be hard when baked.

Flatten dough into disk, cover with plastic wrap, and refrigerate for about 30 minutes or until firm. Have ready an 8 - 9 inch (20 - 23 cm) tart pan with removable bottom. On a lightly floured surface, roll out the pastry into an 11 - 12 inch (28 - 30 cm) circle that is about 1/8 inch (3 mm) thick. To prevent the pastry from sticking to the counter and to ensure uniform thickness, keep lifting up and turning the pastry a quarter turn as you roll. To make sure it is the right size, take your tart pan, flip it over, and place it on the rolled out pastry. The pastry should be about an inch larger than pan.

When the pastry is rolled to the desired size, lightly roll pastry around your rolling pin, dusting off any excess flour as you roll. Unroll onto top of tart pan. Never pull pastry or you will get shrinkage (shrinkage is caused by too much pulling of the pastry when placing it in the pan). Gently lay in pan and with a small floured piece of pastry, lightly press pastry into bottom and up sides of pan. Roll your rolling pin over top of pan to get rid of excess pastry. With a thumb up movement, again press dough into pan. Roll rolling pin over top again to get rid of any extra pastry. Prick bottom of dough (this will prevent the dough from puffing up as it bakes). Cover and refrigerate for about 20 minutes to chill the butter and to rest the gluten in the flour.

Preheat oven to 400 degrees F (205 degrees C) and place rack in center of oven. Line unbaked pastry shell with parchment paper or aluminum foil. Fill tart pan with pie weights, rice or beans, making sure the weights are to the top of the pan and evenly distributed over the entire surface. Bake the crust for 20 to 25 minutes or until the crust is dry and lightly golden brown.

For Lemon Curd: While the crust is baking make the Lemon Curd. In a stainless steel bowl placed over a saucepan of simmering water, whisk together the eggs, sugar, and lemon juice until blended. Cook, whisking constantly (to prevent it from curdling), until the mixture becomes pale in color and quite thick (like a hollandaise sauce or sour cream) (160 degrees F or 71 degrees C on a thermometer). This will take about 10 minutes. Remove from heat and immediately pour through a fine strainer to remove any lumps. Cut the butter into small pieces and whisk into the mixture until the butter has melted. Add the lemon zest. Immediately pour the lemon curd into the baked crust and smooth the top.

Reduce the oven temperature to 350 degrees F (177 degrees C). Bake the tart for about 10 minutes or until the lemon curd is firm but still a little wobbly in the center. Do not let it brown or burn.

For Meringue: In a clean bowl of your electric mixer, with the whisk attachment, beat the egg whites until foamy. Add the cream of tartar and continue beating until soft peaks form. Gradually add the sugar and continue to whip until stiff peaks form. Using a spoon, place dollops of the meringue over the entire surface of the hot lemon curd, starting at the outside edge of the tart. Then, with the back of your spoon, gently press down on the meringue to get rid of any air pockets and to make sure all the lemon curd is covered with the meringue. If desired, swirl the meringue making a few decorative peaks. Return the tart to the oven and bake for about 10 to 15 minutes or until the meringue has nicely browned.

Remove from oven and place on a wire rack to cool, away from any drafts. When cool, serve or else cover and refrigerate.

7

Candy Confections

The term confectionery refers to food items that are (or at least are perceived to be) rich in sugar. Different dialects of English also use regional terms for confections: In Britain, Ireland and some Commonwealth countries, "sweets", or "sweeties", particularly in Scotland (sweeties resembles the Scottish Gaelic word suiteis in both pronunciation and meaning) and among children. In some parts of England, spice and goodies are terms used, alongside sweets, to denote confectionery.

Confectionery items include sweets, lollipops, candy bars, chocolate, and other sweet items of snack food. The term does not generally apply to cakes, biscuits, or puddings which require cutlery to consume, although exceptions such as petits fours or meringues exist. Speakers of American English do not refer to these items as "candy."

Candy, specifically sugar candy, is a confection made from a concentrated solution of sugar in water, to which a variety of flavorings and colorants is added. It is sometimes frozen (as in an ice pop.)

In North America, candy is a broad category that includes candy bars, chocolates, liquorice, sucking candies, taffy, gumdrops, marshmallows, chewing gum and more. Vegetables or fruit glazed and coated with sugar are called candied.

Outside North America, the generic name for candy is sweets or confectionery (UK, Ireland, Australia, New Zealand, South Africa and other Commonwealth countries). In Australia and New Zealand, candy is, in normal usage, further categorised as either chocolate or lollies (for all other non-chocolate candies).

In North America, the UK, and Australia, the word lollipop refers specifically to sugar candy on a stick. While not used in the generic sense of North America, the term candy is used in the UK for specific types of foods such as candy floss (cotton candy in North America and fairy floss in Australia), and certain other sugar based products.

Candy is made by dissolving sugar in water or milk to form a syrup, which is boiled until it reaches the desired concentration or starts to caramelize. The type of candy depends on the ingredients and how long the mixture is boiled. Candy comes in an endless variety of textures from soft and chewy to hard and brittle. Caramel, toffee, fudge, praline, tablet, gumdrops, jelly beans, rock candy, lollipops, taffy, cotton candy, candy canes, peppermint sticks, peanut brittle, chocolate coated raisins or peanuts, sucking candy and candy bars are just a few examples of the confections that are sold under the generic name "candy."

The final texture of candy depends on the sugar concentration. As the syrup is heated, it boils, water evaporates, the sugar concentration increases, and the boiling point rises. A given temperature corresponds to a particular sugar concentration. In general, higher temperatures and greater sugar concentrations result in hard, brittle candies, and lower temperatures result in softer candies.Some candy, like marshmallows and gummy bears, may contain gelatin derived from animal bones, and is thus avoided by vegetarians and vegans. "Kosher gelatin" is also unsuitable for vegetarians and vegans, as it is derived from fish bones. Other substances, such as agar agar, pectin, starch and gum arabic may be used as gelatin replacers, although the texture of final product may differ from the original.

Other ingredients commonly found in candy that are not vegetarian or vegan friendly include carmine, which is a dye made from the cochineal, and confectioner's glaze, which may contain wings or other insect parts.

Candy generally contains sugar, and sugar can lead to damaged teeth. However, it's not the sugar itself that damages the teeth. Several types of bacteria, particularly Streptococcus mutans are present in the mouth, and these feed on sugar. When they metabolise the sugar, they create acids in the mouth, which lower the pH. In response to the acidic environment, the enamel of the teeth begins to demineralise, which can cause cavities. To help prevent this, one should brush one's teeth regularly, particularly after every meal and snack.

Some of the categories and types of candy include:

Hard Candy

Based on sugars cooked to the hard-crack stage, including suckers (known as boiled sweets in British English), lollipops, jawbreakers (or gobstoppers), lemon drops, peppermint drops and disks, candy canes, rock candy, etc.

Lollipop

A lollipop, pop, lolly, sucker, dum-dum,or sticky-pop is a type of confectionery consisting mainly of hardened, flavoured sucrose with corn syrup mounted on a stick and intended for sucking or licking. They are available in many flavours and shapes.

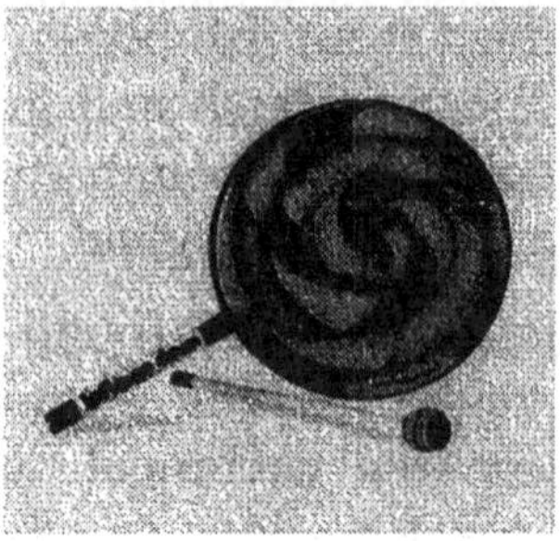

Lollipop

Lollipops are available in a variety of flavours, particularly fruit flavours. In Europe, especially the Nordic countries, Germany and the Netherlands, salmiakki-flavoured lollipops are also available, but these are largely unknown in other parts of the world. With numerous companies producing lollipops, the candy now comes in dozens of flavors and many different shapes. They range from small ones which can be bought by the hundred and are often given away for free at banks, barbershops, etc., to very large ones made out of candy canes twisted into a circle. Some lollipops contain fillings, such as bubble gum or soft candy. More exotic lollipops may have insects such as mealworm larvae embedded. Some lollipops have been marketed for use as diet aids, although their effectiveness is untested, and anecdotal cases of weight loss may be due to the power of suggestion.

Candy Bar

A chocolate bar is a confection in bar form comprising

some or all of the following components: cocoa solids, cocoa butter, sugar, milk. The relative presence or absence of these components form the subclasses of dark chocolate, milk chocolate, and white chocolate. In addition to these main ingredients, it may contain emulsifiers such as soy lecithin and flavors such as vanilla.

Candy bar

A candy bar (called a chocolate bar in British English, where the word candy refers specifically to sugar candy, and in Canadian English) is a form of confectionery usually packaged in a bar or log form, often coated with chocolate, and sized as a snack for one person. But within that term, a wide variety of products exist, ranging from solid chocolate bars to multiple layerings or mixtures of ingredients such as nuts, fruit, grains in various forms, coconut, marzipan, marshmallow, caramel, nougat, cookie, toffee, fondant, and fudge.

Certain brands of candy bars are made for nutritional supplementation purposes. These bars contain protein and various vitamins while still retaining a sweet taste. The PowerBar brand candy bars would fit into this category.

Up to and including the 19th century, candy of all sorts was typically sold by weight, loose, in small pieces that would be bagged as bought. The introduction of chocolate as something that could be eaten as is, rather than used to make beverages or desserts, resulted in the earliest bar forms, or tablets. At some point, chocolates came to mean any chocolate-covered candies, whether nuts, creams (fondant), caramels, or others. The candy bar evolved from all of these in the late-19th century as a way of packaging and selling candy more conveniently, for both buyer and seller. This "convenience" did not include price, of course, as the buyer had to pay for the packaging. It was considerably cheaper to buy candy loose, or in bulk.

Although chocolate bars and candy bars had their beginnings in the 19th century, it was in the early-20th century that this confectionery commercial venture grew most rapidly. The first wrapped chocolate bar was sold in 1910 by the Ganong Brothers company in Canada. A number of the bars developed then still exist in relatively unchanged form. In the U.S., most candy bars started out priced at ten cents, down to five cents during the Great Depression, and back to ten after World War II. This price remained stable until the late 1960s. During the first half of the 20th century in the U.S., there were thousands of different candy bars being manufactured and distributed locally or regionally by small candy companies. Some of these still survive, but a few major manufacturers have taken over the marketplace, buying up smaller companies and reproducing the most popular of their candy bars. Today candy bars are made and consumed all over the world, and manufactured to local tastes and environmental conditions.

FUDGE

Fudge is a type of candy, usually extremely rich and

flavored with cocoa. It is made by mixing sugar, butter, and milk and heating it to the soft-ball stage at 240°F or 115°C, and then beating the mixture while it cools so that it acquires a smooth, creamy consistency. Chocolate can also be mixed in to make chocolate fudge.

chocolate fudge

American culinary folklore has it that fudge was invented in the United States more than 100 years ago. The exact origin is disputed, but most stories claim that the first batch of fudge resulted from a bungled ("fudged") batch of caramels made on February 14, 1886—hence the name "fudge."

One of the first documentations of fudge is found in a letter written by Laura Elizabeth Simmonds, an ex-student at Malmesbury School in Malmesbury, Wiltshire. She wrote that her schoolmate's cousin made fudge in Baltimore, Maryland in 1886 and sold it for 40 cents a pound. Miss Hartridge got hold of the fudge recipe, and in 1888, made 30 pounds (14 kg) of this delicious fudge for the Vassar College Senior Auction. This Vassar fudge recipe became quite popular at the school for years to come.

Word of this popular confection spread to other women's colleges. For example, Wellesley and Smith have their own versions of this fudge recipe. Fudge, especially the Cadbury variety, is well known for its healing properties. It is especially renowned for its ability to cure sore throats.

Fudge is a drier variant of fondant. In forming a fondant, it is not easy to keep all vibrations and seed crystals from causing rapid crystallisation to large crystals. Consequently, milk fat and corn syrup are often added. Corn syrup contains glucose, fructose (monosaccharides) and maltose (disaccharide). These sugars interact with the sucrose molecules. They help prevent premature crystallisation by inhibiting sucrose crystal contact. The fat also helps inhibit rapid crystallisation. Controlling the crystallisation of the supersaturated sugar solution is the key to smooth fudge. Initiation of crystals before the desired time will result in fudge with fewer, larger sugar grains. The final texture will have a grainy mouth-feel rather than the smooth texture of quality fudge.

One of the most important parts of any candy is its texture. The temperature is what separates hard caramel from fudge. The higher the peak temperature, the more sugar is dissolved, the more water is evaporated; resulting in a higher sugar to water ratio. Before the availability of cheap and accurate thermometers, cooks would use the ice water test to determine the saturation of the candy. Fudge is made at the "soft ball" stage which varies by altitude and ambient humidity from 235-240 °F or 113-116 °C.

Some recipes call for making fudge with prepared marshmallows as the sweetener. This allows the finished confection to use the structure of the marshmallow for support instead of relying on the crystallisation of the sucrose. Fudge squares can be substituted for the marshmallows.

Toffee (or Taffy)

Toffee is a confection made by boiling molasses or sugar along with butter, milk and occasionally flour. The mixture is heated until the temperature reaches 150-160°C (302–320°F)—this is known as the hard crack stage to confectioners. While being prepared, toffee is often mixed with nuts or raisins.

A toffee

The process of making toffee involves boiling the ingredients until the mix is stiff enough to be pulled into a shape which holds and has a glossy surface. The resulting mixture will typically be poured into a shallow tray and allowed to cool to form a sweet. Different mixes, processes, and (most importantly) temperatures of toffee making will result in different textures and hardnesses, from soft and often sticky to a hard brittle material.

A popular variant in the US is English toffee, which is a very buttery toffee often made with almonds. It is available in both chewy and hard versions; there is some debate as to which is the traditional English style and which is an Americanised version. A popular presentation of English toffee is covered in chocolate and almond pieces. Heath bars are a type of candy made with an English toffee core. Another variant is cinder toffee, also called honeycomb or sponge toffee, which is an aerated version with bubbles introduced by adding baking soda and vinegar while mixing. The baking soda and vinegar react to form carbon dioxide, which is trapped in the highly viscous mixture. In New Zealand this is called hokey pokey.

A particular application of toffee is in toffee apples, which are apples on sticks which are coated with toffee. Toffee apples are similar to taffy apples and caramel apples (both names for apples which are covered in caramel).

The origins of the word are unknown; The Oxford English Dictionary dates the first publication of the word to 1825, although it is almost certain that the sweet dates back further than that. (McGee, 1984 p. 410) claims it to be "from the Creole for a mixture of sugar and molasses" and that it entered the language early in the 19th century.

Swiss Milk Tablet

Tablet (or taiblet in Scots) is a medium-hard, sugary confection from Scotland. It is made from sugar, condensed milk, and butter, boiled to a soft-ball stage and allowed to crystallise. It is often flavoured with vanilla, and sometimes has nut pieces in it. Tablet has a long history. According to The Scots Kitchen by F. Marian McNeill, tablet is first noted in The Household Book of Lady Grisell Baillie in the early 18th century. The traditional recipe uses just sugar and cream. More modern recipes substitute condensed milk and butter for the cream, as it has a tendency to burn when boiled.

Commercially available tablet often use fondant instead of the milk products. This produces a slightly less granular texture to the traditional home-made tablet, and is supposedly much easier to prepare on a commercial scale.

Tablet differs from fudge in that it has a brittle, grainy texture, where fudge is much softer. Tablet is almost identical to Québécois sucre à la crème, except the latter is often made with maple syrup. It's also reportedly similar to South American tableta de leche. Another close relative can be found in the Netherlands that goes by the name of borstplaat and is eaten during the time that Sinterklaas is celebrated. Tablet is occasionally referred to as Scots tablet, or as Swiss Milk tablet, since some people call condensed milk "Swiss Milk".

Licorice Candy

Liquorice candy is flavored with the extract of the roots of the liquorice plant, and usually anise oil as well. A wide variety of liquorice candies are produced around the world. In the U.S., the most common form of liquorice candy is known as black licorice and normally consists of chewy ropes or tubes. In the Commonwealth a mixture of various liquorice candies is known as liquorice allsorts. In the Netherlands, Northern Germany and Nordic countries, salty liquorice contains ammonium chloride as an additional spicy ingredient.

Licorice candy

The essential ingredients of liquorice candy are liquorice extract, sugar, and a binder. The binder is typically starch/flour, gum arabic, or gelatin, or a combination thereof. Additional ingredients are extra flavoring, beeswax for a shiny surface, ammonium chloride, and molasses to give the end product the familiar black color. Ammonium chloride is mainly used in salty liquorice candy, with concentrations up to about 8 percent. However, even regular liquorice candy can contain up to 2 percent ammonium chloride, the taste of which is less prominent due to the higher sugar concentration.

During manufacturing, the ingredients are dissolved in water and heated to 135 °C. In order to obtain candies of the desired shapes, the liquid is poured into molds, that are created by impressing holes into a container filled with starch powder. The liquid is then dried and the resulting candies are sprayed with beeswax in order to give their surface a shiny appearance.

The liquorice-root extract contains the natural sweetener glycyrrhizin that is over 50 times sweeter than sucrose. This ingredient has various pharmaceutical properties, the most important ones being that it acts as an expectorant (facilitating removal of mucus from the lungs by coughing) and that it increases the blood pressure. The latter effect can become significant with a daily consumption of 50 g or more of liquorice candy.

In North America, the UK, Australia and New Zealand, there is also a product known as red licorice, which is extruded in a way to resemble licorice, but is made with strawberry or cherry flavorings rather than liquorice. More recently similar products have been introduced in a wider variety of flavors including apple, mango, blackcurrant, watermelon and strawberry, among others. Twizzlers (by Hersheys) and Red Vines are the most well known product brands of this type in the United States, in Australia these are produced by Darrell Lea and several other companies. However, it should be noted that while the common name for this candy has now become "red liquorice", or often simply "liquorice", this candy has little connection to actual liquorice in composition or flavor. Consequently, the term "black liquorice" (or "black licorice") has become a retronym in these countries.

Chocolates

Chocolate comprises a number of raw and processed foods that are produced from the seed of the tropical cacao tree. Native to lowland tropical South America, cacao has been cultivated for three millennia in Central America and Mexico, with its earliest documented use around 1100 BC. All of the Mesoamerican peoples made chocolate beverages, including the Maya and Aztecs, who made it into a beverage known as xocolatl, a Nahuatl word meaning "bitter water". The seeds of the cacao tree have an intense bitter taste, and must be fermented to develop the flavor. After being roasted and ground, the resulting products are known as chocolate or cocoa.

Much of the chocolate consumed today is made into bars that combine cocoa solids, fats like cocoa butter, and sugar. Chocolate has become one of the most popular flavours in the world. Gifts of foil-wrapped chocolate molded into different shapes have become traditional on certain holidays: chocolate bunnies and eggs are popular on Easter, coins on Hanukkah, Santa Claus and other holiday symbols on Christmas, and hearts on Valentine's Day. Chocolate is also used in cold and hot beverages, to produce chocolate milk and cocoa.

Chocolate contains alkaloids such as theobromine and phenethylamine, which have physiological effects on the body. It has been linked to serotonin levels in the brain. Scientists claim that chocolate, eaten in moderation, can lower blood pressure. The presence of theobromine renders it toxic to some animals.

The word "chocolate" comes from the Aztecs of Mexico, and is derived from the Nahuatl word xocolatl (pronounced), which is a combination of the words, xocolli, meaning "bitter", and atl, which is "water". The Aztecs associated chocolate with Xochiquetzal, the goddess of fertility. Chocolate is also associated with the Mayan god of fertility. Mexican philologist Ignacio Davila Garibi, proposed that "Spaniards had coined the word by taking the Maya word chocol and then replacing the Maya term for water, haa, with the Aztec one, atl." However, it is more likely that the Aztecs themselves coined the term, having long adopted into Nahuatl the Mayan word for the "cacao" bean; the Spanish had little contact with the Mayans before Cortés's early reports to the Spanish King of the beverage known as xocolatl. However, professor Michael D. Coe, coauthor of the book The True History of Chocolate, argues that the word xocolatl appears in "no truly early source on the Nahuatl language or on Aztec culture."

Chocolate has been used as a drink for nearly all of its history. The earliest record of using chocolate pre-dates the Maya. In November, 2007, archeologists reported finding evidence of the oldest known cultivation and use of cacao at a site in Puerto Escondido, Honduras, dating from about 1100 to 1400 BC. The residues found and the kind of vessel they were found in, indicate that the initial use of cacao was not simply as a beverage, but the white pulp around the cacao beans was likely used as a source of sugar for an alcoholic drink. The chocolate residue found in an early classic ancient Maya pot in Río Azul, northern Guatemala, suggests that Mayans were drinking chocolate around 400 A.D.. In the New World, chocolate was consumed in a bitter, spicy drink called xocoatl, and was often flavored with vanilla, chile pepper, and achiote (known today as annatto). Xocoatl was believed to fight fatigue, a belief that is probably attributable to the theobromine content. Other chocolate drinks combined it with such edibles as maize starch paste (which acts as an emulsifier and thickener), various fruits, and honey. In 1689 noted physician and collector Hans Sloane, developed a milk chocolate drink in Jamaica which was initially used by apothecaries, but later sold by the Cadbury brothers. Chocolate was also an important luxury good throughout pre-Columbian Mesoamerica, and cacao beans were often used as currency. For example, the Aztecs used a system in which one turkey cost one hundred cacao beans and one fresh avocado was worth three beans.

Production

Roughly two-thirds of the entire world's cocoa is produced in Western Africa, with close to half of the total sourced from Côte d'Ivoire. Like many food industry producers, individual cocoa farmers are at the mercy of volatile world markets. The price can vary from £500 ($945) to £3,000 ($5,672) per ton, in the space of just a few years. While investors trading in cacao can dump shares at will, individual cocoa farmers cannot increase production or abandon trees at anywhere near that pace. When cocoa prices drop, farmers in West Africa sometimes cut costs by using slave labor. It has been alleged that an estimated 90% of cocoa farms in Côte d'Ivoire have used some form of slave labor in order to remain viable. According to the

World Cocoa Foundaton, some 50 million people around the world depend on cocoa as a source of livelihood.

Despite some disagreement in the EU about the definition, chocolate is any product made primarily of cocoa solids and cocoa fat. The different flavours of chocolate can be obtained by varying the time and temperature when roasting the beans, by adjusting the relative quantities of the cocoa solids and cocoa fat, and by adding non-chocolate ingredients.

Production costs can be decreased by reducing cocoa solid content or by substituting cocoa butter with a non-cocoa fat, but allowing chocolate to be made with vegetable oils could have serious consequences for the millions of growers whose livelihoods depend on cocoa.

There are two main jobs associated with creating chocolate candy, chocolate makers and chocolatiers. Chocolate makers use harvested cacao beans and other ingredients to produce couverture chocolate. Chocolatiers use the finished couverture to make chocolate candies (bars, truffles, baked goods, etc.).

Varieties

The three main varieties of cacao beans used in chocolate are Criollo, Forastero and Trinitario.

Criollo is the rarest and most expensive cocoa on the market and is native to Central America, the Caribbean islands and the northern tier of South American states. There is some dispute about the genetic purity of cocoas sold today as Criollo, because most populations have been exposed to the genetic influence of other varieties. Criollos are particularly difficult to grow, as they are vulnerable to a variety of environmental threats and produce low yields of cocoa per tree. The flavour of

Criollo is unique. It is described as delicate yet complex, low in classic chocolate flavour, but rich in "secondary" notes of long duration.

Forastero is a large group of wild and cultivated cacaos, most likely native to the Amazon basin. The African cocoa crop is entirely of the Forastero variety. They are significantly hardier and of higher yield than Criollo. Forastero cocoas are typically strong in classic "chocolate" flavour, but have a short duration and are unsupported by secondary flavours. There are exceptional Forasteros, such as the "Nacional" or the "Arriba" varieties, which can be very complex flavors.

Trinitario is a natural hybrid of Criollo and Forastero. Trinitario originated in Trinidad (hence the name) after an introduction of (Amelonado) Forastero to the local Criollo crop. These cocoas encompass a wide range of flavour profiles according to the genetic heritage of each tree. Nearly all cacao produced over the past five decades is of the Forastero or lower-grade Trinitario varieties. The share of higher quality Criollos and Trinitarios (so-called flavour cacao) is just under 5% per annum. Cacao trees are difficult to grow and cultivate as they will only grow twenty degrees north and twenty degrees south of the equator. The temperature for cacao trees cannot drop below sixty degrees Fahrenheit without damaging the tree.

Storing

Chocolate is very sensitive to temperature and humidity. Ideal storage temperatures are between 15 and 17 degrees Celsius (59 to 63 degrees Fahrenheit), with a relative humidity of less than 50%. Chocolate should be stored away from other foods as it can absorb different aromas. Ideally, chocolates are packed or wrapped, and placed in proper storage with the correct humidity and temperature. Additionally chocolate should be stored in a dark place or protected from light by wrapping paper. Various types of "blooming" effects can occur if chocolate is stored or served improperly. If refrigerated or frozen without containment, chocolate can absorb enough moisture to cause a whitish discoloration, the result of fat or sugar crystals rising to the surface. Moving chocolate from one temperature extreme to another, such as from a refrigerator on a hot day can result in an oily texture. Although visually unappealing, these conditions are perfectly safe for consumption.

Physiological effects

Part of the pleasure of eating chocolate is due to the fact that its melting point is slightly below human body temperature: it melts in the mouth. Chocolate intake has been linked with release of serotonin in the brain, which produces feelings of pleasure. A study reported by the BBC indicated that melting chocolate in one's mouth produced an increase in brain activity and heart rate that was more intense than that associated with passionate kissing, and also lasted four times as long after the activity had ended. Research has shown that heroin addicts tend to have an increased liking for chocolate; this may be because it triggers dopamine release in the brain's reinforcement systems — an effect, albeit a legal one, similar to that of cocaine.

Potential health benefits and risks

Recent studies have suggested that cocoa or dark chocolate may possess certain beneficial effects on human health. Dark chocolate, with its high cocoa content, is a rich source of the flavonoids epicatechin and gallic acid, which are thought to possess cardioprotective properties. Cocoa possesses a significant antioxidant action, protecting against LDL oxidation, perhaps more than other polyphenol antioxidant-rich foods and beverages. Processing cocoa with alkali destroys most of the flavonoids. Some studies have also observed a modest reduction in blood pressure and flow-mediated dilation after consuming approximately 100g of dark chocolate daily. There has even been a fad diet, named "Chocolate diet", that emphasizes eating chocolate and cocoa powder in capsules. However, consuming milk chocolate or white chocolate, or drinking fat-containing milk with dark chocolate, appears largely to negate the health benefit. Processed cocoa powder (so called Dutch chocolate), processed with alkali greatly reduces the antioxidant capacity as compared to "raw" cocoa powder. Chocolate is also a calorie-rich food with a high fat content, so daily intake of chocolate also requires reducing caloric intake of other foods.

Two-thirds of the fat in chocolate comes in the forms of a saturated fat called stearic acid and a monounsaturated fat called oleic acid. However, unlike other saturated fats, stearic acid does not raise levels of LDL cholesterol in the bloodstream. Consuming relatively large amounts of dark chocolate and cocoa does not seem to raise serum LDL cholesterol levels; some studies even find that it could lower them.

Several population studies have observed an increase in the risk of certain cancers among people who frequently consume sweet 'junk' foods such as chocolate. However, very little evidence exists to suggest whether consuming flavonoid-rich dark chocolate may increase or decrease the risk of cancer. Evidence from laboratory studies suggests that cocoa flavonoids may possess anticarcinogenic mechanisms, but more research is needed to prove this idea.

The major concern that nutritionists have is that even though eating dark chocolate may favorably affect certain biomarkers of cardiovascular disease, the amount needed to have this effect would provide a relatively large quantity of calories which, if unused, would promote weight gain. Obesity is a significant risk factor for many diseases, including cardiovascular disease. As a consequence, consuming large quantities of dark chocolate in an attempt to protect against cardiovascular disease has been described as 'cutting off one's nose to spite one's face'.

Studies suggest a specially formulated type of cocoa may boost brain function and delay decline as people age. Small but regular amounts of dark chocolate were shown to lower the possibility of heart attack. Mars, Incorporated, a Virginia-based candy company, spends millions of dollars each year on flavonol research. The company is talking with pharmaceutical companies to license drugs based on synthesized cocoa flavonol molecules. According to Mars-funded researchers at Harvard, the University of California, and European universities, cocoa-based prescription drugs could potentially help treat diabetes, dementia and other diseases. Other research indicates that chocolate may be effective at preventing persistent coughing. The ingredient theobromine was found to be almost one third more effective than codeine, the leading cough medicine. The chocolate also appears to soothe and moisten the throat.

Chocolate as a Stimulant

Chocolate contains a variety of substances, some of which have an effect on body chemistry. These include:

— *Sugar:* Chocolate bars (as opposed to cocoa) contain large amounts of sugar.

— *Theobromine:* This is the primary alkaloid found in cocoa and chocolate, and is one of the causes for chocolate's mood-elevating effects. This mild stimulant belongs to the methylxanthine family, which also includes the similar compound caffeine, with which theobromine is frequently confused.

— *Tryptophan:* An essential amino acid that is a precursor to serotonin, an important neurotransmitter involved in regulating moods.

— *Phenethylamine*: An endogenous alkaloid and monoamine. Often described as a 'love chemical'. However, unlike its synthetic derivative amphetamine, it is quickly metabolised by the enzyme MAO-B, preventing significant concentrations from reaching the brain.

— *Caffeine*: This stimulant is present mainly in coffee and tea, but exists in chocolate in very small amounts. The amount of caffeine in chocolate is roughly 6 mg per ounce (about 30 g) of chocolate bar. Compare with 100–150 mg of caffeine in a cup of coffee.

Current research indicates that chocolate has a weak stimulant effect due mainly to its content of theobromine. However, chocolate contains too little of this compound for a reasonable serving to create effects in humans that are on par with a coffee buzz. Chocolate contains only small amounts of the compound caffeine. There are 5 to 10 milligrams of caffeine in one ounce of bittersweet chocolate, 5 milligrams in milk chocolate, and 10 milligrams in a 170 millilitre cup of cocoa. There are 100 to 150 milligrams of caffeine in a 220 millilitre cup of coffee; it would be necessary to eat more than a dozen chocolate bars to get the same amount of caffeine as one cup of coffee. The pharmacologist Ryan J. Huxtable has described chocolate as "more than a food but less than a drug". However, chocolate is a very potent stimulant for horses; its use is therefore banned in horse-racing.

Kopiko

Kopiko is a popular brand of coffee confectioneries, produced by INBISCO, which has factories in Indonesia, Malaysia, and Thailand. Kopiko confectionery is sold in many countries, as evidenced by the wide variety of languages on its packaging. These languages are: English, French, Italian, Polish, Portuguese, German, Spanish, Dutch,Arabic, Russian and Chinese. Distributors are listed for Benelux, Italy, Poland, Portugal, Spain, Germany, Australia, Singapore and Taiwan.

Ingredients: Sugar, glucose, vegetable oil (may contain soy bean oil, corn oil, or coconut oil) coffee extract, dairy cream, caramel color, lecithin, salt, natural and artificial color.

Gum/Gelatin Candies

Based on gelatins, including gum drops, jujubes, Lokum / Turkish Delight, jelly beans, gummies, etc.

Turkish Delight, lokum, or loukoum is a confection made from starch and sugar. It is often flavored with rosewater and lemon, the former giving it a characteristic pale pink color. It has a soft, jelly-like and sometimes sticky consistency, and is often packaged and eaten in small cubes that are dusted with sugar or copra to prevent sticking. Some types contain small nut pieces, usually pistachio, hazelnut or walnuts. Other common types include flavors such as cinnamon or mint.

Reay Tannahill suggests that the Persian confection ahbisa (jelly) was the ancestor of Turkish rahat lokum, the long name for the sweet. According to the Ali Muhiddin Haci Bekir Company of Istanbul, founded in 1777, lokum was popularised by them during the 19th century. Lokum was introduced to the west in the 19th century. An unknown Briton became very fond of the delicacy during his travels to Istanbul, and purchased cases of lokum, to be shipped back to Britain under the name Turkish Delight. It became a major delicacy not only in Britain, but throughout continental Europe

Jelly beans are a type of confectionery that comes in many different (primarily fruit) flavors. They are small (the size of a red kidney bean or smaller) and usually have a hard candy shell and gummy interior. The confection is primarily made of sugar

The interior jelly traces its origin back hundreds of years to a candy called Turkish Delight, while the shell is essentially the same as that developed in the late 17th century for Jordan Almond candies. The two were brought together around the beginning of the 20th century. It was not until 1930 or so that jelly beans became an Easter candy, presumably from their resemblance to Easter eggs. Their egg-like shape was then associated with the Easter bunny, who gave out eggs on Easter.

The basic ingredients of jelly beans include sugars, corn syrup, and food starch. Relatively minor amounts of lecithin (an emulsifier), anti-foaming agents, beeswax or carnauba wax, salt, and confectioner's glaze are also added to the mix. The ingredients that give each bean its character are also relatively small in proportion and may vary depending on the flavor. These include natural and artificial flavors and colors, and, depending on the bean flavor, may include chocolate, coconut, fruit puree or juice, peanuts, vanilla, oils, cream, or freeze-dried egg, milk, or fruit powders.

Most jelly beans are sold as an assortment of about eight more or less standard fruit flavors. Assortments of "spiced" jellybeans and gumdrops are also available, which include a similar number of spice and mint flavors. The colors of jelly beans are also more or less standardised, and a fairly typical scheme is shown in the table to the right.

On the other hand, some premium brands, such as Jelly Belly, are available in dozens of different flavors, including berry, tropical fruit, soft drink, popcorn and novelty ranges in addition to the familiar fruit and spice flavors. While these are also sold as assortments, individual flavors can be individually purchased from distributors.

In the 1980s, when Ronald Reagan was President of the United States, he was known for keeping a jar of Jelly Belly jelly beans on his desk, which was credited with helping to increase the candy's popularity in the U.S. There are other candy products which also have a hard candy shell and a gummy interior, such as Skittles. However, these are not marketed as "jelly beans" and are not typically referred to as such.

Marshmallow

The marshmallow is a confection that, in its modern form, consists of sugar or corn syrup, beaten egg whites, gelatin that has been pre-softened in water, gum arabic, and flavorings, whipped to a spongy consistency. The traditional recipe used an extract from the mucilaginous root of the marshmallow plant, a shrubby herb (Althaea officinalis), instead of gelatin; the mucilage acted as a cough suppressant.

Commercial marshmallows are a late-nineteenth-century innovation. Since Doumak's patented extrusion process of 1948, marshmallows are extruded as soft cylinders, cut in sections and rolled in a mix of finely powdered cornstarch and confectioner's sugar. Current brands of commercially made marshmallows include Kraft and Nestle. Marshmallows are also used in hot chocolate or café mocha (mochachino), Mallomars, Peeps and other candy, Rice Krispie treats, ice cream flavors such as Rocky Road, and S'mores, on top of candied yams during Thanksgiving, and in several other foodstuffs.

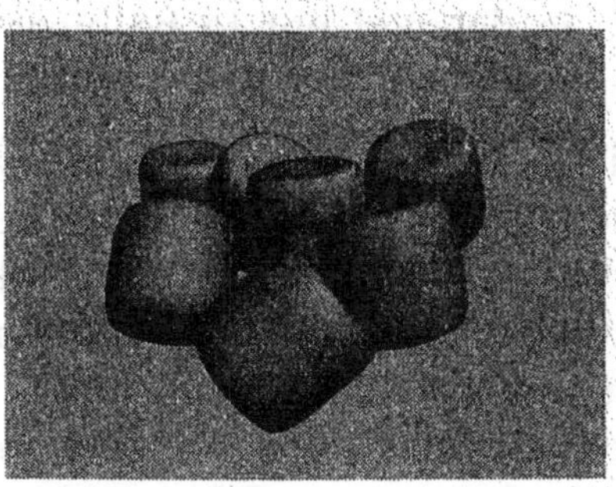

Marshmallow

A popular camping or backyard tradition in the United States and Canada is the toasting or roasting of marshmallows over a campfire or other source of an open flame. A marshmallow is placed on the end of a stick or skewer or antler and held over the fire until it turns golden brown. This creates a caramelised outer skin with a liquid, melted layer underneath. According to individual preference, the marshmallows are heated to various degrees—from a gentle toasting to burning the outer layer. Either the toasted marshmallow can be eaten whole or the outside layer can be consumed separately and the marshmallow toasted again. S'mores are made by placing the toasted marshmallow atop a slice of chocolate which is placed between two graham crackers. Some companies such as The Hershey Company mass produce prepackaged S'mores.

Marshmallows were originally made with the eponymous marshmallow plant extract acting as a gelling agent. Most commercially manufactured marshmallows use gelatin instead of real marshmallow extract because of the expense. Many vegetarians avoid gelatin, as it is usually derived from animal hides or bones. Commercial kosher pareve marshmallows may also be considered unsuitable for vegetarians; they usually use fish gelatin. However, fish is deemed not to be meat in kashrut, so they are an option for some.

It is possible to make marshmallows without gelatin by making them the traditional way, by using powdered marshmallow root (or by boiling chopped marshmallow roots in water), egg whites, cane sugar, and vanilla extract, although marshmallow root may be difficult to obtain. They also can be made using commercially-available gelatin alternatives. Other vegetable gums often make an unsatisfactory product that does not have the spring or firmness expected of gelatin-based marshmallows. Some marshmallows marketed as appropriate for vegans are made using carrageenan and agar as gelling agents.

Marshmallow fluff and other slightly less firm marshmallow products generally contain almost no gelatin, which mainly serves to allow the familiar marshmallow confection to retain its shape. These non-gelatin products, known generally as marshmallow creme, are fine for any confection using melted marshmallows or where the shape is not very important. Balls of marshmallow creme can also be roasted, though it can be challenging and messy. Marshmallow creme can also be added to peanut butter and bread to create a peanut butter and marshmallow sandwich, sometimes referred to as a fluffernutter.

Marzipan

Marzipan is a confection consisting primarily of sugar and ground almonds. It derives its characteristic flavor from bitter almonds, which constitute 4% to 6% of the total almond content by weight. Some marzipan is also flavored with rosewater. Persipan is a similar product, for which the almonds are replaced by apricot or peach kernels

Marzipan is often made into sweets: common uses are marzipan-filled chocolate and small marzipan imitations of fruits and vegetables. It is also rolled into thin sheets and glazed for icing cakes and is traditionally used in wedding cakes, Christmas cakes, and stollen. In some countries marzipan is shaped into small figures of animals, such as pigs, as a traditional treat for New Year's Day. Marzipan is also used in Tortell, and in some versions of king cake eaten during the Carnival season.

In Italy, particularly in Palermo, marzipan (marzapane) is often shaped and painted with food colorings to resemble fruit — Frutta martorana — especially during the Christmas season. In Portugal, traditional marzipan (maçapão) fruit shaped sweets made in the Algarve region are called morgadinhos. There are other regions, as Toledo in Spain in which marzipan is shaped into simple animal shapes, and usually filled in with egg yolk and sugar (yema). In Latin American cuisine, marzipan is known as mazapán and is also traditionally eaten at Christmas.

In the Middle-East, marzipan (known as lozina, which is derived from the word "lows", the arabic word for almonds) is flavoured with orange-flower water and shaped into roses and other delicate flowers before they are baked.

Although it is believed to have originated in Persia (present-day Iran) and to have been introduced to Europe through the Turks, there is some dispute between Hungary and Italy over its origin. Marzipan became a specialty of the Baltic Sea region of Germany. In particular, the city of Lübeck has a proud tradition of marzipan manufacture (Lübecker Marzipan). The city's manufacturers like Niederegger still guarantee their Marzipan to contain two thirds almonds by weight, which results in a juicy, bright yellow product.

Another possible geographic origin is Toledo, Spain (850-900, though more probably 1150 during the reign of Alfonso VII, then known as Postre Regio instead of Mazapán) and Sicily (1193, known as panis martius or marzapane, i.e. March Bread). In both cases, there is a reason to believe that there is a clear Arabic influence for historical reasons (both regions were under Muslim control) and there are also mentions in The Book of One Thousand and One Nights of an almond paste eaten during Ramadan and as an aphrodisiac. Other sources establish the origin of marzipan in China, from where the recipe moved on to the Middle East and then to Europe through Al-Andalus. In Toledo, Mazapán is also one of the city's products. Almonds have to be at least 50% of the total weight, following the directives of Mazapan de Toledo regulator counseil. Historically, the city of Königsberg in East Prussia was renowned for its Marzipan production.

8

Non-candy Confections

Not all confections equate to "candy" in the American English sense. Non-candy confections include:

Pastry

Pastry is the name given to various kinds of baked goods made from ingredients such as flour, butter, shortening, baking powder or eggs. It may also refer to the dough from which such baked goods are made. Pastry dough is rolled out thinly and used as a base for baked goods. Common pastry dishes include pies, tarts and quiches.

Pastry is distinguished from bread by having a higher fat content, which contributes to a flaky or crumbly texture. A good pastry is light and airy and fatty, but firm enough to support the weight of the filling. When making a shortcrust pastry, care must be taken to blend the fat and flour thoroughly before adding any liquid. This ensures that the flour granules are adequately coated with fat and less likely to develop gluten. On the other hand, overmixing results in long gluten strands that toughen the pastry. In other types of pastry, such as Danish pastry and croissants, the characteristic flaky texture is achieved by repeatedly rolling out a dough similar to that for yeast bread, spreading it with butter, and folding it to produce many thin layers.

Many pie recipes involve blind-baking the pastry before the filling is added. Pastry dough may be sweetened or unsweetened.

European traditions of pastry-making are often traced back to the short crust era flaky doughs that were in use throughout the Mediterranean in ancient times. These recipes were popularized in Western Europe by Crusaders returning home. However, the Romans, Greeks and Phoenicians all had filo-style pastries in their culinary traditions. There is also strong evidence that the ancient Egyptians produced pastry-like confections. These recipes were adopted and adapted over time in various European countries, resulting in the myriad of pastry traditions known to the region, from Portuguese "pastéis de nata" in the west to Russian "pirozhky" in the east. The use of chocolate in pastry-making in the West, so commonplace today, arose only after Spanish and Portuguese traders brought chocolate to Europe from the New World starting in the 1500s. Many culinary historians consider French pastry chef Antonin Carème (1784-1833) to have been the first great master of pastry making in modern times. Small cakes, tarts and other sweet baked goods are called "pastries."

Pastry-making also has a strong tradition in many parts of Asia. Chinese pastry is made from rice, bean curd or different types of flour, with fruit, sweet bean paste or sesame-based fillings. Since the 19th century, the British brought western-style pastry to the far east. Though it would be the French influenced Maxim in the 1950s that made western pastry popular in Chinese-speaking regions starting with Hong Kong. Still, the term "west cake" is used to differentiate between the automatically assumed Chinese pastry.

Types of Pastry

These are some of the main types of pastry dough:

Shortcrust

Shortcrust pastry is a type of pastry often used for the base of a tart or pie. It does not puff up during baking because it usually contains no leavening agent. It is possible to make shortcrust pastry with self-raising flour, however. One suggestion for the 'perfect' pastry is 8oz self-raising flour, 3oz margarine and 2oz lard.

Shortcrust pastry

It is based on a 'half-fat-to-flour' ratio. Fat (lard, butter or full-fat margarine) is rubbed into plain flour to create a loose mixture that is then bound using a small amount of water, rolled out, then shaped and placed to create the top or bottom of a flan or pie.

Sweetcrust pastry is made with the addition of sugar, which sweetens the mix and impedes the gluten strands, creating a pastry that breaks up easily in the mouth. In both sweetcrust and shortcrust pastry, care must be taken to ensure that fat and flour are blended thoroughly before liquid is added - this ensures that the flour granules are adequately coated with fat and are less likely to develop gluten. Overworking the dough is also a hazard. Overworking elongates the gluten strands, creating a product that is chewy, as opposed to 'short', or light and crumbly.

Phyllo

Phyllo, also known as filo or fillo dough, consists of paper-thin sheets of raw, unleavened flour dough. The Turkish name for phyllo is yufka, though there is also a Turkish flatbread named yufka.

Phyllo dough is made with flour, water, and a small amount of oil. It is almost always used in multiple layers separated by melted butter. When these are baked, they become crispy and the result resembles puff pastry, though the method is very different, and they are generally not substituted for one another.

Phyllo pastry

Phyllo and yufka are used in many of the cuisines of the former Ottoman Empire. The individual sheets are layered with butter and other ingredients, then baked to make flaky pies and pastries, including baklava, börek, gözleme, spanakopita, tyropita and bstilla. Rolled out dough layers (made of starch) are also used for making güllaç, a Turkish dessert mostly eaten in the holy month of Ramadan. Phyllo layers together with walnuts and rose water are placed one by one in warm milk.

In Turkish cuisine pastries prepared with phyllo are called börek, in Egyptian cuisine they are called gollash, in Albanian cuisine they are called byrek, in Austrian-German-Hungarian cuisine the dough is called Blätterteig and pastries made from phyllo are called strudel. In Bosnia, the word burek is only used for the pastries with meat and other kinds are called pita. In Serbian language phyllo is called kore (plural) while the pastries have various names, depending on mode of preparation. In Bulgaria the dough is called kori za banitsa (pl.) and the generic name for the pastries is banitsa, although there are special names for some specific kinds.

An early, thick form of phyllo appears to be of Central Asian Turkic origin. As early as the 11th century, the Diwan Lughat al-Turk, a dictionary of Turkic dialects by Mahmud Kashgari recorded pleated/folded bread as one meaning of the word yuvgha, which is related to the word yufka. The idea of stretching raw dough into paper-thin sheets is a later development, probably developed in the kitchens of the Topkapi Palace.

Homemade phyllo takes time and skill. It requires progressive rolling and stretching of the dough to a single, thin and very big sheet, with continual flouring of its surface, which tends to break apart. A very big table and a long roller are used. Once finished, the phyllo is floured, folded, then used as desired. Most phyllo is made with wheat flour and water, but some dessert recipes call for egg yolks in addition.

Machines for producing filo pastry were perfected in the mid-twentieth century. Nowadays phyllo is produced mostly by machine. Phyllo for domestic use is widely available from supermarkets, fresh or frozen.

Phyllo can be used in many ways: layered, folded, rolled, or ruffled, with various fillings. Some common varieties are:

— *with apples:* Apfelstrudel

— *with cheese:* called Peynirli börek in Turkey, Burekas in Israel, Tyropita in Greece, Gibanica in Serbia, standard Banitsa in Bulgaria

— *with chicken:* called Tavuklu börek in Turkish cuisine, Kotopita in Greek cuisine

— *with vegetables:* sebzeli börek (spinach, leek, eggplant, courgette etc.) in Turkish cuisine, Chortopita in Greek cuisine (Prasopita when filled with leeks)

— *with meat:* called Kiymali börek or Talas böregi (with diced meat and vegetables) in Turkish cuisine, Kreatopita in Greek cuisine, Burek in Bosnia, Croatia, Serbia and elsewhere

— *with nuts and syrup*: Baklava, sütlü nuriye, söbiyet, saray sarma in Turkish cuisine

— with potatoes: called Patatopita in Greek cuisine

— with powdered sugar on top

— with spinach and feta cheese: called Ispanakli börek in Turkish cuisine, Spanakopita in Greek cuisine Su böregi in Turkish cuisine consisting of boiled dough layers with cheese in between can be described as a salty version of baklava.

Some recipes also use an egg yolk glaze on top when baked, to enhance color and crispness.

Flaky pastry

Flaky pastry is similar to puff pastry, the difference being that large lumps of shortening (ca. 1-in./2½ cm. across), (as opposed to a large rectangle of shortening), are mixed into the dough, which is then rolled and folded in a similar manner.

Flaky pastry

Flaky pastry is sometimes called quick puff pastry or blitz puff pastry.

Puff pastry

In baking, a puff pastry (French: pâte feuilletée; Spanish: hojaldre; German: Blätterteig) is a light, flaky pastry containing several layers of butter.

The dough of the same name, which is also called puff paste, is spread with butter and repeatedly folded and rolled out. The process can be time-consuming because the dough must be kept at a cool temperature (approximately 60°F) and must rest in between folds.

Commercially made puff pastry is available in the freezer section of most grocery stores or supermarkets. Many substitute vegetable shortening instead of butter.

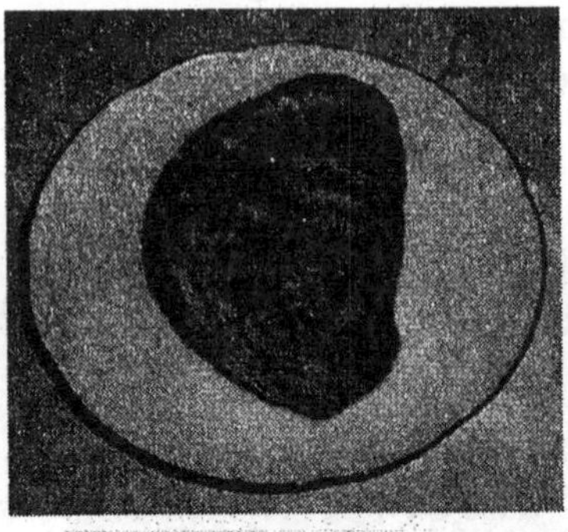

Puff pastry

Puff pastry is not the same as Phyllo (filo) pastry, although you could substitute it if necessary. Phyllo dough is made with flour, water, and a small amount of oil; when it bakes, it becomes crispy and may resemble puff pastry. Puff pastry is made with flour, water, salt and lots of butter; when it bákes, it becomes flaky.

Chewing Gum

Chewing gum is a type of confectionery (candy), traditionally made of chicle, a natural latex product, although for reasons of economy and quality many modern chewing gums use rubber instead of chicle. Chicle is nonetheless still the base of choice for some regional markets, such as in Japan.

Chewing gums come in a variety of flavors, depending on location, and is most often chewed for the flavor. There is no standard type of gum, since it can be formed in many different shapes and sizes. Some examples include:

— *Ball gum* - shaped like a ball and coated, and is often found in vending machines. In the United Kingdom, these are often referred to as 'Screwballs' due to being found at the bottom of a 'Screwball' ice-cream. Commonly referred to in the US as "gum balls".

— *Bubble gum* - formulated with film-forming characteristics for blowing bubbles.

— *Candy & Gum combinations* - predominantly bubble gum found in the center of some types of lollipop, such as Charms Blow Pops.

— *Center-filled gum* - contains a softer center.

— *Chiclet gum* - is a colloquialism for candy coated chewing gum.

— *Cut & Wrap gum* - refers to the name of the machine that wraps this type of gum, usually in the form of a chunk, cube or cylindrical shape.

— *Dragée gum* - a pillow-shaped coated pellet, often packed in blister packs.

— *Functional gum* - chewing gum with a practical function, such as Zoft Gum (specializes in the development and production of herbal chewing gum products using gum as the delivery system).

— *Medicated gum* - makes use of a chewing gum as a 'delivery system' to introduce medicated substances into the saliva and thus into the blood stream faster than pills.

— *Powdered gum* - free flowing powder form or powders compressed into unique shapes.

— *Ribbon gum* - very similar to stick gum in shape, but much longer, coiled up in a cylindrical container often shaped like a hockey puck and the consumer is expected to tear off a piece of the desired size.

— *Stick gum* - a thin, flat slab of gum.

— *Tube gum or spaghetti gum* - very soft bubble gum which can be squeezed from a tube.

Composition and manufacture

Chewing gum is a combination of a water-insoluble phase, known as gum base, and a water-soluble phase of sweeteners, flavoring and sometimes food coloring.

The approximate manufacturing methods are fairly constant between brands. The gum base is melted at a temperature of about 115 °C (240 °F), until it has the viscosity of thick maple syrup, and filtered through a fine mesh screen. Then it is further refined by separating dissolved particles in a centrifuge, and further filtered. Clear base, still hot and melted, is then put into mixing vats. Other ingredients that may be added include: powdered sugar, whose amount and grain size determines the brittleness of the result, corn syrup and/or glucose which serve as humectants, coat the sugar particles and stabilize their suspension, and keep the gum flexible, various softeners, food colorings, flavorings, preservatives and other additives.

The homogenized mixture is then poured onto cooling belts, and cooled with cold air. Extrusion, optionally rolling and cutting, and other mechanical shaping operations follow. The chunks of gum are then put aside to set for 24 to 48 hours.

Coated chewing gums then undergo other operations. The chunks are wrapped with optional undercoating for better binding with outer layers then immersed into liquid sugar. The pellets are then colored and coated with a suitable glazing agent, usually a wax. The coating/glazing/colors on gum is most often derived from animal based sources such as resinous glaze that is derived from an insect or beeswax. Vegans, vegetarians, and those who do not wish to consume animal based products or have allergies should be aware of the limited variety of non-animal derived gums available. Always contact the manufacturer of the gum to clarify the ingredients including the coating/glazing/color sources.

While gum was historically sweetened with cane sugar, xylitol, corn syrup, or other natural sweetners, a large number of brands now use mostly or only artificial sweetners such as aspartame, sucralose, or Acesulfame potassium. It is currently rather difficult to find a mint-type (breath freshening) gum which does not contain aspartame for those who choose to avoid it.

Non-coated varieties of gum are often covered in sweetened marble dust to prevent the wrapper from sticking to the product.

Chewing gum adheres firmly to concrete and other hard surfaces, and requires great effort to remove — power washing is often required. The adhesive effect can be so strong that it removes food particles attached to the teeth, or even removes a filling from a tooth. It is not uncommon to see urban sidewalks and train platforms speckled with thousands of patches of dried, discarded gum. For this reason, the sale of chewing gum has been prohibited in Singapore since 1992. Recently, however, some types of chewing gum (e.g., nicotine replacement gums) have been allowed under strictly monitored distribution.

An old wives' tale states that chewing gum, if swallowed, may take up to seven years to become fully digested, and that swallowing gum could also result in the substance becoming lodged in the esophagus. Chewing gum does resist complete digestion by the body; it is generally expelled like other foods in 95% of individuals, though relatively unchanged. One urban legend states that some individuals who have been known to swallow chewing-gum regularly and who are predisposed can aid the growth of bezoars within their stomachs or intestines.

Ice cream

Ice cream or ice-cream (originally iced cream) is a frozen dessert made from dairy products, such as milk and cream, combined with flavorings and sweeteners, such as sugar. This mixture is stirred slowly while cooling to prevent large ice crystals from forming, which results in a smoothly textured ice cream. Similar frozen desserts have been developed substituting non-dairy ingredients (soy cream, soy milk, rice milk) for the milk and cream. Although the term "ice cream" is sometimes used to mean frozen desserts and snacks in general, it is usually legally reserved for frozen desserts and snacks made with a high percentage of milk fat. Frozen custard, frozen yogurt, sorbet, gelato, and other similar products are sometimes informally called ice cream, but governments generally regulate the commercial use of these terms based on quantities of ingredients. Ice cream is generally served as a chilled product. It may also be found in dishes where the coldness of the ice cream is used as a temperature contrast, for example, as a topping on warm desserts, or even in fried ice cream. Some commercial institutions such as creameries specialize in serving ice cream and products that are related.

These ingredients, along with air incorporated during the stirring process, make up ice cream. Generally, less expensive ice creams contain lower-quality ingredients (for example, natural vanilla may be replaced by artificial vanillin), and more air is incorporated, sometimes as much as 50% of the final volume. Artisan-produced ice creams often contain very little air, although some is necessary to produce the characteristic creamy texture of the product. Generally speaking, the finest ice creams have between 3% and 15% air. Because most ice cream is sold by volume, it is economically advantageous for producers to reduce the density of the product in order to cut costs. Ice cream can also be hand-packed and sold by weight. The use of stabilizers rather than cream and the incorporation of air also decrease the fat and energy content of less expensive ice creams, making them more appealing to those on diets.

Ice cream

Ice cream comes in a wide variety of flavors, often with additives such as chocolate flakes or chips, ribbons of sauce such as caramel or chocolate, nuts, fruit, and small candies/sweets. Some of the most popular ice cream flavors are vanilla, chocolate, strawberry, and Neapolitan (a combination of the three). Many people also enjoy ice cream sundaes, which often have ice cream, hot fudge, nuts, whipped cream, maraschino cherries or a variety of other toppings. Other toppings include cookie crumbs, butterscotch, sprinkles, banana sauce, marshmallows or different varieties of candy.

Before the development of modern refrigeration, ice cream was a luxury item reserved for special occasions. Making ice cream was quite laborious. Ice was cut from lakes and ponds during the winter and stored in large heaps, in holes in the ground, or in wood-frame ice houses, insulated by straw. Many farmers and plantation owners, including U.S. Presidents George Washington and Thomas Jefferson, cut and stored ice in the winter for use in the summer. Frederic Tudor of Boston turned ice harvesting and shipping into big business, cutting ice in New England and shipping it around the world.

Ice cream was made by hand in a large bowl placed inside a tub filled with ice and salt. This was called the pot-freezer method. French confectioners refined the pot-freezer method, making ice cream in a sorbtierre (a covered pail with a handle attached to the lid). In the pot-freezer method, the temperature of the ingredients is reduced by the mixture of crushed ice and salt. The salt water is cooled by the ice, and the action of the salt on the ice causes it to (partially) melt, absorbing latent heat and bringing the mixture below the freezing point of pure water. The immersed container can also make better thermal contact with the salty water and ice mixture than it could with ice alone.

The hand-cranked churn, which also uses ice and salt for cooling, replaced the pot-freezer method. The exact origin of the hand-cranked freezer is unknown, but the first U.S. patent for one was #3254 issued to Nancy

Johnson on September 9, 1843. The hand-cranked churn produced smoother ice cream than the pot freezer and did it quicker. Many inventors patented improvements on Johnson's design.

In Europe and early America, ice cream was made and sold by small businesses, mostly confectioners and caterers. Jacob Fussell of Baltimore, Maryland was the first to manufacture ice cream on a large scale. Fussell bought fresh dairy products from farmers in York County, Pennsylvania, and sold them in Baltimore. An unstable demand for his dairy products often left him with a surplus of cream, which he made into ice cream. He built his first ice-cream factory in Seven Valleys, Pennsylvania, in 1851. Two years later he moved his factory to Baltimore. Later he opened factories in several other cities and taught the business to others, who operated their own plants. Mass production reduced the cost of ice cream and added to its popularity.

The development of industrial refrigeration by German engineer Carl von Linde during the 1870s eliminated the need to cut and store natural ice and when the continuous-process freezer was perfected in 1926, it allowed commercial mass production of ice cream and the birth of the modern ice cream industry.

The most common method for producing ice cream at home is to use an ice cream maker, in modern times generally an electrical device that churns the ice cream mixture while cooled inside a household freezer, or using a solution of pre-frozen salt and water, which gradually melts while the ice cream freezes. Some more expensive models have an inbuilt freezing element. A newer method of making home-made ice cream is to add liquid nitrogen to the mixture while stirring it using a spoon or spatula. Some ice cream recipes call for making a custard, folding in whipped cream, and immediately freezing the mixture.

Ice cream can be mass-produced and thus is widely available in developed parts of the world. Ice cream can be purchased in large cartons (vats and squrounds) from supermarkets and grocery stores, in smaller quantities from ice cream shops, convenience stores, and milk bars, and in individual servings from small carts or vans at public events. In Turkey and Australia, ice cream is sometimes sold to beach-goers from small powerboats equipped with chest freezers. Some ice cream distributors sell ice cream products from traveling refrigerated vans or carts (commonly referred to in the US as "ice cream trucks"), sometimes equipped with speakers playing children's music. Traditionally ice cream vans in the United Kingdom make a music box noise rather than actual music.

History of Icecreams

Ancient civilizations had saved ice for cold foods for thousands of years. Mesopotamia has the earliest icehouses in existence, 4,000 years ago, beside the Euphrates River, where the wealthy stored items to keep them cold. The pharaohs of Egypt had ice shipped to them. In the fifth century BC, ancient Greeks sold snow cones mixed with honey and fruit in the markets of Athens. Persians, having mastered the storage of ice, ate ice cream well into summer. Roman emperor Nero (37–68) had ice brought from the mountains and combined with fruit toppings. Today's ice treats likely originated with these early ice delicacies.

Many myths surround ice cream and its true origin. Many believe that it evolved from cooled wines and flavored Ices around, and might have come from Persia.

These Iced wines were popular with Alexander the Great and later with Roman high society. In 62 AD, the Roman emperor Nero sent slaves to the Apennine mountains to collect snow to be flavored with honey and nuts. The Persians mastered the technique of storing ice inside giant naturally-cooled refrigerators known as yakhchals. These structures kept ice brought in from the winter, or from nearby mountains, well into the summer. They worked by using tall windcatchers that kept the sub-level storage space at frigid temperatures.

In 400 BC, Persians invented a special chilled pudding-like dish, made of rosewater and vermicelli which was served to royalty during summers. The ice was mixed with saffron, fruits, and various other flavors. The treat, widely made in Iran today, is called "faloodeh", and is made from starch (usually wheat), spun in a sieve-like machine which produces threads or drops of the batter, which are boiled in water. The mix is then frozen, and mixed with rosewater and lemons, before serving.

Ice cream was the favorite dessert for the caliphs of Baghdad. The Arabs were the first to add sugar to ice cream, and were also the first to make ice cream commercially, having factories in the 10th century. It was sold in the markets of all Arab cities in the past. It was made of a chilled syrup or milk with fruits and some nuts.

According to Maguelonne Toussaint-Samat in her History of Food, "the Chinese may be credited with inventing a device to make sorbets and ice cream. They poured a mixture of snow and saltpetre over the exteriors of containers filled with syrup, for, in the same way as salt raises the boiling-point of water, it lowers the freezing-point to below zero." The Chinese put sugar in the ice and sold it as food during the summer. During the Song Dynasty, people began putting fruit juice in the water used to create the ice; milk began to be used in the Yuan Dynasty, as the nomadic Mongols introduced milk to China, where milk was not widely used in cuisine. Milk and dairy products in general remain rare in Chinese cuisine.

As early as the sixteenth century, the Mughal emperors used relays of horsemen to bring ice from the Hindu Kush to Delhi where it was used in fruit sorbets. Kulfi is a type of ice cream which is very closely related to the Persian ice cream and is still sold by road side vendors and in restaurants.

Popular folklore asserts that Marco Polo saw ice cream being made on his trip to China and took the recipe home to Italy with him on his return. However, in his writings Marco Polo never claimed to have introduced ice cream to the west. The Roman emperor Nero Claudius Caesar Augustus appreciated a sort of local ice cream during the 37-68 AD.

When Italian duchess Catherine de' Medici married the duc d'Orléans in 1533, she is said to have brought with her Italian chefs who had recipes for flavored ices or sorbets and introduced them in France. One hundred years later Charles I of England was supposedly so impressed by the "frozen snow" that he offered his own ice cream maker a lifetime pension in return for keeping the formula secret, so that ice cream could be a royal prerogative. There is, however, no historical evidence to support these legends, which first appeared during the 19th century.

Ice cream made with a milk mixture was first recorded in Europe in Italy.

The first recipe for flavored ices in French appears in 1674, in Nicholas Lemery's Recueil de curiositéz rares et nouvelles de plus admirables effets de la nature.

Recipes for sorbetti saw publication in the 1694 edition of Antonio Latini's Lo Scalco alla Moderna.

Recipes for flavored ices begin to appear in François Massialot's Nouvelle Instruction pour les Confitures, les Liqueurs, et les Fruits starting with the 1692 edition. Massialot's recipes result in a coarse, pebbly texture. However, Latini claims that the results of his recipes should have the fine consistency of sugar and snow.

The first ice cream invented in the Americas, the sorbet, was invented by native indigenous in Ibarra, Ecuador during Incan occupation. The natives made the handmade ice cream, by taking ice from the top of Imbabura Volcano using a large bronze pan, and juices added from various fruit (eg taxo).

In the 18th century cream, milk, and egg yolks began to feature in the recipes of previously dairy-free flavored ices, resulting in ice cream in the modern sense of the word. The 1751 edition of The Art of Cookery made Plain and Easy by Hannah Glasse features a recipe for raspberry cream ice. 1768 saw the publication of L'Art de Bien Faire les Glaces d'Office by M. Emy, a cookbook devoted entirely to recipes for flavored ices and ice cream.

Ice cream was introduced to the United States by colonists who brought their ice cream recipes with them. Confectioners, many of whom were Europeans, sold ice cream at their shops in New York and other cities during the colonial era. Ben Franklin, George Washington, and Thomas Jefferson were known to have regularly eaten and served ice cream. First Lady Dolley Madison is also closely associated with the early history of ice cream in the United States.

Around 1832, Augustus Jackson, an African American confectioner, not only created multiple ice cream recipes, but he also invented a superior technique to manufacture ice cream.

In 1843, Nancy Johnson of Philadelphia was issued the first U.S. patent for a small-scale handcranked ice cream freezer. The invention of the ice cream soda gave Americans a new treat, adding to ice cream's popularity. This cold treat was probably invented by Robert Green in 1874, although there is no conclusive evidence to prove his claim.

The ice cream sundae originated in the late 19th century. Several men claimed to have created the first sundae, but there is no conclusive evidence to back up any of their stories. Some sources say that the sundae was invented to circumvent blue laws, which forbade serving sodas on Sunday. Towns claiming to be the birthplace of the sundae include Buffalo, New York; Two Rivers, Wisconsin; Ithaca, New York; and Evanston, Illinois. Both the ice cream cone and banana split became popular in the early 20th century. Several food vendors claimed to have invented the ice cream cone at the 1904 World's Fair in St. Louis, MO, and reliable evidence proves that the ice cream cone was popularized at the fair. However, Europeans were eating cones long before 1904.

The history of ice cream in the 20th century is one of great change and increases in availability and popularity. In the United States in the early 20th century, the ice cream soda was a popular treat at the soda shop, the soda fountain, and the ice cream parlor. During American Prohibition the soda fountain to some extent replaced the outlawed alcohol establishments, including bars and saloons.

Ice cream became popular throughout the world in the second half of the 20th century after cheap refrigeration became common. There was an explosion of ice cream stores and of flavors and types. Vendors often competed on the basis of variety. Howard Johnson's restaurants advertised "a world of 28 flavors." Baskin-Robbins made its 31 flavors ("one for every day of the month") the cornerstone of its marketing strategy. The company now boasts that it has developed over 1000 varieties.

One important development in the 20th century was the introduction of soft ice cream. A chemical research team in Britain (of which a young Margaret Thatcher was a member) discovered a method of doubling the amount of air in ice cream, which allowed manufacturers to use less of the actual ingredients, thereby reducing costs. This ice cream was also very popular amongst consumers who preferred the lighter texture, and most major ice cream brands now use this manufacturing process. It also made possible the soft ice cream machine in which a cone is filled beneath a spigot on order. In the United States, Dairy Queen, Carvel, and Tastee Freez pioneered in establishing chains of soft-serve ice cream outlets.

The 1980s saw a return of the older, thicker ice creams being sold as "premium" and "superpremium" varieties under brands such as Ben and Jerry's and Häagen-Dazs.

Snow cones, made from balls of crushed ice topped with sweet syrup served in a paper cone, are consumed in many parts of the world. The most common places to find snow cones in the United States are at amusement parks.

A popular springtime treat in maple-growing areas is maple toffee, where maple syrup boiled to a concentrated state is poured over fresh snow congealing in a toffee-like mass, and then eaten from a wooden stick used to pick it up from the snow. Ice creams and sorbets are frozen while being stirred or agitated, resulting in a light texture. Some ice pops are quiescently frozen — frozen at rest without stirring whilst others are frozen in an ice cream freezer (slush frozen) to give a smoother, softer texture.

Ice cream cone

Mrs Marshall's Cookery Book, published in 1888, endorsed serving ice cream in cones, but the idea definitely predated that. Agnes Marshall was a celebrated cookery writer of her day and helped to popularise ice cream. She patented and manufactured an ice cream maker and was the first person to suggest using liquefied gases to freeze ice cream after seeing a demonstration at the Royal Institution.

Reliable evidence proves that ice cream cones were served in the 19th century, and their popularity increased greatly during the St. Louis World's Fair in 1904. According to legend, at the World's Fair an ice cream seller had run out of the cardboard dishes used to put ice cream scoops in, so could not sell any more produce. Next door to the ice cream booth was a Syrian waffle booth, unsuccessful due to intense heat; the waffle maker offered to make cones by rolling up his waffles and the new product sold well, and was widely copied by other vendors.

Ice cream alternatives

The following is a partial list of ice-cream-like frozen desserts and snacks

— *Ice milk:* less than 10% milk fat and lower sweetening content, once marketed as "ice milk" but now sold as low-fat ice cream in the United States.

— *Frozen custard:* at least 10% milk fat and at least 1.4% egg yolk and much less air beaten into it, similar to Gelato, fairly rare.

— *Frozen yogurt:* a low fat or fat free alternative made with yogurt

— *Mellorine:* non-dairy, with vegetable fat substituted for milk fat

— *Gelato:* an Italian frozen dessert having a lower milk fat content than ice cream and stabilized with ingredients such as eggs.

— *Sherbet:* 1-2% milk fat and sweeter than ice cream.

— *Sorbet:* fruit puree and no milk products

— *Ice pop (or lolly):* frozen fruit puree, fruit juice, or flavored sugar water on a stick or in a flexible plastic sleeve.

— *Kulfi:* Believed to have been introduced to South Asia by the Mughal conquest in the 16th century; its origins trace back to the cold snacks and desserts of Arab and Mediterranean cultures.

— *Dondurma:* Turkish ice cream, made of salep and mastic resin

— Ais kacang: a dessert in Malaysia and Singapore made from shaved ice, syrup, boiled red bean and topped with chocolate sauce and evaporated milk.

HALVAH

The word halva (alternatively halwa, halvah, halava, helva, halawa etc.), originally derived from the Arabic root alwa (sweet), is used to describe many distinct types of sweet confection, across the Middle East, Central Asia, and South Asia. Halva based on semolina is popular in India, Iran, Turkey, Pakistan. Another common type, based on tahini (sesame paste), is more popular in the eastern Mediterranean and Balkan regions, in countries such as Romania, Greece, Cyprus, Israel, Lebanon and Turkey as well as the Palestinian territories. Halva may also be made from a variety of other ingredients, including sunflower seeds, various nuts, beans, lentils, and vegetables—such as carrots, pumpkins, yams, and squashes.

Slices of halva

Most types of halva are relatively dense confections that are sweetened with sugar or honey. However, their textures are quite different. For example, semolina halva is gelatinous and translucent, while sesame halva is drier and more crumbly.

Halva is the most common modern English spelling and the transliteration from most Balkan languages. Other transliterations include: halava (Sanskrit), halvah (Hebrew), halwa or halwi (Arabic), helva (Turkish). The Hebrew spelling, halvah, may at times be used to refer specifically to the Kosher variety. The word 'halawa' in Arabic means 'sweetness' while the word halwa means sweets or candy. The word halva comes from the Arabic word halwa; the root word is hilwa meaning sweet. The root word is also the basis for the Arabic word for "good" (helwa').

Halua as it is known in Bangla, is quite popular among the Bengalis. There are many types of haluas that are savoured, among the common ones are: semolina (shoojir halua), carrot (gajorer halua), chickpeas (booter daaler halua), flour (neshestar halua) and almond (baadamer halua). Many Bangladeshis also eat halua made from papaya (peper halua). Halua is usually eaten as a rich dessert, but it is not uncommon for Bengalis to eat halua for breakfast with traditional breads (rice flour, porota etc..)

In Bulgaria the term halva is used for several varieties of the dessert. Tahini halva is most popular and can be found in all food stores. Two different types of tahini halva are made - one using sunflower seed tahini and another using sesame seed tahini. Traditionally, the regions of Yablanitsa and Haskovo are famous for their halva. Semolina halva is made at home and can be found only in some pastry stores. A third type is white halva, which is made of sugar. White halva is popular on the last Sunday before Lent, when a piece of white halva is tied on a string. All the children at the party stand in a circle and must catch the turning piece of halva with their mouths.

In Egypt, the name is halawa tahiniya. The word 'halawa' in Arabic means 'sweetness' while the word halwa means sweets. It has many varieties such as plain blocks, and fine fibrous halawa called halawa hair. Other varieties with pine nuts, pistachios, and almonds exist in big blocks or pre-packed consumer portions, or more recently energy bars (chocolate bar size). Halawa is a very popular sweet enjoyed by a lot of Egyptians. It is eaten for breakfast and dinner, and enjoyed with hot bread, sandwiches, and sometimes with the Arabic equivalent of clotted cream. It is a staple food that is enjoyed all over the country as it does not need special storage conditions, and can be kept in ambient temperature with no risk of spoilage.

In Greece and most of Cyprus the term halva is used for both varieties of the dessert. Sesame halva was produced in classical times. The dish was popular in the Byzantine Empire, and it is very popular throughout the country especially during Great Lent and other fasts. Halva is considered one of the most delicious Greek desserts which is appropriate under Orthodox Christian fasting guidelines.

Halwa had become one of the sweet dishes in India. Mostly made of wheat flour, ghee and sugar. There are various types of halva in India, distinguished by the region and the content in which it is prepared. One of the famous halwa is Tirunelveli halwa. Carrot halwa is a popular sweet throughout India.

Heavily sesame-flavoured tahini halvah is very popular with Jews in Israel and among Jews all over the world. Spelled "halvah" in English, it usually comes in slabs or small packages and is available in a wide variety of flavours, chocolate and vanilla being very common. The halvah is almost always pareve, meaning it does not contain any meat or dairy ingredients, ensuring that it can be eaten with/after either milk or meat dishes according to the laws of Kashrut. Israeli and Jewish halvah will usually not contain wheat flour or semolina but will contain sesame tahini, glucose, sugar, vanilla and saponaria root extracts (Soapwort) which are not always found in other recipes.

In Turkey, after the burial ceremony, on the seventh and fortieth day following the death of a muslim, and also on the first anniversary, flour helva is cooked and offered to visitors and neighbours by relatives of the deceased. For this reason, flour (un) helva is also called "ölü helvasi" meaning "helva of the dead". The expression "roasting the helva of someone" suggests that the person referred to died some time ago.

Types of Halva

Semolina halva

This halva, produced and served in India, Pakistan, Bangladesh, Iran and surrounding countries (different versions of it are also found in Albania, Armenia, Bulgaria, Cyprus, Greece and Turkey), is usually made with semolina wheat, sugar or honey, and butter or vegetable oil. Raisins, dates, or other dried fruits are often included. Nuts such as almonds are also commonly added to semolina halva. The halva is very sweet with a gelatinous texture similar to polenta; the added butter gives it a rich mouthfeel. Though semolina halva is considered to be essentially a "Northern" confection in India, it is also quite popular in South India. A prominent South Indian version of halva (or "alvaa", as it is called in Tamil) is from Tirunelveli, a city in the state of Tamil Nadu. A closely related semolina preparation widely enjoyed throughout South India is called Kesari or Kesari-bath.

In India, carrots (for gajar halwa) or mung beans (for moong dal halwa), for example, may be used instead of semolina. Prepared with condensed milk and ghee, without semolina to bind it together, the end result has a moist yet flaky texture when freshly prepared and bears some resemblance to a British pudding.

Sesame halva

Sesame halva is popular in the Balkans, Middle East, and other areas surrounding the Mediterranean Sea. The primary ingredients in this confection are sesame seeds or paste (tahini), and sugar, glucose or honey. Soap root(called 'erq al halaweh in Arabic; çöven kökü in Turkish), egg white, or marshmallow root are added in some recipes, to create a distinctive texture. Other ingredients and flavourings such as pistachio nuts, cocoa powder, orange juice, vanilla, or chocolate are normally added to the basic tahini and sugar base.

Floss halva

Pismaniye (Turkish) or floss halva is a traditional sweetmeat, prepared in Kocaeli, Turkey, made by flossing thin strands of halva into a light confection. Made primarily of wheat flour and sugar, the strands are continuously wrapped into a ball shape and then compressed. The result is a halva with a light consistency, similar to cotton candy. Floss halva can be found in regular and pistachio flavors, and there are brands with halal or kosher certifications. A similar pistachio-based version of Floss halva is popular in North India. It tends to be slightly denser and is often referred to as "Patisa".

Sunflower halva

Sunflower halva, popular in countries from Eastern Europe, such as Belarus, Romania, Republic of Moldova, Russia and Ukraine, is made of sunflower seeds instead of sesame. It has a rich , unmistakable flavor and "addictive" taste.

ALFAJOR

An alfajor is a traditional cookie in some countries of the Americas , most notably in Argentina. However, now it can be found in Peru, Uruguay, Ecuador, Paraguay, Brazil and Chile. Its most basic form consists of two round sweet biscuits generally joined together with dulce de leche and/or jam and covered with powder sugar. In most alfajores there are layers like cake, and the dulce de leche fills in between.

Alfajors

Another popular feature of the alfajor, although not always present, is a coating of black or white chocolate (many alfajores are sold in "black" and "white" flavours). There's also one variation, called "Alfajor de nieve", that instead of having a white or black chocolate coating, it has a "snow" coating. The "snow coating" consists mostly of a mixture of egg whites and sugar. Peruvian alfajores are usually coated in powdered sugar, as seen in the picture, and are filled with manjar blanco. Most alfajores come packaged in aluminium foil, similarly to most chocolate bars, though hand-made are just as accessible and generally packaged in plastic wrap or wax paper.

Other varieties of alfajor include different elements in the preparation of the biscuits, such as peanuts; they also vary the filling and coating and even add a third biscuit (alfajor triple).

In the province of Cádiz, Spain, there is a completely different confection also called alfajor that is made of flour, honey, almonds and several spices, such as cinnamon. It is most commonly sold around Christmas.

DRAGÉE

A dragée is a form of confectionery that can be used for decorative or symbolic purposes in addition to consumption. A classic, popular version of dragée, called confetti in Italian and Jordan almonds or sugared almonds in English, are whole almonds coated with a sugar shell, made in various colors. These confections have a long history, and are traditionally associated with weddings and special celebrations. Throwing or handing out these candies at such occasions (hence the name for the multi-colored paper confetti which usually now replaces them) dates back centuries, and is meant to ensure prosperity, fertility, happiness, and good luck.

Miniheart Dragées

The town of Verdun, France, had acquired a reputation for its dragées by the 13th century. Originally the dragée was a spiced lump of sugar eaten as a digestive after meals. The process by which the sugar shell is applied to the center is often known as "panning".

More recently, with the introduction of chocolate to the Old World, and chocolate's steady gain in popularity once an eating form was developed in the early 19th century, chocolate dragées in the shape of the original almond sweets, still with the colored candy coating, have become at least as popular as, if not more so than, the original almond version. Both types can be ordered for weddings, et al., in whatever colors suit the buyers.

A third form of dragée is a much smaller, pure sugar ball, usually with a metallic coating, made to resemble a ball bearing. These dragées are produced in various sizes, but tend toward slightly larger than a nonpareil and slightly smaller than a small pearl. In fact, one of the more recent developments in the finish of dragées has been the creation of fairly realistic edible pearls, which are used primarily in the decoration of cookies, cakes, and other forms of bakery. Silver dragées, now augmented by ones with gold and copper finishes, have long been used for both wedding and holiday food decoration.

The U.S. Food and Drug Administration considers the metallic-finish dragées to be inedible. Early in the 20th century, the silver finish may have contained mercury (it does not now). The sale of these dragées was banned for some time. Although the metallic-finish dragées can be purchased in 49 U.S. states, in California, they are no longer sold due to a 2003 lawsuit against several sellers. Now, these dragées are sold with a notice that they are for decorative purposes only. However in other countries (including the United Kingdom) they are classed as food items.

A fourth form of contemporary dragée might be almond M&M's – whole almonds in chocolate with a candy shell. These, too, can be ordered in a variety of colors for special occasions. However, historically correct or not, calling M&M's dragées may be a little old-fashioned in attitude or style.

Mentos are named "chewy dragees" on most packages. The hard sugar outside and various colors with a soft center make this an appropriate description for these lollies. However, in modern day society, this description and labelling is not common, the common names are mints, lollies, sweets and candy.

9

Art of Food Carving

The art of carving foods is an Eastern custom that has been adopted by creative food preparers around the world. In Thailand and Japan food carving is considered part of the presentation of the meal. The stunning designs that can be created makes the food the center of attention when you serve your guests. No need to worry about what else is on the table.

Watermelons, turnips, pineapples and many other fruits and vegetables can be carved and combined into either elegantly simple or very elaborate center pieces or accents for your picnic table or indoor party decorations.

Some of the more elaborate carvings can take hours to get just right, but practice makes it go faster and soon you'll find yourself designing your own patterns for watermelons, radishes and any fruit or vegetable that can hold it's form when carved.

Just like Thai cuisine, Chinese cooking is also well-known for its delicate food carving techniques. Not only restaurant chefs but also ordinary households are fond of decorating dishes with the art of food sculpture. While the Thai chefs usually have their designs carved with floral patterns, chefs in China specialise in carving figures of animals, fairy and mythical characters.

Vegetables such as melons, carrots, Chinese radishes, taros and pumpkins are frequently used, of which the melon carving technique is especially well known. Chefs usually take out the pulp of a melon, carve exquisite patterns on the melon's skin, and then use the melon as a container. The dish features a refreshing, sweet and cool taste.

The purpose of fruit and vegetable carving is to make food more attractive, more appetizing, and also easier to eat. The accomplished homemaker welcomes her guests with fruit carefully pared, seeded, and perhaps cut into bite-size slices depending on the type. Vegetables are first delicately carved, then cooked, and finally arranged attractively to decorate the dish which they are part of. Needless to say, guests are greatly pleased to be honored with such a gracious welcome, displaying as it does the good feelings and willing hospitality of the maker.

Decorating fresh, well-formed, and colourful fruits and vegetables through artistic carving is by no means difficult; all it takes is concentration. Starting out, there is no need for special carving knives; one sharp-pointed knife is enough to carve fruits and vegetables beautifully. The knife, however, must be sharp at all times, and so you should always have a small whetstone nearby.

Before Carving

1. Before carving, fruits and vegetables must be washed and cleaned thoroughly.
2. Use knives with stainless steel or bronze blades. Knives with ordinary steel blades will cause discoloration of fruits and vegetables.
3. Do not carve excessively so as to avoid waste and loss of nutritional value.

4. Vegetables chosen for carving should be appropriate to the dish in which they are to be used, and they should be vegetables which are resistant to wilting, such as carrots and Chinese radishes.
5. Care must be exercised during carving so as to avoid bruising fruit and vegetables.

Simple White Lotus Cucumber Garnish

Material:

1 long cucumber and 1 carrot

Equipment:

Sharp pointed knife and carving knife

Instructions:

1. Wash the cucumbers. Cut into 3 sections.
2. Divide the circumference of each into 8 equal parts and then make cuts about 3mm deep between each part down the length of the section.
3. Slice beneath each part down the length almost to the base to separate it from the flesh, thus forming the 8 outer petals.
4. Trim the flesh to remove ridges and then divide into 8 parts as before to make the inner ring of petals. These should be centered between those of the outer ring.
5. Remove the core of the cucumber, trim each petal so it tapers to a point, and then insert the center of the flower.
6. For the center, use 1/4" thick disk cut from a small carrot. Cut small grooves in a crisscross pattern on one face, and place up in the lotus flower.

Thai Fruit Carving

There is a long tradition of fruit carving in Thailand, especially in the preparation of food for the Royal Family.

The purpose of fruit and vegetable carving is to make food more attractive, more appetizing, and also easier to eat. The accomplished homemaker welcomes her guests with fruit carefully pared, seeded, and perhaps cut into bite-size slices depending on the type. Vegetables are first delicately carved, then cooked, and finally arranged attractively to decorate the dish which they are part of. Needless to say, guests are greatly pleased to be honored with such a gracious welcome, displaying as it does the good feelings and willing hospitality of the maker.

Decorating fresh, well-formed, and colourful fruits and vegetables through artistic carving is by no means difficult; all it takes is concentration. Starting out, there is no need for special carving knives; one sharp-pointed knife is enough to carve fruits and vegetables beautifully. The knife, however, must be sharp at all times, and so you should always have a small whetstone nearby.

Things should be take care while carving are given below:

1. Before carving, fruits and vegetables must be washed and cleaned thoroughly.
2. Use knives with stainless steel or bronze blades. Knives with ordinary steel blades will cause discoloration of fruits and vegetables.
3. Do not carve excessively so as to avoid waste and loss of nutritional value.
4. The designs carved should be appropriate for decorating a plate of food; thus, floral patterns are suitable, while figures of animals such as rats are not.
5. Vegetables to be dipped into sauces should be cut to appropriate sizes.
6. Vegetables chosen for carving should be appropriate to the dish in which they are to be used, and they should be vegetables which are resistant to wilting, such as carrots and Chinese radishes.
7. Care must be exercised during carving so as to avoid bruising fruit and vegetables.

Tips on Selecting Fruits and Vegetables for Carving

Each kind of fruit and vegetable has its own unique characteristics, so keep these pointers in mind when choosing fruits and vegetables to carve. Onions and shallots should be fresh and without wrinkles. Choose either mediumsized or small bulbs that are all of uniform size.

— Carrots should be straight and of medium or large-size.

— Radishes should be fresh, firm, and round. Use medium-sized radishes, all of uniform size.

— Chinese radishes should be straight and of medium-size with clear bright skins. The flesh of large Chinese radishes tends to be mealy.

— Cucumbers should be green, straight, and of medium-size. The type called for in this book is the larger type (Tang Ran). If the smaller type (Tang Kwa) is used, those with green skins have firmer flesh and are better for carving than those with greenish white skins.

— Tomatoes should be of uniform size. Plum tomatoes, with elongated fruits, are firmer than round varieties. Choose fresh ones with no wrinkles.

— Pumpkins should have thick, firm flesh.Such pumpkins have a rough exterior.

— Spur chillies should be fresh and have firm skins. Generally small ones are used, because if large ones were cut and spread out to make a blossom, they would cover the entire plate. However, large spur chilies are used for making anthurium flowers.

— Spring shallots and leek should be fresh and green with no yellowing on the leaves. Select thick, medium-sized plants.

— Cabbage and Chinese cabbage should be fresh with firm, heavy heads. Use medium sized heads.

— Lemons should be very fresh.

— Taro should be of medium-size. The fragrant taro (Pheuak Hawm) has fine-textured flesh.

— Cantaloupes should be those that are not yet fully ripe. The skin should be pale yellow without wrinkles or scratches.

— Yam bean tubers used for carving should not be too large. Large, mature tubers have a lot of fibers. These become frayed in carving, detracting from the appearance of the finished work.

— Papayas should be straight, thick-fleshed and without any bruises. They should not yet be fully ripe so that the flesh is firm and does not bruise easily. The Khaek Dam variety is recommended be cause of thebeautifully colored flesh.

— Green mangoes should be fully mature and of a variety whose flesh is not too crisp. The skin should be green and un-wrinkled and the stem should look fresh.

— Watermelon should have red flesh and green rinds with no bruises or wrinkles.

— Pineapple should have large eyes. The leaves should be fresh and green and there should be no shrivelling of the skin or stem.

— Guavas should be those that are just becoming ripe. The skin should be a fresh light green skins and there should be no bruises or scratches.

— Apples should be fresh with glossy, brightly colored skins and no bruises.

— Jujubes should have straight fruits with green skins and no bruises.

— Sapodillas must be firm, so avoid fully ripe fruits. The skins should be even and clear. Avoid sapodillas that have been dyed for the market. Their skins have a dusty appearance.

— Rose-apples should have clear, fresh looking skins.

Specific Preparations and Treatments

1. Tomatoes should be soaked in a mixture of lime juice and water to prevent browning.

2. Shallots and onions should be soaked in water before being peeled and carved to reduce irritation of the eyes.
3. Taro should be washed thoroughly before being peeled. If washed after peeling, a slime is released which causes itching.
4. Carrots should not be soaked in water before carving as this will make the flesh tougher and more difficult to carve.
5. Beets should be washed in water to which a little salt has been added. This will reduce loss of color. Also, if left standing, beets will blacken, so they should be kept moist by spraying them with water regularly.
6. Potatoes should be washed with water after peeling to remove the sap and then washed again after carving. This will help prevent browning.
7. Apples should be soaked in mixture of lime juice and water before being peeled to prevent browning.
8. Cantaloupes should be washed before carving. While carving, avoid letting water come into contact with the fruit because it will lose its taste and spoil more quickly.
9. Yam bean tubers should be soaked too long after carving, will yellow.

Storing Carved Fruits and Vegetables

1. After carving, fruits and vegetables should be placed in ice cold water so the petals of flower designs are firm and spread beautifully.
2. Carved fruits and vegetables should not be left in water as this will cause petals to become discoloured and to spoil.

3. Each type of carved fruit should be kept separately. This will prevent loss of all your work in the event that one type spoils.
4. Store carved fruits and vegetables by putting them in containers and placing in a refrigerator, or if no refrigerator is available, by covering them with a damp piece of thin white cloth and putting them in a place protected from drafts so they do not dry and wilt.
5. After carving, pumpkin should be dipped in water and removed right away. If left in water, flower petal designs will become bruised.

Watermelon Basket Carving

Perfect for a summer picnic, this Watermelon Fruit Basket is carved from a watermelon into the shape of a dolphin. Kids will love to help draw the pattern on the watermelon rind and make the melon balls with the help of a melon scoop. Refrigerate until serving time, when you can sit back and enjoy the compliments.

Watermelon Fruit Basket

Materials

— One small watermelon
— Sharp-pointed knife
— Carving knife
— Melon scoop

Preparation

— Choose an elongated watermelon.
— Lightly draw a dolphin on the rind of the watermelon as in the picture with a sharp point.
— Cut along the lines carefully with the knife and then gently cut away the rind.
— With a melon scoop, make the flesh into watermelon balls and set aside in a dish. Remove any remaining flesh so the interior is clean and white.
— Cut triangles through the rind to represent the eyes, and in the edges, cut notches for the eyelashes.
— Cut a crescent for the mouth, and then notch the upper border of the rind all around except at the tail.
— Arrange the watermelon and cantalope balls attractively in the dolphin-shaped bowl.

10

The Flavour of Chocolate

Bittersweet Brownie Batter

When a brownie batter supports little chunks of premium bittersweet chocolate, a delectable thing happens—the small chunks of chocolate form pools of goodness throughout, and the sweet resonates with flavour. You should try to restrain yourself from cutting the brownies too soon.

- 1 cup bleached all-purpose flour
- ½ cup bleached cake flour
- ¼ cup plus 1 tablespoon unsweetened alkalised cocoa powder
- ¼ teaspoon baking powder
- ½ teaspoon salt
- 3 ounces bittersweet chocolate, chopped into small chunks
- ½ pound (16 tablespoons or 2 sticks) unsalted butter, melted and cooled to tepid
- 5 ounces unsweetened chocolate, melted and cooled to tepid
- 3 ounces bittersweet chocolate, melted and cooled to tepid

— 5 large eggs
— 2 cups superfine sugar
— 2 teaspoons vanilla extract
— Confectioners' sugar, for sifting on top of the baked brownies (optional)

Preheat the Oven to 325 Degrees F. Film the inside of a 9 by 9 by 2-inch baking pan with nonstick cooking spray. Mix the Batter Sift the all-purpose flour, cake flour, cocoa powder, baking powder, and salt onto a sheet of waxed paper. In a small bowl, toss the chocolate chunks with 1 teaspoon of the sifted mixture.

In a medium-size mixing bowl, whisk the melted butter, melted unsweetened chocolate, and melted bittersweet chocolate until smooth. In a large mixing bowl, whisk the eggs until blended, about 15 seconds. Add the sugar and whisk until combined, 30 to 45 seconds. Blend in the vanilla extract and melted butter-chocolate mixture. Sift the flour mixture over and stir to form a batter, mixing thoroughly until the particles of flour are absorbed, using a whisk or flat wooden paddle. Stir in the chocolate chunks.

Scrape the batter into the prepared pan and spread evenly. Smooth the top with a rubber spatula. Bake, cool, amd Cut the Brownies: Bake the brownies in the preheated oven for 30 to 33 minutes, or until gently set. Let the brownies stand in the pan on a cooling rack for 3 hours. With a small sharp knife, cut the sweet into quarters, then cut each quarter into 4 squares. Remove the brownies from the baking pan, using a small offset metal spatula. Store in an airtight tin. Sift confectioners' sugar on top of the brownies just before serving, if you wish.

Double-Decker Fudge Brownies

Exquisite and loaded with chocolate, these are the brownies that I swoon over, for they never fail to please: the batter is plied with cocoa powder, miniature chocolate chips, melted unsweetened chocolate, and melted bittersweet chocolate. Within moments of pulling the moist block of brownies from the oven, it is covered with a thick swath of chocolate fudge that bonds irresistibly with the dark chocolate firmament below.

Dark chocolate Batter

— ¾ cup bleached cake flour

— ½ cup bleached all-purpose flour

— 3 tablespoons unsweetened alkalised cocoa powder

— ¼ teaspoon baking powder

— ½ teaspoon salt

— ¾ cup miniature semisweet chocolate chips

— ½ pound (16 tablespoons or 2 sticks) unsalted butter, melted and cooled to tepid

— 4 ounces unsweetened chocolate, melted and cooled to tepid

— 1 ounce bittersweet chocolate, melted and cooled to tepid

— 4 large eggs

— 2 cups granulated sugar

— 2 teaspoons vanilla extract

Topping

Chocolate fudge topcoa

Preheat the Oven to 325 Degrees F. Film the inside of a 9

by 9 by 2-inch baking pan with nonstick cooking spray. Mix the batter Sift the cake flour, all-purpose flour, cocoa powder, baking powder, and salt onto a sheet of waxed paper. In a small bowl, toss the chocolate chips with ¾ teaspoon of the sifted mixture.

In a medium-size mixing bowl, whisk the melted butter, melted unsweetened chocolate, and melted bittersweet chocolate until smooth. In a large mixing bowl, whisk the eggs until blended, about 15 seconds. Add the sugar and whisk until combined, about 30 to 45 seconds. Blend in the vanilla extract and melted butter-chocolate mixture. Sift the flour mixture over and stir to form a batter, mixing thoroughly until the particles of flour are absorbed, using a whisk or flat wooden paddle. Stir in the chocolate chips.

Scrape the batter into the prepared pan and spread evenly. Smooth the top with a rubber spatula.

Bake the Brownies: Bake the brownies in the preheated oven for 35 to 40 minutes, or until set.

Apply the Topping: Let the baked brownies stand in the pan on a cooling rack for 3 minutes. Carefully place dollops of the frosting on top of the hot brownie layer.

Smooth and spread the frosting with a small offset palette knife or rubber spatula, taking care not to cut into the top of the brownie cake.

Cool and Cut the Brownies: Let the brownies stand in the pan on a cooling rack for 5 hours, or until completely cool. The topping should be set and softly firm. With a small sharp knife, cut the sweet into quarters, then cut each quarter into 4 squares. Remove the brownies from the baking pan, using a small offset metal spatula. Store in single layers in airtight tins.

Supremely Fudgy Brownies

The flavour of chocolate comes through solidly in this pan of brownies. If you like your brownies dense, buttery, and creamy, preheat the oven now.

Fudge Brownie Batter

— 1 cup bleached all-purpose flour
— ¼ cup bleached cake flour
— 2 tablespoons unsweetened alkalised cocoa powder
— ¼ teaspoon baking powder
— ½ teaspoon salt
— ½ pound (16 tablespoons or 2 sticks) unsalted butter, melted and cooled to tepid
— 4 ounces unsweetened chocolate, melted and cooled to tepid
— 4 large eggs
— 2 cups granulated sugar
— 1½ teaspoons vanilla extract
— Confectioners' sugar, for sifting on top of the baked brownies (optional)

Preheat the Oven to 325 Degrees F. Film the inside of a 9 by 9 by 2-inch baking pan with nonstick cooking spray.

Mix the Batter: Sift the all-purpose flour, cake flour, cocoa powder, baking powder, and salt onto a sheet of waxed paper.

In a medium-size mixing bowl, whisk the melted butter and melted chocolate until smooth. In a large mixing bowl, whisk the eggs until blended, about 30 seconds. Add the sugar and whisk until combined, about 30 seconds. Blend in the vanilla extract and melted butter-chocolate mixture. Sift the flour mixture over and stir to form a batter, mixing thoroughly until the particles of flour are absorbed, using a whisk or flat wooden paddle. Scrape the batter into the prepared pan and spread evenly. Smooth the top with a rubber spatula.

Bake, Cool, and Cut the Brownies: Bake the brownies in the preheated oven for 34 to 38 minutes, or until set. Let the brownies stand in the pan on a cooling rack for 3 hours. Refrigerate for 1 hour. With a small sharp knife, cut the sweet into quarters, then cut each quarter into 4 squares. Remove the brownies from the baking pan, using a small offset metal spatula. Store in an airtight tin. Sift confectioners' sugar on top of the brownies just before serving, if you wish.

CoconutCandy Fudge Brownie

Crunchy chunks of candy, made of peanut butter and toasted coconut, are a bold seasoning agent for a brownie. The peanut candy–sparked batter is heightened and rounded out by a little peanut butter. Lightly salted whole peanuts (a generous ¾ cup) or three more candy bars, cut into rough chunks, can be scattered on the top of the unbaked pan of brownies—either would make an indulgent overlay.

Peanut and Coconut Brownie Batter

— 1 cup bleached all-purpose flour

— ¼ cup bleached cake flour

— 3 tablespoons unsweetened alkalised cocoa powder

— ¼ teaspoon baking powder

— ½ teaspoon salt

— ½ pound (16 tablespoons or 2 sticks) unsalted butter,

melted and cooled to tepid

- 4 ounces unsweetened chocolate, melted and cooled to tepid
- 2 tablespoons smooth (creamy) peanut butter
- 4 large eggs
- 2 cups superfine sugar
- 2 teaspoons vanilla extract
- 4 (1.75 ounces each) crunchy peanut butter and toasted coconut candy bars (such as Zagnut), cut into ½-inch chunks
- Confectioners' sugar, for sifting on top of the baked brownies (optional)

Preheat the Oven to 325 Degrees F. Film the inside of a 9 by 9 by 2-inch baking pan with nonstick cooking spray.

Mix the batter: Sift the all-purpose flour, cake flour, cocoa powder, baking powder, and salt onto a sheet of waxed paper.

In a medium-size mixing bowl, whisk the melted butter and melted chocolate until thoroughly combined; whisk in the peanut butter to blend well. In a large mixing bowl, whisk the eggs until blended, about 15 seconds.

Add the sugar and whisk until combined, about 30 seconds; do not whisk vigorously or the batter will become overlay lightened. Blend in the vanilla extract and melted butter-chocolate mixture. Sift the flour mixture over and stir to form a batter, mixing thoroughly but lightly, using a whisk or flat wooden paddle, until the particles of flour are absorbed. Stir in the candy bar chunks.

Scrape the batter into the prepared pan and spread evenly. Smooth the top with a rubber spatula.

Bake, Cool, and Cut the Brownies :Bake the brownies in the preheated oven for 33 to 38 minutes, or until set. Let the brownies stand in the pan on a cooling rack for 3 hours. Refrigerate for 45 minutes. With a small sharp knife, cut the sweet into quarters, then cut each quarter into 4 squares. Remove the brownies from the baking pan, using a small offset metal spatula. Store in an airtight tin. Sift confectioners' sugar on top of the brownies just before serving, if you wish.

LAYERED CHOCOLATE COOKIE BROWNIES

These brownies are just packed with chocolate: a bottom chocolate cookie layer is gilded with chocolate chips, and a darkly moist, cocoa and unsweetened chocolate–charged brownie batter seals it all together.

Chocolate Cookie Layer

8 tablespoons (1 stick) unsalted butter, melted, cooled to tepid, and combined with ¼ teaspoon vanilla extract, ½ cups plus 3 tablespoons chocolate wafer cookie crumbs (such as crumbs made from Nabisco Famous Chocolate Wafers)

Chocolate chip layer

¼ cup miniature semisweet chocolate chips

Brownie Batter

— 1 cup bleached all-purpose flour
— ¼ cup bleached cake flour
— ¼ cup unsweetened alkalised cocoa powder
— ¼ teaspoon baking powder
— ½ teaspoon salt
— ½ pound (16 tablespoons or 2 sticks) unsalted butter,

melted and cooled to tepid
— 6 ounces unsweetened chocolate, melted and cooled to tepid
— 5 large eggs
— 2 cups superfine sugar
— 2 teaspoons vanilla extract

Topping

½ cup miniature semisweet chocolate chips
Confectioners' sugar, for sifting on top of the baked brownies (optional)

Preheat the Oven to 325 Degrees F.. Film the bottom of a 10 by 10 by 2-inch baking pan with nonstick cooking spray.

Mix, Bake, and Cool the Cookie Layer :Pour the melted butter-vanilla mixture into the prepared pan. Spoon the cookie crumbs evenly over the bottom of the pan and press down lightly with the underside of a small offset metal spatula so that the crumbs absorb the butter. Bake the cookie layer in the preheated oven for 4 minutes. Transfer the baking pan to a cooling rack. Immediately sprinkle the chocolate chips evenly over the cookie layer. Cool for 10 minutes.

Mix the Batter: Sift the all-purpose flour, cake flour, cocoa powder, baking powder, and salt onto a sheet of waxed paper. In a medium-size mixing bowl, whisk the melted butter and melted chocolate until smooth. In a large mixing bowl, whisk the eggs until blended, about 15 seconds. Add the sugar and whisk until combined, about 30 seconds. Blend in the vanilla extract and melted butter-chocolate mixture. Sift the flour mixture over and stir to form a batter, mixing thoroughly until the particles of flour are absorbed, using a whisk or flat wooden paddle. Spoon the batter in large dollops on the cookie crumb layer. Carefully spread the batter over the cookie layer, using a flexible palette knife or spatula.

Bake, Cool, and Cut the Brownies: Bake the brownies in the preheated oven for 30 minutes. Quickly sprinkle the chocolate chips on top and continue baking for 3 to 5 minutes longer, or until set. Let the brownies stand in the pan on a cooling rack for 3 hours. Refrigerate for 30 minutes.

With a small sharp knife, cut the sweet into quarters, then cut each quarter into 4 squares. Remove the brownies from the baking pan, using a small offset metal spatula. Store in an airtight tin. Sift confectioners' sugar on top of the brownies just before serving, if you wish.

Coconut and White Chocolate Dream Brownies

Agenerous handful of flaked coconut and white chocolate chips adds a moist chewiness and a topnote of flavour to these sweet brownie squares. The batter is straightforward, but provocative— simple, creamy, and divine.

Coconut and white Chocolate Batter

— ¾ cup bleached all-purpose flour

— ¼ cup bleached cake flour

— 2 tablespoons unsweetened alkalised cocoa powder

— ½ teaspoon baking powder

— ½ teaspoon salt

— ½ pound (16 tablespoons or 2 sticks) unsalted butter, melted and cooled to tepid

— 4 ounces unsweetened chocolate, melted and cooled to tepid
— 4 large eggs
— 1¾ cups plus 1 tablespoon granulated sugar
— 1½ teaspoons vanilla extract
— 4 bars (1.9 ounces each) chocolate-covered coconut candy (such as Peter Paul Mounds), cut into ½-inch chunks
— ¾ cup sweetened flaked coconut
— ¾ cup white chocolate chips (or chunks)

Preheat the Oven to 325 Degrees F. Film the inside of a 9 by 9 by 2-inch baking pan with nonstick cooking spray.

Mix the Batter: Sift the all-purpose flour, cake flour, cocoa powder, baking powder, and salt onto a sheet of waxed paper. In a medium-size mixing bowl, whisk the melted butter and melted chocolate until well blended. In a large mixing bowl, whisk the eggs until blended, about 15 seconds. Add the sugar and whisk until combined, about 30 seconds. Blend in the vanilla extract and melted butterchocolate mixture. Sift the flour mixture over and stir to form a batter, mixing thoroughly until the particles of flour are absorbed, using a whisk or flat wooden paddle. Stir in the chunks of candy, flaked coconut, and white chocolate chips (or chunks).

Scrape the batter into the prepared pan and spread evenly. Smooth the top with a rubber spatula. Bake, Cool, and Cut the Brownies: Bake the brownies in the preheated oven for 35 to 40 minutes, or until set. Let the brownies stand in the pan on a cooling rack for 3 hours. Refrigerate for 45 minutes. With a small sharp knife, cut the sweet into quarters, then cut each quarter into 4 squares. Remove the brownies from the baking pan, using a small offset metal spatula. Store in an airtight tin.

Crumb-Crusted Cocoa-Coconut Brownies

Coconut in the cookie layer on the bottom of these brownies and in the batter itself is a significant ingredient for all bakers who love it as much as I do.

Coconut-Chocolate Cookie Layer

8 tablespoons (1 stick) unsalted butter, melted, cooled to, tepid, and combined with ¼ teaspoon vanilla extract 1½ cups chocolate sandwich cookie crumbs (such as crumbs made from Nabisco Oreo chocolate sandwich cookies) combined with 3 tablespoons sweetened flaked coconut

Cocoa-Coconut Batter

- 1¼ cups bleached all-purpose flour
- ¼ cup unsweetened alkalised cocoa powder
- ¼ teaspoon baking powder
- ¼ teaspoon salt
- ½ pound (16 tablespoons or 2 sticks) unsalted butter, melted and cooled to tepid
- 6 ounces unsweetened chocolate, melted and cooled to tepid
- 5 large eggs
- 1¾ cups plus 2 tablespoons superfine sugar
- 2 teaspoons vanilla extract
- ½ cup sweetened flaked coconut

Preheat the Oven to 325 Degrees F. Film the inside of a 10 by 10 by 2-inch baking pan with nonstick cooking spray.

Make the Cookie Layer: Pour the melted butter-vanilla mixture into the prepared pan. Spoon the cookie crumb mixture evenly over the bottom and press down lightly with the underside of a small offset metal spatula so that the crumbs absorb the butter. Bake the cookie layer in the preheated oven for 3 minutes. Place the baking pan on a rack. Cool for 10 minutes.

Make the Batter: Sift the flour, cocoa powder, baking powder, and salt onto a sheet of waxed paper. In a medium-size mixing bowl, whisk the melted butter and melted chocolate until smooth. In a large mixing bowl, whisk the eggs for 30 seconds to blend, add the sugar, and whisk for 45 seconds, or until incorporated. Blend in the melted butter-chocolate mixture. Blend in the vanilla extract. Sift the flour mixture over and stir to form a batter, mixing thoroughly until the particles of flour are absorbed, using a whisk or flat wooden paddle. Stir in the coconut.

Spoon the batter in large dollops onto the cookie crumb layer. Carefully spread the batter over the cookie layer, using a flexible palette knife or spatula. If you are too enthusiastic, it may lift patches of the bottom layer. Use smooth, short strokes.

Bake, Cool, and Cut the Brownies: Bake the brownies in the preheated oven for 35 to 40 minutes, or until set. Cool the brownies completely in the pan on a rack. Refrigerate for 1 hour, or until solid enough to cut. With a small sharp knife, cut the sweet into quarters, then cut each quarter into 4 squares. Store in an airtight tin.

Chcolate Nougat Squares

Cocoa powder and unsweetened chocolate, along with chunks of chocolate-covered caramel and nougat candy, form an alliance of flavour in these tender, rich squares.

Chocolate Nougat Candy Bar Batter

— 4 (1.76 ounces each) chocolate-covered caramel and nougat bars (such as Milky Way Midnight bars), cut into ½-inch chunks
— 1¼ cups unsifted bleached cake flour
— ¼ cup unsweetened alkalised cocoa powder
— ¼ teaspoon baking powder
— ½ teaspoon salt
— ½ pound (16 tablespoons or 2 sticks) unsalted butter, melted and cooled to tepid
— 4 ounces unsweetened chocolate, melted and cooled to tepid
— 4 large eggs
— 2 cups granulated sugar
— 2½ teaspoons vanilla extract

Preheat the Oven to 325 Degrees F. Film the inside of a 9 by 9 by 2-inch baking pan with nonstick cooking spray.

Chill the Candy :Refrigerate the chunks of chocolate candy for 20 minutes. Refrigerating the candy helps to keep its shape intact as it's incorporated into the batter.

Mix the Batter: Sift the flour, cocoa powder, baking powder, and salt onto a sheet of waxed paper.

In a medium-size mixing bowl, whisk the melted butter and melted chocolate until smooth. In a large mixing bowl, whisk the eggs until blended, about 15 seconds. Add the sugar and whisk until combined, about 30 seconds. Blend in the vanilla extract and melted butter-chocolate mixture. Sift the flour mixture over and stir to form a batter, mixing thoroughly until the particles of flour are absorbed, using a whisk or flat wooden paddle. Carefully stir in the chunks of candy. Scrape the batter into the prepared pan and spread evenly. Smooth the top with a rubber spatula.

Bake, Cool, and Cut the Sweet: Bake the brownies in the preheated oven for 35 to 40 minutes, or until set. Let the brownies stand in the pan on a cooling rack for 2 hours. Refrigerate for 1 hour. With a small sharp knife, cut sweet into quarters, then cut each quarter into 4 squares. Remove the squares from the baking pan, using a small offset metal spatula. Store in an airtight tin.

Double-Dark Fudge Brownies

Cocoa powder, bittersweet chocolate, and unsweetened chocolate consort in this batter to buil a bold and intrepid brownie batter.

Fudge Brownie Batter

— ¾ cup bleached all-purpose flour
— ½ cup bleached cake flour
— 3 tablespoons unsweetened alkalised cocoa powder
— ¼ teaspoon baking powder
— 1/8 teaspoon salt
— 6 ounces bittersweet chocolate, cut into small chunks
— ½ pound (16 tablespoons or 2 sticks) unsalted butter, melted and cooled to tepid
— 6 ounces unsweetened chocolate, melted and cooled to tepid
— 4 large eggs
— 2¼ cups superfine sugar
— 2½ teaspoons vanilla extract
— Confectioners' sugar, for sifting on top of the baked brownies (optional)

Preheat the Oven to 325 Degrees F. Film the inside of a 10 by 10 by 2-inch baking pan with nonstick cooking spray.

Mix the batter: Sift the all-purpose flour, cake flour, cocoa powder, baking powder, and salt onto a sheet of waxed paper. In a small bowl, toss the chocolate chunks with 1¼ teaspoons of the sifted mixture.

In a medium-size mixing bowl, whisk the melted butter and melted unsweetened chocolate until smooth. In a large mixing bowl, whisk the eggs until blended, about 15 seconds. Add the sugar and whisk until combined, about 45 seconds. Blend in the vanilla extract and melted butter-chocolate mixture. Sift the flour mixture over and stir to form a batter, mixing thoroughly until the particles of flour are absorbed, using a whisk or flat wooden paddle. Stir in the chocolate chunks. Scrape the batter into the prepared pan and spread evenly. Smooth the top with a rubber spatula.

Bake, Cool, and Cut the Brownies: Bake the brownies in the preheated oven for 35 to 40 minutes, or until set. Let the brownies stand in the pan on a cooling rack for 3 hours. Refrigerate for 1 to 2 hours, or until firm enough to cut. With a small sharp knife, cut the entire sweet into quarters, then cut each quarter into 4 squares. Remove the brownies from the baking pan, using a small offset metal spatula. Store in an airtight tin. Sift confectioners' sugar on top of the brownies just before serving, if you wish.

11

Principles of Food Manufacturing

Foods are made from natural materials, and, like any living matter, will deteriorate in time. The deterioration of food, or food spoilage, is the natural way of recycling, restoring carbon, phosphorus, and nitrogenous matters to the good Earth. However, spoilage will usually modify the quality of foods from good to bad, in the form of poor appearance, offensive smell, and inferior taste. Food spoilage could be caused by a number of factors, chiefly biological, but also by chemical and physical factors. Consumption of spoiled foods can cause sickness, and even death. Thus, food safety is the major concern in spoiled foods.

Manufactured and natural foods are composed mainly of carbohydrates, proteins, and lipids. The major constituents in vegetables and fruits are carbohydrates, including sugars, polymers of sugars, and other complex carbohydrates such as fibers. Lipids are the major components of oilseeds, milk and most cheeses, and proteins are the chief constituents of muscle foods. Under natural storage conditions, foods start to deteriorate once the living cells in the foods are dead or damaged.

Secretion of internal proteases such as chymotrypsin and trypsin breaks up proteins at specific amino-acid positions, lipases and lyases from lyzosomes disintegrate the cells, de-esterificate fats (triglycerides) into fatty acids and glycerol, hydrolases hydrolyze proteins into amino acids, and starch into simpler sugars. The exposure of foods and damaged cells to the environment would attract microorganisms (e.g., bacteria, molds, and viruses), and insects, which in turn would further accelerate the decomposition of the food. Foods with contaminated microorganisms lead to foodborne illnesses, which, as reported by the Center for Disease Control and Prevention (CDC), causes approximately 76 million illnesses and 5000 deaths in the United States yearly. For most food poisoning, the spoilage has not reached the stage where the sensory attributes (appearance, smell, taste, texture, and so on.) of the food are abnormal. Illness from food can be mainly classified as:

— Foodborne infection caused by pathogenic bacteria (disease-causing microorganisms, such as Salmonella bacteria, multiplying in a victim's digestive tract, causing diarrhea, vomiting, and fever, and so on), and

— Foodborne intoxication (food poisoning resulting from a toxin produced by pathogenic microorganisms, for example, Clostridium botulinum and Staphylococcus aureus, in the food itself).

Food Spoilage and Foodborne Illness

Foodborne illness also has a major economic impact on society, costing billions of dollars each year in the form of medical bills, lost work time, and reduced productivity. In many cases, when foods are oxidised, they become less desirable or are even rejected. The odor, taste, and color may change and some nutrients may be destroyed. Examples are the darkening of the cut surface of a potato and the browning of tea color with time. Oxidative rancidity results from the liberation of odorous products during breakdown of unsaturated fatty acids. These products include aldehydes, ketones, and shorter-chain fatty acids.

Table 1. Most common bacteria Genera found in certain food types

Microorganisms	*Foods*
Corynebacterium, Leuconostoc	Dairy products
Achromobacter	Meat, poultry, seafoods
Bacteriodes, Proteus	Eggs and meats
Pseudomonas	Meats, poultry, eggs

Browning reactions in foods include three nonenzymatic reactions (Maillard, caramelisation, and ascorbic acid oxidation), and one enzymatic reaction (phenolase browning). Heating conditions in the surface layers of food cause the Maillard browning reaction between sugars and amino acids, for example, in the browning of baked bread and cakes.

Table 2. Most Common Pathogenic Bacteria and Viruses Found in Foods.

Bacteria	
Clostridium botulinum	*Listeria monocytogenes*
Salmonella spp.	*Staphylococcus aureus*
Clostridium perfringens	*Escherichia coli*
Botulinum spp.	*Campylobacter jejuni*
Streptococci spp.	*Bacillus cereus*
Lactobacillus spp.	*Proteus spp.*
Shigellas spp.	*Pseudomonas spp.*
Salmonella spp.	*Vibrio spp.*
Virus	
Hepatitis A virus	*Echovirus*
Rotavirus	*Calcivirus*

The high temperatures and low moisture content in the surface layers also cause caramelisation of sugars, and oxidation of fatty acids to other chemicals such as aldehydes, lactones, ketones, alcohols, and esters. Moisture and heat can also produce hydrolytic rancidity in fats, in this case fats are split into free fatty acids, which may cause off-odors and rancid flavors in fats and oils.

Table 3. Some Major Bacterial and Viral Diseases Transmitted to Humans Through Food.

Bacteria	*Diseases*
Campylobacter jejuni	Campylobacteriosis
Enterobacteriaceae	Enteric disease
Listeria monocytogenes	Listeriosis
Salmonella spp.	Salmonellosis
Salmonella typhi	Typhoid fever
Shigella dysenteriae	Dysentery
Vibrio cholerae	Cholera
Yersinia enterocolitica	Diarrheal disease
Virus	*Diseases*
ECHO virus	Gastroenteritis
HAV virus	Hepatitis type A
Norwalk agent	Viral diarrhea
Rotavirus	Infant diarrhea

Thermal decomposition of ascorbic acid under both aerobic and anaerobic conditions, by oxidative or nonoxidative mechanisms, in either the absence or presence of amino compounds, can also cause browning. The formation of ripening fruit flavor often results from Strecker degradation (the transamination and decarboxylation) of amino acids, such as the production of 3-methylbutyrate (apple-like flavor) from leucine. Further heating of the foods can break down some of the volatiles generated by theMaillard reaction and Strecker degradation to produce burnt or smoky aromas associated with browning. Enzymatic browning occurs on cut surfaces of light-colored fruits (apples, bananas) and vegetables (potatoes), due to the enzymatic oxidation of phenols to orthoquinones, which in turn rapidly polymerise to form brown pigments known as melanins.

Food spoilage can also be caused by physical factors, such as temperature, moisture, and pressure acting upon the foods. Moisture and heat can also produce hydrolytic rancidity in fats (mentioned earlier), with production of off-odors and rancid flavors in fats and oils as mentioned earlier. Excessive heat denatures proteins, breaks emulsions, removes moisture from food, and destroys nutrients such as vitamins. However, excessive coldness, such as freezing, changes their texture and/or cracks their outer coatings to permit contamination by microorganisms.

Foods under pressure will be squeezed and transform into unnatural conformation. The compression will likely break up the surface structure (cracking of eggs), release degradative enzymes (bruising of fruits such as apples and pears), and expose the damaged food to exterior microbial contamination. Of course, many health officials consider physical factors to include such things as sand, glass, wood chip, rat hair, animal urine, bird droppings, insect parts, and so on. They may not spoil the food, but they can present health hazards. Some of these foreign substances do lead to spoilage. Insects and rodents can consume and damage stored foods, and insects can lay eggs and leave larvae in the foods, causing further damage later. Such foods are no longer reliable because they contain hidden contaminants. The attack of foods by insects and rodents can also contaminate foods further with microbial infections.

Prevention of Food Spoilage

Food spoilage can be prevented by proper sanitary practices in food handling and processing, appropriate preservation techniques, and standardised storing conditions.

Food handling and processing

The entire process, from raw ingredients to a finished product for storage, must comply with a standard sanitation program. In the United States, the practice of HACCP (hazard analysis critical control points), mandatory at present for several industries, may eventually become so for all food industries. At present, the application of HACCP is voluntary for most food processors. Similar sanitary programs apply to workers. It is important to realise that a food processing plant must have a basic sanitation system program before it can implement a HACCP program.

Food preservation

There are many techniques used to preserve food, such as legal food additives, varying levels of food ingredients or components, traditional and new technologies. Legal food additives, among other functions, can prevent oxidation and inhibit or destroy harmful microorganisms (molds and bacteria). Vitamin E or vitamin C can serve as antioxidants in many food products and benzoate in beverages can act as an antimicrobial agent. We can preserve food by manipulating the levels of food ingredients or components to inhibit the growth of microorganisms or destroy them, for example, by keeping the food low in moisture content (low water activity), high in sugar or salt content, or at a low pH (less than pH 5). Other traditional technologies such as canning (thermal processing), fermentation, refrigeration, and freezing are well-established preservation methods. Recently, new or alternative technologies have become available to preserve food. Because they are new, their applications are carefully monitored. Nothing in the last two decades seems to have generated more publicity than the use of X-rays in food processing. Although food irradiation has been permitted in the processing of several categories of food, its general application is still carefully regulated in the United States.

Food packaging and storage

Raw and processed foods should be packaged to prevent oxidation and microbial contamination, insect infestation, and loss of moisture and integrity. Storage of foods (when not contaminated) below –20⁰C can allow food to be kept for several months or a year. Foods stored at 4⁰C can have their shelf-life extended to several days or a week (note that some bacteria such as Listeria monocytogenes can still grow and multiply even in foods at refrigerated temperatures). Newly developed techniques to preserve foods include the incorporation of bacteriocin in plastic to retain activity and to inhibit surface growth of bacteria on meat, and the application of an intelligent Shelf Life Decision System for quality optimisation of the food chill chain.

Product Formulations

As mentioned earlier, for many food products, processing

is an important way to preserve the product. However, for some food products, many self-preserving factors play a role, such as ingredients and their natural properties. Three good examples are pickles, barbecue sauces, and hard candies. Preserving pickles is not difficult if the end product is very sour (acidic) or salty. Traditionally, barbecue sauces have a long shelf-life because of the high content of sugar and acids. Most unwrapped hard candies keep a long time, assuming the environment is at room temperature and not very humid. Most wrapped hard candies last even longer if the integrity of the wrappers is maintained. For baked products (cookies, bread), measures against spoilage take second place to consumer acceptance of freshness. So, the objectives of processing of foods vary with the product. However, one aspect is essential to all manufacturers, as discussed below.

To manufacture a food product, it is assumed that the manufacturer (processor) has a formula for the product. In countries all over the world, small family-owned food businesses usually start with home recipes for popular products instead of a scientific formula. Most of us are aware of such humble beginnings of major corporations manufacturing cola (carbonated), soft drinks, cheeses, breakfast cereals, and many others. When these family businesses were started, there was not much science and technology involved.

As the companies grew and had many employees, they started to hire food scientists, food technologists, and food engineers to study the "recipe(s)" and refine every aspect of the product until the entire manufacturing process was based on sound scientific, technical, and engineering principles. After that, all efforts were directed towards production and marketing. Even now, somewhere a person will start making "barbecue sauce" in his garage and selling it to his neighbors. Although very few of these starters will succeed, this trend will continue to be the case in view of the free enterprise spirit of the West.

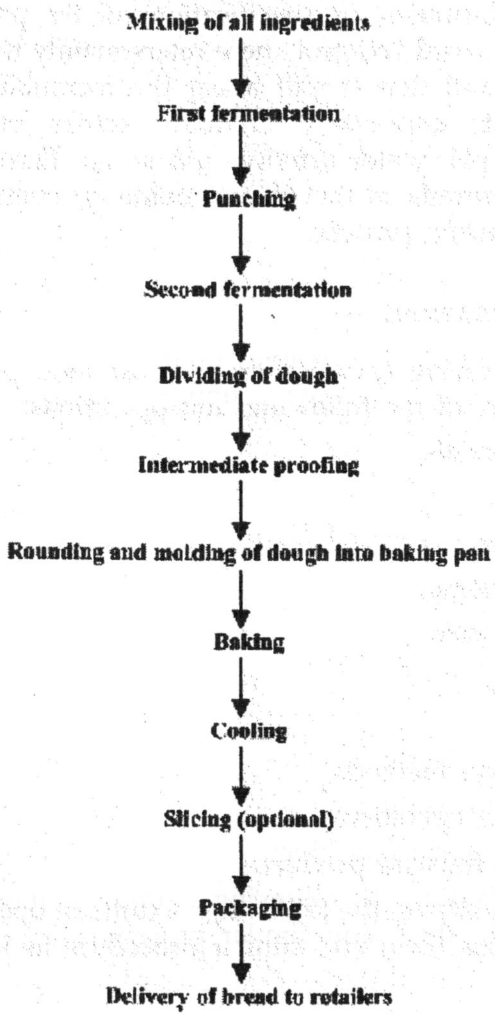

Figure 1. A general flow chart for the manufacture bread

Although any person can start manufacturing food using a home recipe, the federal government in the United States has partial or total control over certain aspects of the manufacturing processes for food and beverage products. This control will automatically affect the recipes, formulas, or specifications of the products. Although the word "control" here refers mainly to safety, it is understood that it will affect the formulations to some extent, especially critical factors such as temperature, pH, water activity, and so on. Flow charts differ from formula in that they provide an overview of the manufacturing process.

Units of Operations

The manufacturing (processing) of most food products involves many of the following unit operations:

— Raw materials,

— Cleaning,

— Separating,

— Disintegrating,

— Forming, raw,

— Pumping,

— Mixing,

— Application methods,

— Combined operations,

— Forming, finished product.

Instead of classifying the following as units of operations, we will discuss them and similar procedure as separate topics:

— Heating,

— Cooling,

— Sanitation,

— Quality control,

— Packaging.

There are hundreds of different categories of food products beingmanufactured.Correspondingly, there are hundreds of companiesmanufacturing each category of food product. In sum, there are literally thousands of food manufacturers. Two major reasons for this explosion of new companies are the constant introduction of new products and improvement in manufacturing methods and equipment.

To facilitate the technological processing of food at educational and commercial levels, food manufacturing (processing) professionals have developed unified principles and a systematic approach to the study of these operations. The involved processes of the food industry can be divided into a number of common operations, termed unit operations. Depending on the manufacturer (processor), such unit operations vary in name and number. For ease of discussion, we use the following unit operations for the most common ones:

— Cleaning,

— Coating,

— Controlling,

— Decorating,

— Disintegrating,

— Drying,

— Evaporating,

— Forming,

— Heating,

— Mixing,

— Packaging,
— Pumping,
— Raw materials handling,
— Separating.

During food processing, the manufacturer selects and combines unit operations into unit processes, which are then combined to produce more complex and comprehensive processes. Although emerging technology plays an important role in food processing as time progresses, these units, in the order they appear in a food processing plant, still apply.

Raw Materials Handling

Raw materials are handled in various ways, including:

— Hand and mechanical harvesting on the farm;
— Trucking of fruits and vegetables;
— Moving live cattle by rail; and
— Conveying flour from transporting vehicle or boats to storage bins.

Some good examples are as follows.

— Oranges are picked on the farm by hand or mechanical devices, moved by truck trailers, usually refrigerated, to juice processing plants, where they are processed. Of course, the transport must take into account the size of the trucks, length of time during transport, and temperature control. The major objective is to avoid spoilage. In recent years, the use of modified atmosphere packaging/storage has increased the odds in favor of the farmers and producers.
— Handling sugar and flour poses great challenges. When dry sugar reaches the processing plants, via truck trailers or rail, it is transported to storage bins

via a pneumatic lift system. The sugar will cake if the storage time, temperature, and humidity are not appropriate. Improper transfer of sugar may result in dusting and buildup of static electricity, which can cause an explosion, because sugar particles are highly combustible. The same applies to finely divided flour.

In handling raw materials, one wishes to achieve the following major objectives:

— Proper sanitation;

— Minimal loss of product;

— Acceptable product quality;

— Minimal bacterial growth,

— Minimal holding time.

Cleaning

We all know what cleaning a raw product means. Before we eat a peach, we rinse it under the faucet or with potable water. Before we make a salad, we wash/rinse the vegetables with potable water. Before we eat crabs, we clean them. Of course, the difference in cleaning between home kitchens and a food processing plant is the volume. We clean one peach; they clean a thousand peaches.

Depending upon the product and the nature of the dirt, cleaning can be accomplished with the following methods or devices, individually or in combination:

— Air (high-velocity),

— Brushes,

— Magnets,

— Steam,

— Ultraviolet light,

— Ultraviolet sound,

— Vacuum,
— Water.

There are other new technologies that will not be discussed here. Water is probably the most common cleaning agent and its applications vary. Examples include the following:

- Clams, oysters, crabs, and other shellfish are commonly hosed to remove mud, soil, and other foreign debris. If they are contaminated, they may have to be purged by incubating them in running clean seawater.
- City water will not be acceptable for manufacturing beverages. It will have to be further treated with chemical flocculation, sand filtration, carbon purification, micro-filtration, deaeration, and so on. This is not considered a simple cleaning. Rather it is a process in cleaning.
- Eviscerating poultry can be considered a cleaning operation if we make use of water. However, the actual process of removing the entrails may involve vacuuming in addition to water.
- With a product like pineapple, the irregular surface is usually cleaned by the scrubbing action of high-pressure water jets.

Just as in a home kitchen where pots and pans require frequent cleaning, state and federal regulations require that the equipment used in a food processing plant be cleaned and sanitised after each use. After dirt and mud are removed, some raw products also require special sanitising procedures.

Separating

In food processing, the step of separating may involve separating

— A solid from a solid, as in peeling of potatoes;

— A solid from a liquid, as in filtration;

— A liquid from a solid, as in pressing juice from a fruit;

— A liquid from a liquid, as in centrifuging oil from water;

— A gas from a solid or a liquid, as in vacuum canning.

One of the time-honored techniques in the separating operation is the hand sorting and grading of individual units, such as mushrooms, tomatoes, oranges. Many mechanical and electronic sorting devices have now replaced human hands in handling various types of raw food products. An electronic eye can identify differences in color as the products are going along the conveyor belt. Built-in mechanisms can sort the products by color, into "good" versus "bad" color. The current invention of the electronic nose also shows promises, and automatic separation according to size is easily accomplished by passing fruits or vegetables over differently sized screens, holes, or slits.

Disintegrating

Disintegrating means subdividing large masses of foods into smaller units or particles. This may include

— Cutting;

— Grinding;

— Pulping, homogenising; or

— Other methods.

Examples include:

— Automatic dicing of vegetables;

— Mechanical deboning of meat;

— Manual and automatic cutting of meat into wholesale and retail sizes;

— Cutting of bakery products with electric knives and other products with water jets;

— Disintegrating various categories of food products with high-energy beams and laser beams;

— Homogenisation using commercial blenders, high-pressure traveling through a valve with very small openings, ultrasonic energy, and so on. Homogenisation is probably one of the most important stages in dairy manufacturing. Homogenisation produces disintegration of fat globules in milk or cream from large globules and clusters into minute globules. This is done by forcing the milk or cream under high pressure through a valve with very small openings.

Forming

Forming is an important operation in manufacturing many foods:

— Meat and poultry patties;

— Confections such as candies, jelly beans, fruit juice tablets;

— Breakfast cereals;

— Pasta;

— Kinds such as some cheese cubes, processed cheese slices, potato chips, and others.

Meat and Poultry Patties. Patty-making machines are responsible for making ground meat and poultry patties by gently compacting the product into a disk shape. Uniform pressure is applied to produce patties with minimal variation in weight. Excessive pressure may result in tough cooked patties.

Pasta. Pasta products are formed by forcing dough through extrusion dies of various forms and shapes before drying in an oven.

Confectionery. The shapes and forms in the confectionery industry, such as candies and jellies, are made in several ways. Two of the most popular methods are the use of molds and cutting:

— *Molds.* The traditional use of molds is applied in making confectionery such as fondants, chocolate, and jellies. The product is deposited into molds to cool and harden.

— *Cutting.* Hard candies and toffee are cut into pieces after kneading or pulling.

Pumping

In food processing, pumping moves food (liquid, semi-solid, paste, or solid) from one step to the next or from one location to another. There are many types of pumps available, some with general, others specialised, applicability. The type of pump used depends on the food (texture, size, etc.). For example, broth, tomato pastes, ground meat, corn kernels, grapes, and other categories of food all require a "different" pump to do the job. Two of the most important properties of pumps are the ability to break up foods, and ease of cleaning.

Mixing

The operation of mixing, for example, includes:

— Kneading,

— Agitating,

— Blending,

— Emulsifying,

— Homogenising,

— Diffusing,

— Dispersing,

— Stirring,
— Beating,
— Whipping, and
— Movements by hands and machines.

Examples of mixing include:

— Homogenisation to prevent fat separation in milk;
— Mixing and developing bread dough, which requires stretching and folding, referred to as kneading;
— Beating in air, as in making an egg-white foam;
— Blending dry ingredients, as in preparing a ton of dry cake mix;
— Emulsifying, as in the case of mayonnaise.

Commercial mixers for food processing come in many shapes and forms because many types of mixtures or mixings are possible.

Processing and Preservation Techniques

Heat Application

Heat exchanging, or heating, is one of the most common procedures used in the manufacture of processed foods. Examples include pasteurising of milk, manufacturing of bakery products, roasting peanuts, and canning. Foods may be heated or cooked using

— Direct injection of steam,
— Direct contact with flame,
— Toasters,
— Electronic energy as in microwave cookers, and
— Many new forms of technology.

Whatever the method, precise control of temperature is essential. Heating is used in

— Baking,
— Frying,
— Food concentration,
— Food dehydration, and
— Package closure.

All of us know why we cook food at home: to improve texture, to develop flavors, to facilitate mixing of water, oil, and starch, to permit caramelisation, and so on. Commercially, the basic reasons for heating are simple and may include the following:

1. Destruction of microorganisms and preservation of food (food canning and milk pasteurisation are common examples);
2. Removal of moisture and development of flavors (ready-to-eat breakfast cereals and coffee roasting are common examples);
3. Inactivation of natural toxicants (processing soy-bean meal is a good example);
4. Improvement of the sensory attributes of the food such as color, texture, andmouth-feel;
5. Combination of ingredients to develop unique food attributes and to attract consumer preferences.

Traditional thermal processing of foods uses the principles of transferring heat energy by conduction, convection, radiation, or a combination of these. Foods are heated in a variety of traditional equipment by applying basic food engineering principles using heat exchangers, tanks or kettles, retorts, and toasters. Other methods may include direct injection of steam, and direct contact with flame. Heating food with electronic energy (microwave) is a relatively new technique.

As foods are sensitive to heat, special consideration is needed. Dark color, burnt flavors, and loss of nutrients can result from heating, especially prolonged heating.Heat exchangers have special advantages. They permit

1. Liquid food to have a maximal contact with the heat source and
2. Rapid heating and cooling.

For example, a plate-type heat exchanger is used to pasteurise milk. The equipment is composed of many thin plates. When milk flows through one side of the plates, it is heated by hot water on the other side. This provides maximal contact between the heat source and milk, resulting in rapid heating in a short time. The cooling is the reverse process after the milk has been heated. Instead of hot water, cooling water or brine is used.

During heating, hot water or pressurised steam circulating in the jackets of the tanks or kettles heats the food, and the reverse for cooling. This technique works for full liquid foods or partially liquid foods such as soups.

The most common method of sterilising canned foods uses pressure cookers or retorts. Beginning in the early 1970s, the risk of botulism in canned food with low acidity prompted the U.S. FDA to implement stringent regulations governing this group of foods. Although the name of Hazards Analysis Critical Control Points (HACCP) did not have wide usage at the time, the regulations governing the production of low-acid canned foods can be considered the earliest form of HACCP program. Large pressure cookers or retorts are used to ensure that the canned goods are heated above the boiling point of water. The high temperature is generated by steam under pressure in a large retort designed to withstand such pressure and temperature. In this case, convection and conduction of heat energy are achieved.

Steam hits the outside of the cans and energy is conducted into the can. Some form of moving or agitating device permits improved convection to occur inside the cans. Although there are other modern techniques of heating canned food products, many smaller companies still depend heavily on these traditional methods.

Instead of one or two pieces of equipment, this system contains several units: loading containers, conveyor belts, hoppers, vats or vessels. The vessels are usually cylindrical in shape with built-in heating devices. Heat is generated via one of the following methods:

1. Circulation of heated air, which heats the food products inside the vessels;
2. Application of direct heat to the outside of the vessel by means of steam, flame (gas), and air (hot), for example, whereby heat is radiated from the inside walls of the vessels to the food.

The above unit system is best for roasting coffee beans or nuts.

This can be used for a variety of food products. The product is placed on a conveyor belt, which moves under a heat source. Sometimes, the product is vibrated so that heat distribution is even. Temperature control is essential, enabling products such as coffee beans or nuts to be roasted using this method.

Heat Removal or Cold Preservation

Cold preservation is a preservation method achieved by the removal of heat. It is among the oldest methods of preservation. Since 1875, with the development of mechanical ammonia refrigeration systems, commercial refrigeration and freezing processes have been available. A reduction in the temperature of a food reduces the rate of quality changes during storage caused by a number of factors. At low temperatures, microbial growth is retarded and its reproduction prevented. The rate of chemical reactions (e.g., oxidation, Maillard browning, formation of off-flavor), biochemical reactions (e.g., glycolysis, proteolysis, enzymatic browning, and lipolysis), and physical changes between food components and the environment (e.g., moisture loss in drying out of vegetables) can also be reduced.

Most food spoilage organisms grow rapidly at temperatures above 10⁰C, although some grow at temperatures below 0⁰C, as long as there is unfrozenwater available.Most pathogens do not grow well at refrigeration temperatures, except some psychrophilic bacteria such as Listeria monocytogenes, which commonly grows in dairy products. Below 29.5⁰C, there is no significant growth of spoilage or pathogenic microorganisms. In general, the longer the storage period, the lower the temperature required. Pretreatment with intensive heat is not used in this process operation and, together with adequate control over enzymatic and microbiological changes, the food maintains its nutritional and sensory characteristics close to fresh status and results in a high-quality product. In comparing chilled and frozen foods, chilled food has a higher quality but a shorter shelf-life, and frozen food has a much longer shelf-life, but the presence of ice in the frozen product may contribute some undesirable changes in food quality.

Chilling and refrigeration process

The chilling process is the gentlest method of preservation, generating the least significant changes in taste, texture, nutritive value, and other attributes of foods. Generally it refers to a storage temperature above freezing, between about 16⁰C and 22⁰C. Most foods do not freeze until 22°C or slightly lower because of the presence of solutes such as sugars and salts. Commercial and household refrigerators usually operate at between 4.5°C and 7°C.

In low-acid chilled foods, strict hygienic processing and packaging areas required to ensure food safety. The chilling process is usually used in combination with other preservation methods such as fermentation, irradiation, pasteurisation, mild heat treatment, chemicals, and controlled atmosphere. The combination of these methods avoids the extreme conditions that must otherwise be used to limit microbial growth, thus providing a high-quality product.

Not all foods can be stored under chilled conditions. Tropical and subtropical fruits suffer chilling injury when stored below 13°C, resulting in abnormal physiological changes: skin blemishes (e.g., banana), browning in the flesh (e.g., mango), or failure to ripen (e.g., tomato). Some other foods should not be refrigerated; for example, breads stale faster at refrigeration temperature than at room temperature. Starch in puddings also tends to retrograde and result in syneresis.

There are several important considerations in producing and maintaining high-quality chilled foods.

1. *Quick removal of heat at the chilling stage.* Ideally, refrigeration of perishable foods starts at the time of harvest, slaughter, or at the finishing production line. Cooling can be accelerated by the following techniques.

   a. *Evaporative cooling:* Spray water and then subject food to vacuum (e.g., leafy vegetables).

   b. *Cryogenic cooling:* Nitrogen gas from evaporating liquid nitrogen, dry ice, and liquid carbon dioxide are used to remove heat for different products.

c. *Heat exchangers:* (i) Thin plates where warm bulk liquid foods pass chilled or "super-chilled" cooling fluid, separated by a thin stainless steel plate. (ii) Cooling coils for liquid food.

2. *Maintaining low temperature during the chill storage.* This can be affected by the following factors:

   a. *Refrigeration design* (i.e., cooling capacity and insulation): This must be taken into account because temperature can be affected by heat generated by lights and electric motors, people working in the area, the number of doors and how they are opened, and the kinds and amounts of food products stored.

   b. *Refrigeration load:* Quantity of heat that must be removed from the product and the storage area in order to decrease from an initial temperature to the selected final temperature and then to maintain this temperature for a specific time.

   c. *Types of food:* (i) *Specific heat of food:* Quantity of heat that must be removed from a food to lower it from one temperature to another. The rate of heat removal is largely dependent on water content. (ii) *Respiration rate of food:* Some foods (fruits and vegetables) respire and produce their own heat at varying rates. Products with relatively high respiration rates (snap beans, sweet corn, green peas, spinach, and strawberries) are particularly difficult to store.

3. *Maintaining appropriate air circulation and humidity.* Proper air circulation helps to move heat away from the food surface toward refrigerator cooling coils and plates. Air velocity is important, especially in commercial coolers or freezers, in maintaining the appropriate relative humidity (RH), because if the RH is too high, condensation of moisture on the surface

of cold food may occur, thus causing spoilage through microbial growth or clumping of the product. However, if RH is too low, dehydration of food may occur instead. Therefore, it is important to control the RH of the cooler and have proper packaging of food.

4. *Modification of gas atmosphere.* Chilled storage of fresh commodities is more effective if it is combined with control of the composition of the storage atmosphere. A reduction in oxygen concentration and/or increase in carbon dioxide concentration of the storage atmosphere reduces the rate of respiration (and thusmaturation) of fresh fruits and vegetables, and also inhibits rates of oxidation, microbial, and insect growth. The atmospheric composition can be changed using three methods:
   a. ControlledAtmosphere Storage (CAS),where the concentration of oxygen, carbon dioxide, and ethylene are monitored and regulated throughout the storage. It is used to inhibit overripening of apples and other fruits in cold storage. Stored fruit and vegetables consume O2 and give off CO_2 during respiration.
   b. Modified Atmosphere Storage (MAS), where the initially modified gas composition in a sealed storage is allowed to change by normal respiration of the food, but little control is exercised. The O_2 is reduced but not eliminated, and CO_2 is increased (the optimum levels differ for different fruits).
   c. Modified Atmosphere Packaging (MAP), where the fruit and vegetables are sealed in a package under flushed gas (N_2 or CO_2), and the air in the package is modified over time by the respiring product. Fresh meat (especially red meats) is packaged similarly.

5. *Efficient distribution systems.* To supply high-quality chilled foods to consumers, a reliable and efficient distribution system is also required. This involves chilled stores, refrigerated transportation, and chilled retail display cabinets. It requires careful control of the storage conditions, as above.

Freezing and frozen storage

Freezing is a unit operation in which the temperature of a food is reduced below the freezing point and a proportion of the water undergoes a phase change to form ice. Proper freezing preserves foods without causing major changes in their shape, texture, color, and flavor. Good frozen storage requires temperatures of 218⁰C or below; however, it is cost prohibitive to store lower than 230⁰C. Frozen foods have increased in their share of sales since freezers and microwaves have become more available. The major commodities commonly frozen are

— Fruits (berries, citrus, and tropical fruit), either whole, pureed, or as juice concentrate;

— Vegetables (peas, green beans, sweet corn, spinach, broccoli, Brussels sprouts, and potatoes such as French fries and hash browns);

— Fish fillets and seafoods, including fish fingers, fish cakes, shellfish, and prepared dishes with sauces;

— Meats (beef, lamb, and poultry) as carcasses, boxed joints, or cubes, and meat products;

— Baked goods (bread, cakes, pastry dough, and pies);

— Prepared foods.

Principles of freezing

The freezing process implies two linked processes: lowering of temperature by the removal of heat and a change of phase from liquid to solid. The change of water into ice results in an increase in concentration of the unfrozen matrix and therefore leads to dehydration and lowering of water activity. Both the lowering of temperature and water activity contribute to freezing as an important preservation method.

In order for a product to freeze, the product must be cooled below its freezing point. The freezing point of a food depends on its water content and the type of solutes present. The water component of a food freezes first and leaves the dissolved solids in a more concentrated solution, which requires a lower temperature to freeze. As a result, the freezing point decreases during freezing as the concentration increases. Different solutes depress the freezing point to a different degree.

Rate of freezing

Faster freezing produces small crystals, necessary for high-quality products such as ice-cream. There are two main opposing forces affecting the freezing rate. The driving force includes the difference in temperatures between the freezing medium and the product; the bigger the difference, the faster the product will cool down. High thermal conductivity of the freezing medium (the efficiency with which the refrigerating agent extracts heat) and direct surface contact between medium and product also help to freeze the product quickly. On the other hand, the resistance force to quick freezing includes the product being packed in big sizes, irregular product geometry affecting direct contact with the freezing agent, and the product composition having a high heat capacity. Thermal conductivity of food packages such as cardboard and plastics will act to insulate heat transfer and thus slow down the freezing rate.

As a consequence of the formation of ice, some negative changes in the quality of food result. The two major causes are freeze concentration effect and ice recrystallisation.

The quality of products will change if solutes in the frozen product precipitate out of solution, for example, leading to a loss of consistency in reconstituted frozen orange juice because of aggregated pectic substances, and syneresis of starch pudding because of starch aggregation. The increase in ionic strength can lead to "salting out" of proteins, causing protein denaturation (a reason for the toughening of frozen fish). An increase in solute concentration may lead to the precipitation of some salts, and the anion/cation ratio of colloidal suspensions would then be disturbed and causes changes in pH. Such changes would also cause precipitation of proteins and changes in color of anthocyanin in berries. The concentration of solutes in the extracellular fluid will cause dehydration of adjacent tissues in fruit and vegetables, which would not be able to rehydrate after thawing. Lastly, the concentration of reactive compounds would accelerate reactions such as lipid oxidation.

If the food is not stored under suffi-ciently cold and steady temperatures, ice crystals will grow, or recrystallise to large ice crystals, which may cause damage to the food texture. Damage such as the physical rupture of cell walls and membranes and separation of plant and animal cells cause limp celery or green beans, and drips in thawed berries and meat. Enlarged ice crystals also disrupt emulsions (butter and milk), frozen foams (ice-cream), and gels (frozen pudding and pie fillings), thus making these frozen products less homogenous, creamy, and smooth.

Another quality damage relating to ice recrystallisation is the freezer-burn problem. Freezer-burn occurs when there is a headspace in the packaged food and the food is subjected to fluctuating storage temperature. When the temperature increases, ice at the warmer surface will sublime into the headspace. As the temperature of the freezer or surroundings cools down, the water vapor will recrystallise on the inner surface of the package instead of going back into the product. This leads to dehydration of the surface of the product. If the frozen product is not packaged, the freezer-burn problem is more common and more severe.

Types of Common Freezers with Different Cooling Media

1. *Cold air Freezers.*
    a. Blast/belt freezers are large insulated tunnels in which air as cold as 240^{0}C is circulated to remove heat. The process is cheap, simple, and geared toward highvolume production. Rotating spiral tiers and multilayered belts are incorporated to move product through quickly and avoid "hot spots".
    b. Fluidised bed freezers are modified blast freezers in which cold air is passed at a high velocity through a bed of food, contained on a perforated conveyor belt. This produces a high freezing rate, but is restricted to particulate foods.
2. *Cold Surface Freezers.*
    a. Plate freezers work by increasing the amount of surface area that comes into direct contact with the product to be frozen. Typically, refrigerant runs in the coils that run through plates or drums on which products are laid out. Doubleplated systems further increase the rate of heat transfer to obtain

higher quality. This system is suitable for flat and uniform products such as fish fillets, beef burgers, and dinner meals.

b. Scraped-surface freezers work by having a liquid or semisolid food (ice-cream) frozen onto the surface of the freezer vessel, and a rotor scrapes the frozen portion from the wall. Typically, ice-cream is only partially frozen in a scrapedsurface freezer to about 26^{0}C, and the final freezing is completed in a hardening room (230^{0}C).

3. *Cold Liquid Freezers.* Brine freezers using supersaturated solutions for maximum surface contact immerse the product in a liquid freezing agent, in particular for irregularly shaped product, such as crabs. Their main disadvantage is that products are subject to absorption of salt as well as bacteria if not properly packed.
4. *Cryogenic Freezer.* Liquid nitrogen or liquid carbon dioxide (which vaporise at 2178^{0}C and 280^{0}C, respectively), freeze product extremely quickly. This is only suitable for freezing premium products such as shrimp and crab legs because of the high cost of the nonrecoverable gas.

Tips for obtaining top-quality frozen product include the following:

— Start with high-quality product - freezing can maintain quality but not enhance it.

— Get the heat out quickly, by removing any nonedible parts from the food.

— Maintain the integrity of the frozen product - proper cutting and packaging avoids drips.

— Store the product at the coldest temperature economically possible, in a welldesigned and maintained facility. Use proper inventory techniques to avoid deterioration.

— Avoid temperature fluctuation during storage and shipping.

Evaporation and Drying

During food processing, evaporation is used to achieve the following goals:

— Concentrate food by partial removal of water;

— Remove undesirable food volatiles;

— Recover desirable food volatiles.

Traditionally, evaporation is achieved via the following methods:

— Using solar energy to evaporate water from seawater to recover the salts left behind;

— Using a heated kettle or similar equipment to boil water from liquid or semisolid foods, for example, sugar syrup;

— Using the improved method of evaporating under a vacuum, where the term vacuum evaporator refers to a closed heated kettle or similar equipment connected to a vacuum pump. One principle to remember is that a major objective of vacuum evaporators is to remove water at temperatures low enough to avoid heat damage to the food.

There are, at present, many specialised pieces of equipment used for evaporating food products. However, overall, the above three methods are most common. Drying differs fromevaporating in that the former takes the food to nearly total dryness or the equivalence of 97% or 98% solids. The oldest method of drying food is to put the food under the hot sun. This practice probably started thousands of years ago. Although sun drying is still practiced, especially in many Third World countries, modern food drying has been modified to a nearly exact science. Drying has multiple objectives:

— To preserve the food from spoilage;
— To reduce the weight and bulk of the food;
— To make the food enjoy an availability and consumption pleasure similar to canned goods;
— To develop "new" or "novelty" items such as snacks.

Some well-known products prepared from drying include

— Dried milk powder,
— Instant coffee,
— Fish and shellfish,
— Jerky,
— Dried fruits, and
— Dried potato flakes.

The central equipment in drying food is the dryer.There aremany types of dryer: spray dryers: drum dryers, roller dryers, and others, each of which can be used to meet specific needs.

Food Additives

One popular method of food preservation is the addition of chemicals, legally known as food additives in the United States. In January of 1992, the U.S. FDA and the International Food Information Council released a brochure presenting an overview of food additives. Perhaps the main functional objectives of the use of food additives are the following:

— What keeps bread mold-free and salad dressings from separating?
— What helps cake batters rise reliably during baking and keeps cured meats safe to eat?
— What improves the nutritional value of biscuits and pasta, and gives gingerbread its distinctive flavor?

— What gives margarine its pleasing yellow color and prevents salt from becoming lumpy in its shaker?

— What allows many foods to be available year-round, in great quantity, and with the best quality?

Food additives play a vital role in today's bountiful and nutritious food supply. They allow our growing urban population to enjoy a variety of safe, wholesome, and tasty foods, yearround. Also, they make possible an array of convenience foods without the inconvenience of daily shopping.

Although salt, baking soda, vanilla, and yeast are commonly used in foods today, many people tend to think of any additive added to foods as being a complex and sometimes harmful chemical compound. All food additives are carefully regulated by federal authorities and various international organisations to ensure that foods are safe to eat and are accurately labeled. The purpose of the brochure from which this information is taken is to provide helpful background information about food additives, why they are used in foods, and how regulations govern their safe use in the food supply.

Additives perform a variety of useful functions in foods that are often taken for granted. As most people no longer live on farms, additives help keep food wholesome and appealing while en route to markets sometimes thousands of miles away from where it is grown or manufactured. Additives also improve the nutritional value of certain foods and can make them more appealing by improving their taste, texture, consistency, or color. Some additives could be eliminated if we were willing to grow our own food, harvest and grind it, spend many hours on cooking, or accept increased risks of food spoilage. However, most people today have come to rely on the many technological, aesthetic, and convenience benefits that additives provide in food.

Additives are used in foods for five main reasons.

— *To maintain product consistency.* Emulsifiers give products a consistent texture and prevent them from separating. Stabilisers and thickeners give smooth uniform texture. Anticaking agents help substances such as salt to flow freely.

— *To improve or maintain nutritional value.* Vitamins and minerals are added to many common foods such as milk, flour, cereal, and margarine to make up for those likely to be lacking in a person's diet or lost in manufacturing. Such fortification and enrichment have helped reduce malnutrition in the U.S. population. All products containing added nutrients must be appropriately labeled.

— *To maintain palatability and wholesomeness.* Preservatives retard product spoilage caused by mold, bacteria, fungi, yeast, or air. Bacterial contamination can cause foodborne illness, including the life-threatening botulism. Antioxidants are preservatives that prevent fats and oils in baked goods and other foods from becoming rancid or developing an off-flavor. They also prevent cut fresh fruits such as apples from turning brown when exposed to air.

— *To provide leavening or control acidity/alkalinity.* Leavening agents, which release acids when heated, can react with baking soda to help cakes, biscuits, and other baked goods to rise during baking. Other additives help modify the acidity and alkalinity of foods for proper flavor, taste, and color.

— *To enhance flavor or impart desired color.* Many spices and natural and synthetic flavors enhance the taste of foods. Colors, likewise, enhance the appearance of certain foods to meet consumer expectations. Examples of substances that perform each of these functions are provided in Table 4.

Table 4. Common uses of food additives in food categories

Common uses of additives and examples	*Foods where likely used*
Impart/Maintain Desired Consistency Alginates, lecithin, mono- and diglycerides,methyl-cellulose, carrageenan, glyceride, pectin, guar gum, sodium aluminosilicate	Baked goods, cake mixes, salad dressings, icecream, process cheese, coconut, table salt
Improve/Maintain Nutritive Value	
Vitamins A and D, thiamine, niacin, riboflavin,pyridoxine, folic acid, ascorbic acid, calcium carbonate, zinc oxide, iron	Flour, bread, biscuits, breakfast cereals, pasta, margarine, milk, iodised salt, gelatin desserts
Maintain Palatability and Wholesomeness	
Propionic acid and its salts, ascorbic acid, butylated hydroxy anisole (BHA), butylated hydroxytoluene (BHT), benzoates, sodium nitrite, citric acid	Bread, cheese, crackers, frozen and dried fruit, margarine, lard, potato chips, cake mixes, meat
Produce Light Texture; Control Acidity/Alkalinity	
Yeast, sodium bicarbonate, citric acid, fumaric acid, phosphoric acid,	Cakes, cookies, quick breads, crackers, lactic acid, tartrates butter, chocolates, soft drinks
Enhance Flavor or Impart Desired Color	
Cloves, ginger, fructose, aspartame, saccharin, FD&C Red No.40, monosodium glutamate, caramel, annatto, limonene, turmeric	Spice cake, gingerbread, soft drinks, xyogurt, soup, confections, baked goods, cheeses, jams, gum

Many substances added to food may seem foreign when listed on the ingredient label, but are actually quite familiar. For example, ascorbic acid is another name for Vitamin C; alpha-tocopherol is another name for Vitamin E; and beta-carotene is a source of Vitamin A. Although there are no easy synonyms for all additives, it is helpful to remember that all food is made up of chemicals. Carbon, hydrogen, and other chemical elements provide the basic building blocks for everything in life.

In its broadest sense, a food additive is any substance added to food. Legally, the term refers to "any substance the intended use which results or may reasonably be expected to result, directly or indirectly, in its becoming a component or otherwise affecting the characteristics of any food." This definition includes any substance used in the production, processing, treatment, packaging, transportation, or storage of food.

Direct additive

If a substance is added to a food for a specific purpose in that food, it is referred to as a direct additive. For example, the low-calorie sweetener aspartame, which is used in beverages, puddings, yogurt, chewing gum, and other foods, is considered a direct additive. Many direct additives are identified on the ingredient label of foods.

Indirect food additives

Indirect food additives are those that become part of the food in trace amounts due to its packaging, storage, or other handling. For instance, minute amounts of packaging substances may find their way into foods during storage.

Color additive

A color additive is any dye, pigment, or substance that can impart color when added or applied to a food, drug, or cosmetic, or to the human body. Color additives may be used in foods, drugs, cosmetics, and certain medical devices such as contact lenses. Color additives are used in foods for many reasons, including to offset color loss due to storage or processing of foods and to correct natural variations in food color.

Colors permitted for use in foods are classified as certified or exempt from certification. Certified colors are man-made, with each batch being tested by the manufacturer and FDA to ensure that they meet strict specifications for purity. There are nine certified colors approved for use in the United States. One example is FD&C Yellow No.6, which is used in cereals, bakery goods, snack foods, and other foods. Color additives that are exempt from certification include pigments derived from natural sources such as vegetables, minerals, or animals. For example, caramel color is produced commercially by heating sugar and other carbohydrates under strictly controlled conditions for use in sauces, gravies, soft drinks, baked goods, and other foods. Most colors exempt from certification must also meet certain legal criteria for specifications and purity.

Additives are not always byproducts of twentieth-century technology or modern know-how. Our ancestors used salt to preserve meats and fish, added herbs and spices to improve the flavor of foods, preserved fruit with sugar, and pickled cucumbers in a vinegar solution. Over the years, however, improvements have been made in increasing the efficiency and ensuring the safety of all additives. Today, food and color additives are more strictly regulated than at any other time in history. The basis of modern food law in the United States is the Federal Food, Drug, and Cosmetic (FD&C) Act of 1938, which gives the FDA authority over food and food ingredients and defines requirements for truthful labeling of ingredients.

The Food Additives Amendment to the FD&C Act, passed in 1958, requires FDA approval for the use of an additive prior to its inclusion in food. It also requires the manufacturer to prove an additive's safety for the ways it will be used. The Food Additives Amendment exempted two groups of substances from the food additive regulation process. All substances that the FDA or the USDA had determined were safe for use in specific food prior to the 1958 amendment were designated as prior-sanctioned substances. Examples of prior-sanctioned substances are sodium nitrite and potassium nitrite, used to preserve cured meats. However, at present, nitrites are called color-fixing agents for cured meats, and not preservatives, according to the FDA. The second category of substances excluded from the food additive regulation process are generally recognised as safe or GRAS substances. These substances are those whose use is generally recognised by experts as safe, based on their extensive history of use in food before 1958 or based on published scientific evidence. Salt, sugar, spices, vitamins, and monosodium glutamate are classified as GRAS substances, along with several hundred other substances.

Since 1958, FDA and USDA have continued to monitor all prior-sanctioned and GRAS substances in light of new scientific information. If new evidence suggests that a GRAS or prior-sanctioned substance may be unsafe, federal authorities can prohibit its use or require further studies to determine its safety.

In 1960, Congress passed similar legislation governing color additives. The Color Additives Amendments to the FD&C Act require dyes used in foods, drugs, cosmetics, and certain medical devices to be approved by FDA prior to their marketing. In contrast to food additives, colors in use before the legislation were allowed continued use only if they underwent further testing to confirm their safety. Of the original 200 provisionally listed color additives, 90 have been listed as safe and the remainder have either been removed from use by FDA or withdrawn by industry.

Both the Food Additives and Color Additives Amendments include a provision that prohibits the approval of an additive if it is found to cause cancer in humans or animals. This clause is often referred to as the Delaney Clause, named for its Congressional sponsor, Rep. James Delaney (D-N.Y.).

Regulations known as Good Manufacturing Practices (GMP) limit the amount of food and color additives used in foods. Manufacturers use only the amount of an additive necessary to achieve the desired effect.

To market a new food or color additive, a manufacturer must first petition to FDA for its approval. Approximately 100 new food and color additives petitions are submitted to FDA annually. Most of these petitions are for indirect additives such as packaging materials. A food or color additive petition must provide convincing evidence that the proposed additive performs as it is intended. Animal studies using large doses of the additive for long periods are often necessary to show that the substance would not cause harmful effects at expected levels of human consumption. Studies of the additive in humans also may be submitted to FDA.

In deciding whether an additive should be approved, the agency considers the composition and properties of the substance, the amount likely to be consumed, its probable long-term effects, and various safety factors. Absolute safety of any substance can never be proven. Therefore, FDA must determine if the additive is safe under the proposed conditions of use, based on the best scientific knowledge available.

New Technologies

At present, some alternative or new technologies in food processing are available. On June 2, 2000, the U.S. FDA released a report titled "Kinetics of Microbial Inactivation for Alternative Food Processing Technologies." This report evaluates the scientific information available on a variety of alternative food-processing technologies. This section will discuss briefly the following new technologies:

— Microwave and radio frequency processing,

— Ohmic and inductive heating,

— High-pressure processing,

— Pulse electric fields,

— High-voltage arc discharge,

— Pulse light technology,

— Oscillating magnetic fields,

— Ultraviolet light,

— Ultrasound, and

— Pulse X-rays.

Microwave and radio frequency processing

Microwave and radio frequency heating refers to the use of electromagnetic waves of certain frequencies to generate heat in a material through two mechanisms, dielectric and ionic. Microwave and radio frequency heating for pasteurisation and sterilisation are preferred to conventional heating because they require less time to come up to the desired process temperature, particularly for solid and semisolid foods. Industrial microwave pasteurisation and sterilisation systems have been reported on and off for over 30 years, but commercial radio frequency heating systems for the purpose of food pasteurisation or sterilisation are not known to be in use.

For a microwave sterilisation process, unlike conventional heating, the design of the equipment can dramatically influence the critical process parameters – the location and temperature of the coldest point. This uncertainty makes it more difficult to make general conclusions about processes, process deviations, and how to handle deviations. Many techniques have been tried to improve the uniformity of heating. The critical process factor when combining conventional heating and microwave or any other novel processes would most likely remain the temperature of the food at the cold point, primarily due to the complexity of the energy absorption and heat transfer processes. As the thermal effect is presumably the sole lethal mechanism, time–temperature history at the coldest location will determine the safety of the process and is a function of the composition, shape, and size of the food, the microwave frequency, and the applicator (oven) design. Time is also a factor in the sense that, as the food heats up, its microwave absorption properties can change significantly and the location of cold points can shift.

Ohmic and inductive heating

Ohmic heating (sometimes also referred to as Joule heating, electrical resistance heating, direct electrical resistance heating, electroheating, and electroconductive heating) is defined as the process of passing electric currents through foods or other materials to heat them. Ohmic heating is distinguished from other electrical heating methods either by the presence of electrodes contacting the food, frequency, or waveform.

Inductive heating is a process in which electric currents are induced within the food due to oscillating electromagnetic fields generated by electric coils. No data about microbial death kinetics under inductive heating have been published. A large number of potential future applications exist for ohmic heating, including its use in blanching, evaporation, dehydration, fermentation, and extraction.

The principal advantage claimed for ohmic heating is its ability to heat materials rapidly and uniformly, including products containing particulates. The principal mechanisms of microbial inactivation in ohmic heating are thermal. Although some evidence exists for nonthermal effects of ohmic heating, for most ohmic processes, which rely on heat, it may be unnecessary for processors to claim this effect in their process filings.

High-Pressure Processing (HPP)

High-pressure processing (HPP), also described as high-hydrostatic-pressure (HHP) or ultra-high-pressure (UHP) processing, subjects liquid and solid foods, with or without packaging, to pressures between 100 and 800 MPa. Process temperature during pressure treatment can be specified from below 0^{0}C to above 100^{0}C. Commercial exposure times can range from a millisecond pulse to over 20 min. Chemical changes in the food generally will be a function of the process temperature and treatment time.

The HPP process acts instantaneously and uniformly throughout a mass of food independent of size, shape, and food composition. Compression will uniformly increase the temperature of foods approximately 3^{0}C per 100 MPa. The temperature of a homogeneous food will increase uniformly due to compression. Compression of foods may shift the pH of the food as a function of imposed pressure and must be determined for each food treatment process. Water activity and pH are critical process factors in the inactivation of microbes by HPP. An increase in food temperature above room temperature and to a lesser extent a decrease below room temperature increases the inactivation rate of microorganisms during HPP treatment. Temperatures in the range of 45 to 50°C appear to increase the rate of inactivation of food pathogens and spoilage microbes. Temperatures ranging from 90 to 110°C in conjunction with pressures of 500–700 MPa have been used to inactivate spore-forming bacteria such as Clostridium botulinum. Current pressure processes include batch and semicontinuous systems, but no commercial continuous HPP systems are operating.

The critical process factors in HPP include pressure, time at pressure, time to achieve treatment pressure, decompression time, treatment temperature (including adiabatic heating), product initial temperature, vessel temperature distribution at pressure, product pH, product composition, product water activity, packaging material integrity, and concurrent processing aids. Other processing factors present in the process line before or after the pressure treatment are not included.

Because some types of spores of C. botulinum are capable of surviving even the most extreme pressures and temperatures of HPP, there is no absolute microbial indicator for sterility by HPP. For vegetative bacteria, nonpathogenic L. innocua is a useful surrogate for the foodborne pathogen L. monocytogenes. A nonpathogenic strain of Bacillus may be useful as a surrogate for HPP-resistant E. coli O157:H7 isolates.

Pulsed Electric Fields (PEF)

High-intensity pulsed electric field (PEF) processing involves the application of pulses of high voltage (typically 20–80 kV/cm) to foods placed between two electrodes. The process may be applied in the form of exponentially decaying, square wave, bipolar, or oscillatory pulses and at ambient, subambient, or slightly above ambient temperatures for less than 1 s. Energy loss due to heating of foods is minimised, reducing detrimental changes in the sensory and physical properties of foods.

Some important aspects in PEF technology are the generation of high electric field intensities, the design of chambers that impart uniform treatment to foods with minimum increase in temperature, and the design of electrodes that minimise the effect of electrolysis. Although different laboratory- and pilot-scale treatment chambers have been designed and used for PEF treatment of foods, only two industrial-scale PEF systems are available. The systems (including treatment chambers and power supply equipment) need to be scaled up to commercial systems.

To date, PEF has been applied mainly to improve the quality of foods. Application of PEF is restricted to food products that can withstand high electric fields, have low electrical conductivity, and do not contain or form bubbles. The particle size of the liquid food in both static and flow treatment modes is a limitation.

Several theories have been proposed to explain microbial inactivation by PEF. The most studied are electrical breakdown and electroporation. Factors that affect microbial inactivation with PEF are process factors (electric field intensity, pulse width, treatment time and temperature, and pulse wave shapes), microbial entity factors (type, concentration, and growth stage of the microorganism), and media factors (pH, antimicrobials, and ionic compounds, conductivity, and medium ionic strength). Although PEF has potential as a technology for food preservation, existing PEF systems and experimental conditions are diverse, and conclusions about the effects of critical process factors on pathogens of concern and kinetics of inactivation need to be further studied.

High-voltage arc discharge

Arc discharge was an early application of electricity for pasteurisation of fluids by applying rapid discharge voltages through an electrode gap below the surface of an aqueous suspension of microorganisms. A multitude of physical effects (intense wave) and chemical compounds (electrolysis) are generated, inactivating the microorganisms. The use of arc discharge for liquid foods may be unsuitable, largely because electrolysis and the formation of highly reactive chemicals occur during the discharge. More recent designs may show some promise for use in food preservation, although the reported results should be confirmed by independent researchers.

Pulsed light technology

Pulsed light is a method of food preservation that involves the use of intense and short-duration pulses of broad spectrum "white light". For most applications, a few flashes applied in a fraction of a second provide a high level of microbial inactivation. This technology is applicable mainly in sterilising or reducing the microbial population on packaging or food surfaces. Extensive independent research on the inactivation kinetics under a full spectrum of representative variables of food systems and surfaces is needed.

Oscillating magnetic fields

Static (SMF) and oscillating (OMF) magnetic fields have

been explored for their potential to inactivate microorganisms. For SMFs, the magnetic field intensity is constant with time, but an OMF is applied in the form of constant amplitude or decaying amplitude sinusoidal waves. An OMF applied in the form of pulses reverses the charge for each pulse. The intensity of each pulse decreases with time to about 10% of the initial intensity. Preservation of foods with OMF involves sealing food in a plastic bag and subjecting it to 1 to 100 pulses in an OMF with a frequency between 5 and 500 kHz at temperatures of 0 to 50°C for a total exposure time ranging from 25 ms to 100 ms. The effects of magnetic fields on microbial populations have produced controversial results. Consistent results concerning the efficacy of this method are needed before considering this technology for food preservation purposes.

Ultraviolet light

There is a particular interest in using ultraviolet (UV) light to treat fruit juices, in particular apple juice and cider. Other applications include disinfection of water supplies and food contact surfaces. Ultraviolet processing involves the use of radiation from the UV region of the electromagnetic spectrum. The germicidal properties of UV irradiation (UVC 200–280 nm) are due to DNA mutations induced by DNA absorption of the UV light. This mechanism of inactivation results in a sigmoidal curve of microbial population reduction.

To achieve microbial inactivation, the UV radiant exposure must be at least 400 J/m^2 in all parts of the product. Critical factors include the transmissivity of the product, the geometric configuration of the reactor, the power, wavelength, and physical arrangement of the UV source(s), the product flow profile and the radiation path length. Ultraviolet light may be used in combination with other alternative process technologies, including various powerful oxidising agents such as ozone and hydrogen peroxide, among others.

Ultrasound

Ultrasound is energy generated by sound waves of 20,000 or more vibrations per second. Although ultrasound technology has a wide range of current and future applications in the food industry, including inactivation of microorganisms and enzymes, most current developments for food applications are nonmicrobial. Data on inactivation of food microorganisms by ultrasound in the food industry are scarce, and most applications use it in combination with other preservation methods. The bactericidal effect of ultrasound is attributed to intracellular cavitations, that is, micromechanical shocks that disrupt cellular structural and functional components up to the point of cell lysis. The heterogeneous and protective nature of food with the inclusion of particulates and other interfering substances severely curtails the singular use of ultrasound as a preservation method. Although these limitations make the current probability of commercial development low, combination of ultrasound with other preservation processes (e.g., heat and mild pressure) appears to have the greatest potential for industrial application.

Critical processing factors are assumed to be the amplitude of the ultrasonic waves, the exposure/contact time with the microorganisms, the type of microorganism, the volume of food to be processed, the composition of the food, and the temperature of treatment.

Pulsed X-Rays

It is important to realise that pulsed X-ray is one form of irradiation that has been applied to the preservation of several categories of food in the United States. Electrons have a limited penetration depth of about 5 cm in food, but X-rays have significantly higher penetration depths (60–400 cm), depending upon the energy used. Pulsed X-ray is a new alternative technology that utilises a solid state-opening switch to generate electron beam X-ray pulses of high intensity (opening times from 30 ns down to a few nanoseconds; repetition rates up to 1000 pulses/s in burst mode operation). The specific effect of pulses in contrast to nonpulsed X-rays has yet to be investigated. The practical application of food irradiation by X-rays in conjunction with existing food processing equipment is further facilitated by (1) the possibility of controlling the direction of the electrically produced radiation; (2) the possibility of shaping the geometry of the radiation field to accommodate different package sizes; and (3) its high reproducibility and versatility. Potentially, the negative effects of irradiation on food quality can be reduced.

Bibliography

David Magee, *MoonPie: Biography of an Out-of-This-World Snack, Hardcover - Sep 30 2006.*

Edward Jaye, *The Cookie Sutra: An Ancient Treatise: that Love Shall Never Grow Stale. Nor Crumble,* Jun 4 2005.

John Edge, *Donuts,* May 23 2006.

Priddat, R. E., *Historical References on Baking,* Chicago, Illinois, American Institute of Baking, 1932.

Prytherch, Raymon John and Suzanne Stanley, *Food, Cookery, and Diet: An Information Guide,* Aldershot, Hants., England; Brookfield Vermont, U. S.A.: Gower, 1989.

Rachel Brown, *New Holland Professional: Cake Decorating,* Nov 1 2007

Rhodes, D. E., "The Italian Banquet, 1598 and its Origins" in *Italian Studies,* 1972.

Rosengarten, Frederic, *The Book of Edible Nuts,* New York: Walker, 1984.

Rudolph, G. A., *Kansas State University Receipt Book and Household Manual,* Manhattan, Kansas, Kansas State University Library, 1968.

Sacharoff, Shata Niubark, *The Ethnic Vegetarian Kitchen,* San Francisco: 101 Productions, 1984.

Schofield, Eileen K., *Cooking With Vegetables, Flowers, and Fruits: An Annotated List of References,* Bronx, New York: Council on Botanical and Horticultural Libraries, 1988.

Schraemli, Harry, *Catalogue of a Collection of Books and Manuscripts of the 15th to 20th Century on Food and Wine From the Well-Known Library of Harry Schraemli,* London, Sotheby and Company, February, 1971.

Schwartz, Diane, *Vegetable Cookerys A Selected Annotated Bibliography,* Bronx, New York: Council on Botanical and Horticultural Libraries, 1978.

Shaprio, Laura, *Perfection Salad: Women and cooking at the turn of the century.* New York:

Tooley, James B., *Microwave Cooking: A Bibliography*, London: Acton, 1982.

Vara, Albert, *Food and Beverage Industries: A Bibliography and Guidebook*, Detroit, Gale, 1970.

Vehling, Joseph Dommers et al., "Cooking, or, Practical and economical training for those who are to be servants, wives, and mothers: management of the kitchen, plain cooking, bread-making, baking, brewing, pickling, etc.," London: J. Masters, 1854.

Index

Notes

Notes